SOMEONE, NO ONE

SOMEONE, NO ONE

An Essay on Individuality

KENELM BURRIDGE

PRINCETON UNIVERSITY PRESS
PRINCETON, NEW JERSEY

Copyright © 1979 by Princeton University Press

Published by Princeton University Press, Princeton, New Jersey
In the United Kingdom: Princeton University Press, Guildford,
Surrey

Library of Congress Cataloging in Publication Data will be found on
the last printed page of this book

This book has been composed in VIP Bembo

Clothbound editions of Princeton University Press books are
printed on acid-free paper, and binding materials are chosen for
strength and durability

Printed in the United States of America by Princeton University
Press, Princeton, New Jersey

TO THE MEMORY OF
N.A.R. AND E.E.E-P.

CONTENTS

PREFACE

This essay both summarizes the gist of several talks given on a variety of occasions over a number of years and develops themes appearing in other publications of mine. Faced with the choice between a large volume studded with references and one that would read more smoothly if idiosyncratically, I have opted for the latter. Though so much has been written about the individual and individuality that it would be difficult to say anything original, it seemed to me that a short contextual summary might serve the purpose of opening new avenues. And these tend to lead into areas of contingency where by definition rules and principles are not to be found.

Still, these areas need to be identified, and I have sought to bring them together in the notion of individuality. For, appealing though they are in positive instances, the familiar theoretical constructs purporting to explain or account for the how and why of what happens in social life tend to wilt in the face of negative instances. Why in this or that case, given the circumstances, did the supposedly inevitable consequences not occur? Why are we so often taken by surprise? Why in the event do we so frequently fail to recognize what is happening? The most general and obvious answer is that we do not know sufficient clearly enough. And it is an easy discretion to doubt whether new but currently unimaginable paradigms would take us much further. But perhaps we have missed what is too close to our noses. Are those supposedly hapless creatures of circumstances, people, really so helpless? Do prisoners not corrupt their guards? The contingencies and opportunities between the constraints we so habitually polish claim attention. Though the chaos or areas of nonrestraint beside or beneath the rules or constraints and principles which we use to describe society are not susceptible to order, and more certainly produce the noxious and destructive than the creative, they are surely the fount of most of our becomings and, in large part, seem to be engendered by particular constellations of constraints. These last, therefore, become peculiarly significant. If we could see ourselves not so much in the stasis of identities, situated, as in limbos of becoming other we might break out of the images that science necessarily impresses on us. Hence this essay: an attempt to sketch a part of our authenticity.

My debts are too many to articulate in full. The bibliography contains works which, while not specifically referred to in the text, have, I think, been influential. I gladly acknowledge the influence of the work and thought of, particularly, Louis Dumont, Mary Douglas, and Victor Turner, upon whose systematic and imaginative applications this essay greatly relies. I apologize if I have misunderstood them; I could not have done without them. The influence of Claude Lévi-Strauss may not be obvious, but it is there, absorbed into the general discourse, and, like most anthropologists writing today, I have been acutely conscious of it. I thank Julian Wake and John LeRoy for the stimulus of their conversation and graduate theses on related topics, and Professor Gianfranco Poggi, Dr. Yunshik Chang, Cathy Wylie, and Allan Salo who were kind enough to read and comment upon drafts of the typescript. Financial grants from the Canada Council enabled me to travel overseas and engage in short periods of fieldwork. The award of a Fellowship by the John Simon Guggenheim Foundation provided me with an abundantly rewarding sabbatical year, some of the fruits of which are contained herein. I acknowledge with gratitude their help and support. I also thank the Council of the Humanities of Princeton University for their generosity in inviting me to be a Visiting Fellow, an opportunity I took to broach some of the themes developed in this essay. The kind hospitality and comments of members of the Departments of Anthropology and Religious Studies at Princeton remain a most happy memory. To Noel Ross and Sir Edward Evans-Pritchard, individuals both, and to whose memory this essay is dedicated, I owe more than I can say.

KENELM O. L. BURRIDGE
UNIVERSITY OF BRITISH COLUMBIA
JANUARY 1979

PART I
INDIVIDUALITY
EXPLORED

1 INTRODUCTION

Within the European or Western experience the thought which invests the human organism with individuality has been the home of many disparate and contradictory ideas. Whether in the here-now, this or that historical period, or in relation to other cultures or civilizations, residues from the past mingle with the present, and shades of understanding and lines of demonstration defy the clean chop of precision. Continually in flux, changing, developing, falling back into the past to metamorphose anew, thoughts about the individual and individuality—accreting into a variety of -isms—spell out the history of European thought: love, conscience, free will, morality, equality before the law, property, liberty; the restless desire to capture and contain in new social forms the moral significance of the truth or goodness in otherwise existential events. Moving then from the constituted abstraction to the concrete reality, sitting individuality on a specific human being in relation to others poses questions of being and identity. Who or what is this he or she whose actuality has been supposed to rest on an equation between "being" and "thinking"; whose verity is wont to melt in the heat of others' images; who moves between the poles of a supposed sovereignty, alone and in dread of the freedom it might provide, and an idealized participation in the being of others; whose despair and cheer lies in every hair being counted and cared for; who is supposed to be as a god, made in His image; who is exhorted both to love and be just; who is enjoined to the crisis of willing and realizing freedom and truth, who is pricked into transcending the norm when happiness flows in comforting conformities?

"A single instance of the species" reads the dictionary. "Distinguished by special attributes" it goes on. We contain in the one notion the ordinary or common and general and the special or peculiar. In opposing the individual to society and the collective forms, we tend to forget that in one aspect the individual represents or replicates them and in the other is opposed to them and may renew or recreate them. Caught as we are in history where time is measured less by the cycles of the celestial bodies than by changing universes of social orders and relationships, the permanence of the individual and individuality as principles that both conserve the past and unfold new futures often escapes us—until, that is, we begin to recollect, describe, and write. Then the individual in one or other aspect becomes a point of departure, and wheresoever we journey in thought or deed we return to the same landfall. And we do so because whether as categories or actual living people the individual and individuality lie at the center of our civilization. Working out the varied implications of the fertile and institutionalized ambiguity and contradiction that is the individual is, so to speak, our business: the stuff of history and social relations, of virtue and ideals, exhortation and reprimand, ridicule, protest, injured dignity, love, the psychiatric couch, and social and political action. Is it in similar manner the business of other cultures? Is this central dynamic of Western civilization, this two-faced eudaemon whose varieties of expressions will presently be pursued, the development of a universal in human experience, or is it in some sense culturally specific?

Within the European or Western tradition we tend to think of ourselves as unique beings in whom others, a computer, and God perhaps, take a particular interest. Yet in practice each one of us *is*, not necessarily because we think or because thoughts come or even because somewhere there are papers which say who and what we are. We *are* because in immediate objectivity in relation to others each one of us is life: genes in movement, a nervous system, a mouth to be fed. In interaction with a sociocultural environment and through a mind or brain capable of a variety of operations we *become*. Not so far from Mead (G. H. Mead 1967), but reformulating, take the energy of the peculiar integration of these features as, provisionally, constituting the self. Whether God-given, in which case this energy becomes the soul journeying back to its creator, or gene-given, or simply intuited, the fact of integration—some sort of coherence or coordination of the parts or constituents of being—does not detach the integrative energy or self from its constituents, but still makes it more than the sum of the parts and, in that sense, conceptually and empirically distinct.

In its integration of animal and sociocultural parts, a self may show forth the person: a "single instance of the species," the conformist who, in reproducing in word and deed the norms of the given traditional social order, manifests the relations of that tradition. Put another way, the constitutive relations of one who conforms to the given social tradition reveal the person. Going further, the self may also integrate the parts into the individual: not merely the nonconformist or one who has the qualities or attributes of the "single instance" in greater degree—one who can run faster, talk better, or work harder or the like—but, giving the "special attributes" and the inherent ambiguity of the word their full force, one who manifests relations opposed to those indicated by the person. That is, the moral critic who envisages another kind of social or moral order, the creative spark poised and ready to change tradition. Or, one might say, the individual is one who manifests relations potentially capable of changing the given or traditional moral order. Yet if some people are wholly individuals and others are persons, it is matter of common observation that most people are in some respects and most frequently persons while in other respects and at other times they can appear as individuals. And this apparent oscillation or movement between person and individual—whether in a particular instance the movement is one way or a return is made—may be identified as individuality. Or, individuality refers to the opportunity and capacity to move from person to individual and/or vice versa. The self now becomes an integrative/disintegrative energy which gathers particular relations either into the person or into the individual and, also, an energy which either inhibits or makes possible the movement between person and individual.

A conversation between person and individual, whether the relations are contained in the same or separate human beings, is likely to be argumentative. The first is content with things as they are, the second posits an alternative set of moral discriminations. And because, corresponding with the ambiguity in the individual and individuality of ordinary discourse, the idea of morality also contains an ambiguity between what is and what ought to be, the conversation is likely to be confusing as well as lively. Nevertheless, because the self is capable of moving toward an integration of now one and then the other, the interplay between person and individual can yield either a dilemma—indicative of a self in disintegrative mode—or an apperception of own being in relation to traditional or alternative categories. Without this interplay and apperception, sociology and social or cultural anthropology would not be possible. Which makes of the self a necessary if mute assumption.

From within a culture, emically or subjectively, the categories and basic assumptions of the social order are, generally speaking, taken to indicate a sufficient approximation to the truth of things, reality. The discriminations between what is good or efficient and what is bad or evil or inefficient in social relations and the world are viable. But the actual truth of things, reality itself—again generally speaking—is usually and sensibly regarded as discrete from that ordering and the expectations that derive from it. The relations manifested by a society and the truth of things fit each other only loosely and approximately: expectations can be disappointed or surprised by events or relations that are not, or do not seem to be, predicated or accommodated by the structure. Then, perhaps, if the disappointments or surprises are sufficiently severe or occur sufficiently often, adjustments are made and the moral discriminations change. An individual is not overtly necessary. If, however, any weight or value is to be assigned to the notion of a positive moral critique, we are more or less forced into saying that while, among ourselves at least, the person reproduces the structure of the given tradition in a stream of rationalizations,* intellectualizations, and symbolic representations—statements in words, paint, sculpture, and formal and informal ritual and symbolic activities which, taken together, make up a semantic environment assigning meaning and relevance to events and relations—the individual, using similar modes but transcending the given categories, rerationalizing and arguing antithetically, provides a moral critique and, ideally, seeks a closer fit with the goodness in the truth of things as he or she perceives them. Which does not deny that, subjectively and particularly in the view of a person, an individual's rerationalizations may seem bad, an evil.

The opportunity to rerationalize is provided by events and by the social structure itself. The capacity to use the opportunity is what makes an individual. Becoming aware of a gap between the person's reproductions and the truth of things by seizing on or being seized by peculiarly significant events, the self is moved to a transcendence of the traditional categories, to a reintegration of the event in a new rationalization assigning new meaning and relevance. In this transcendence and reintegration, manifest in the new rationalization, the self realizes the individual.

In opposition to such a model, sociology and social or cultural anthropology regard reality and the truth of things as tied to those predicates of a given social order which, after analysis in relation to a particular theoretical framework (itself

---

*The word "rationalization" is not used here in its restricted psychological sense of, essentially, falsification—though of course something of the sort is usually entailed. In the matter which follows, "intellectualizations and symbolic representations" is sometimes added to "rationalizations," sometimes not. It makes little difference. What is being referred to is the (parts of) the semantic environment which assign meaning and relevance to what occurs.

a peculiarly stringent set of interrelated rationalizations predicating a semantic environment) cannot be gainsaid. If it be
claimed that there is a truth or reality discrete from the analyzed structure, it is either not cognizable by the disciplines,
or it will, in time, be discovered to be part of the structure in
the light of a more efficient theoretical framework. The necessary working assumption that social relations are predicative,
and the dogma that the structure of those relations constitutes
truth, are enlivened by the faith—characteristic of individuality—that in penetrating to the truth the structure will be made
more complete. But although social or cultural anthropologists seek that theoretical framework or set of universals
which would contain or account for all possible emic or
homemade models, they have not yet found it. Consequently, they remain bound to a cultural and moral relativ-
ism, and so to conceptions of relative truths: truth—or reality—becomes that which, in a particular culture, mediates and
manifests social relationships. Truth and truths are to be discovered in the properties of the machine. Beyond that, illusion gobbles the gullible.

On the other hand, were it not for the imaginative but
covert intuitions of the investigating self in relation to the
selves being investigated—a communication and cohesiveness
between human selves which first uses and then probes further than the person's reproductions—anthropologists might
the more easily have been able to find the framework they
seek. As it is, the varied integrations of selves raise subtle but
major barriers of understanding which idioms of explicit
communication cannot vault: no culture is accurately communicated in the terms of another. The fieldworker's apprehension of the fruitlessness of epistemological confrontation,
and that respect for ontological truth which is gained in the
communication between selves while learning another culture
and then participating in that culture's linguistic categories,
come together to deter most from the use of what would be
purely mechanical techniques. The properties of the machine
become an illusion, then reassert themselves as indicative of

the deeper truths in which they are embedded. Hence the importance of the self and interacting selves as loci of truth perception. They are Archimedean points from which, albeit momentarily, structures do not exist and truth or reality are perceived—only to be recloaked with cultural idioms when and if that reality is articulated or rationalized. The self and a respect for truth mediate the discussion at all levels and point to that praxis of the event which, caught between history (what, existentially, actually seems to have occurred) and the rationalizations which assign meaning and significance or nonmeaning or nonsignificance, anthropologists attempt to grasp. For the core of the anthropological endeavor is not so much the ordering and reordering of rationalizations—though this is what mostly occurs—nor even the difference between what is done and what is said—though this must be a byproduct—but the relationship between what *actually happens to people*, events, and the forms and modes by which those events are articulated and made communicable by rationalizations, intellectualizations, and symbolic representations.

As the systemic reach into other cultures, social and/or cultural anthropology are unique to the European or Western intellectual tradition which, in spite of perverse ethnocentricities, has characteristically applied itself to the study of man wherever he may be. Reaching out from the home environment to examine the variety of physical and cultural conditions under which man exists or has existed, the tradition can be defined by the ways in which it has fed on and absorbed other ways of life and traditions. It is also a tradition which, stretching itself into a conceived otherness, has always been intent on creating different conditions for itself. Never content with the present, thinkers, writers, and reformers have not simply dreamed or imagined different kinds of worlds—though this might be thought sufficient—but have themselves or in combination with the politically able striven to create and realize them. If much of this reach into what might or should be has been born of the resources contained within the native tradition itself, it has also been sustained by the ongoing conversation with and investigation of other cultures and traditions. The primary questions have been not, "Who or what am I?"—though this must follow—but, "What is man, What are his conditions of life, How should he live?"

In part, this tradition of reaching into otherness, this venture into other social forms and experience to discover a general human ontology tied to moral universals, stems from the Greeks who brought other worlds into the native cognizance, marrying other cultural and intellectual traditions to their own. They gave us the logos, a means by which, through an intellectual construct, we could, ideally, look at ourselves and others objectively and not from a merely subjective or ethnocentric standpoint. The Roman empire, composed of diverse cultures, provided the conditions in which actual experience and an intellectual appreciation of otherness could develop and take firm root. Even so, an inertial tendency toward ethnocentricity, toward creating a single secure world safe from outside interference, intellectual or otherwise, would probably have asserted itself had it not been for the impact of Christianity. For the latter introduced complex notions of love whose varied aspects Western civilization is still trying to work out. At its most general if not always simple level, love entailed, as it still does, that participation in the beings of others which, ideally realized through and by means of the triune Godhead, is opposed to the rational objectivity of the logos, and defies and transcends structural oppositions to reach into an awareness of oneness. Working within the Roman ambience, the precarious synthesis between Greek and Christian put the seal on what was to become an inbuilt and continuing endeavor. The spirit of a new heaven and a new earth, containing the instruction to transcend the given categories of a social order and extend one's love across cultural and political boundaries, peculiarly appropriate to the conditions of the Roman hegemony, found in Plato the intellectual soil on which a City of God could be built.

Partly through St. Paul but mainly through St. Augustine, platonic moral idealism and the idea of an alternative social order inherent in *The Republic* became informed with Christian values. In turn, these were assimilated to the logos or intellectual construct yielding a rational objectivity to become a theology. Not measuring human acts and achievements against some statistical mean, normative mode, or traditional usage—though these criteria must necessarily have played their parts—Christianity went to a relation between the here-now, the historical past, and a totality of knowledge and achievement rationally and objectively contained in a triune Godhead "out there." Access to this knowledge as well as to a moral and spiritual wholeness was formally promised in the Father, assured in the Son, the Christ, who was both God and man, and implemented through the workings of the Holy Spirit. Man was made in God's image, was as a god. The logos was subsumed in revelation. Man was given at least formal access not only to the objective and intellectual knowledge yielded by the logos, but also to the further wisdoms contained in the Godhead.*

Long evoked by some of the prophets of the Old Testament and the events and teachings of the gospels, the lineaments of the individual began to emerge from the Graeco-Christian synthesis. We can, too, trace to the same sources the intellectual and moral roots of what was to become social or cultural anthropology. For going together with the Platonic and Augustinian heritage was the injunction to go and teach all nations—the missionary purpose and endeavor exemplified by St. Paul. Shouldering that obligation implied that the teachers should learn from others: a necessary corollary to extending one's love and making oneself understood. Formally and ideally denying political and cultural exclusivisms, the invitation to development in universal terms was explicit whatever the practice in many instances may have turned out to be. Other cultural traditions were contained in God's will

*A fuller exposition of these themes is contained in Burridge 1973a: 1-38.

and purpose. God was for all of mankind. Moreover, the face of God was not to be sought in contemplation of own being, or the abstract, nor yet in a conversation with the native tradition. It could only be found in realizing love of and for others, and in imprinting on heart and mind the import of the sacred scriptures: the history, images, events, figures, and religious experience of the Hebrews, a people distanced from the European both in space and in time. The Old and New Testaments were, indeed, the centerpiece of a triptych which included on either hand a knowledge of, and familiarity with, the history, customs, languages, and experience of the ancient Greeks and Romans. The measure of intellectual worth lay in the penetration of other social spaces, in exploring and making intelligible the categories of other cultures in terms of one's own. The study of other cultures, the individual, and individuality are intimately entwined. Each is an aspect, phase, or transformation of the other. Each is also infused with a common dilemma: an opposition between the intellectual orderliness of a logos, as in a *Republic*, which entails distancing, and the participatory values of love conjoined, so often, with the anomie of disconcerting events and interventions.

Familiarity with the languages and customs of other peoples always was, and to some extent still is, the mark of the educated European. Historical works, utopian constructions, the novel, science fiction, travel books, and descriptions of strange cultures, systematic or otherwise, all attest the reach across both time and space into existing, imagined, monstrous, or ideal kinds of otherness which is intrinsic to European civilization. Imperial designs and the occurrence of many hundreds of millenarian, enthusiastic, revolutionary, and similar movements in European history point to the same characteristic features. A new heaven and a new earth are either explicit or implied. And this sense of the social order as flux, as a present about to realize a new future—corresponding to the way we think of what is in relation to what ought to be—is inherent in the individual, is indeed the central expression of that tension between the here-now and otherness which seems peculiar to European or Western civilization. By contrast, other cultures appear to us to have a wholeness and authenticity that is as almost autogenetic as makes no matter. We know that this is not quite true, that other cultures and civilizations learn from and adopt the practices of strangers, making portions of otherness their own. Yet this seems curiously unimportant. The model for them is the intellectual orderliness and integration of *The Republic*. The notion of the alternative and ideal social order contained in the same exemplar combined with the sense of an unfolding purpose derived from the Biblical experience point to the authentic in the European or Western heritage: a new heaven and new earth through the exploration and absorption of otherness.

Studying other cultures and moving from the person to the individual and back again in relation both to our own tradition and other cultures are integral to European or Western being. Though the question "Who or what am I?" requires an awareness of the self and person as well as a movement into the individual if the bounded cultural tradition is to be transcended, "Who or what is man?" carries the peculiar insecurity of a continuing thrust into the unknown or strange. Own identity wavers. Not only the native but other cultural categories have to be transcended in relation to each other. In this limbo of the ethnographic act, with being in metamorphosis as the self attempts to integrate quite different epistemologies, other traditions must appear as secure and whole. Our own wholeness can only be discovered and realized through all of mankind. This indeed is the gist of the Christian message. And contained within or corresponding with that message is the anthropological search for a theoretical framework or set of universals in terms of which all cultures and their ontologies can be described.

There have been phases in Western history, to be sure, when the dominant feeling has been to call a halt—Wholeness now! Enough of otherness! And movements of millenarian or utopian kind evidence the attempt to realize a wholeness in an immediate here-now. But inevitably the dialectic continues. Wholeness here-now is permeated by the historical past, by wholeness in the future, by wholeness as ought or ideal. Whether or not we think of ourselves as believing Christians, and whether translated into the idioms and activities of theology, psychology, morality, economics, or politics, the antitheses between being content with ourselves in the here-now, making wholeness out of what we have and are at a particular moment in time, and reaching out into others and otherness to make wholeness a true universal, are indelibly stamped into our cultural being. As parasites or altruists, in greed or generosity, selfish cynicism or love, enthusiastically or reluctantly, we are impelled to realize ourselves by going out beyond the peripheries as initially presented to us. These features are as distinctive of the individual as they are of European or Western scholarship in general and of social or cultural anthropology in particular. The scientific study of society or culture becomes suffused with moral purpose and modified by the search for a logos or intellectual construct that will communicate the ideas and activities of one culture to another.

Traditionally in sociology or in social or cultural anthropology the single instance has been thought of as the unit of experience by which the lineaments of a society may be discovered. Empirical work in the field makes necessary what can be avoided in purely documentary studies. Still, not always aware of, and for the most part at least blurring the distinction between person and individual—opposed categories which may be present in the same single instance or biological organism—investigators tend to focus on that which to them reveals normalcy and the normative: the person. Single instance, biological organism, person, and individual are rolled into equivalences. Then, as the investigation moves from the field to the study, the experience of people and events begins to sink under the weight of rationalizations. The latter become the data; analysis orders rationalizations, categories, and the catalogue of constraints which, making up society, are susceptible to generalization as principle. The mess of events and real lives is sacrificed to intellectual elegance. As indeed it must be. The principles of order underlying or informing events, activities, and social relationships are what is being sought. The opportunities grasped by people become contingencies which have no place in an order.

Nevertheless, the initial focus on the single instance is not simply due to the circumstances of fieldwork but is characteristically European or Western. Traditionally attributed with an immortal soul, the biological organism or single instance, each mouth, was and remains sacred. And translating "soul" into secular idiom, the single instance remains sacred because of the creative possibilities inherent in the opposition between person and individual. Nor are the distinctions blurred into equivalences simply because social scientists seek the general and normative, eschew the soul, and take fright at uniqueness. The relationship between self and other courses lightly through the elementary other-self, and, from author-people, becomes in virtue of a given theoretical construct, author-analysis: a relationship corresponding to individual-person. Transforming an experience of people into an experience of society requires first participation and conformity, then critique. The author, whose self has communicated with other selves and from there has been moved to translate the terms of one epistemology into the terms of another, has moved from person to individual. Further, because ideology is that which evokes the transformation of one order into another preferred order, the intellectual construct which has brought order tends to become ideology. And at that point the selves of the investigator and subjects become constrained in the elegantly destructive rules of a *Republic*. Without the anomie of the disconcerting event or intervention—and the Bible and fieldwork experience are replete with them—there can be no invitation to rerationalize. Without the disorderly but creative confusion given in a soul that is both person and individual the mouth loses significance and becomes as expendable as idle thought.

Though it can be said (cf. Dumont 1967: 237; Nakamura 1967: 8-11) on several grounds that the great Eastern cultures do not have a notion of the individual that corresponds with the European—concentrating here on that aspect of the individual which is focused on the single instance, the biological organism—this biological organism is not as simple and straightforward as it seems. A man, a woman, a child: single instances of the species. But neither we nor anyone else live in a purely biologically bounded world. All live in an environment of dreams, thoughts, speech, images, emotions, stories, awarenesses, continuities and discontinuities, and explicit categories and articulate rules which govern interrelations and address to the world. When we say that husband and wife are one flesh, we deny the biological simplicity and enter the ambiguities of symbol and metaphor. Dressed thus with an awareness of being and meaning, we return to a quite different animal. Each spatially bounded organism may contain the world, and is taken to be able to become not only a person, realizing the given, but an individual, creating anew. We hold to this because, traditionally, each was both life and soul which, proceeding from the Godhead, was held capable of that love and creativity which indicated the divine presence.

Secularized and attenuated though the soul has become, and despite varieties of attempts to subordinate single instances to the state or social order, the sacral character of the single instance still lingers in our apprehensions as something creative, divine, capable of overcoming or transcending the deadening rules and regulations of a given social order. That these apprehensions are contained in and nourished by institutionalized individuality there can be little doubt. Equally, if there were no selves—not the same as souls but running behind on a parallel track—with their varied integrations to revivify it continually, the institution would become moribund and die.

2 THE SELF AND THE SOCIAL

Integrating the animal into a coherence with the sociocultural environment, the self reveals itself as particular or peculiar in its mode of integration. Capable of that integration which manifests the person, the self may also claim or be credited with an integration of those special attributes or relations which evoke the individual. Folded into the social categories and images of others, the *I* that is the self's image of itself can either reflect the light of others or strive to cut the coils and bid others note a new light. The more we suffer the sight and sound of uniformed masses, directly encountered or figured in the bland tones of the media as the statistics and categories which make us single and abstract instances, the more tightly we cling to those who embrace us as refractions of their own uniqueness, perceive our special attributes. These hear the same bell, share the events from which life and being spring, are persons certainly, but also individuals like ourselves.

You know that some who know you and others whom you know are only persons, embodiments of the categories prescribed by tradition and the social order. Only you can continually know the *I am*, the self, grasped in snatches by those others who perceive that distorted image of the *I* which is your you-ness. The shared event, the dive into truth—these are quickly buried in differing and competing rationalizations which, sadly, are your only hold on what happened. And when you talk, or take direction from the words that tumble around you, you may well wonder what "really" happened, and who or what you are. If your face and being are not your fault, which of all those encountered others have made you? If culture and tradition have molded you—what saints and heroes measure you, small though you be? What artist's perceptions showed you the way? Filling a niche or a slot machined by an intersection of the common and general categories provides identity; and the self's integration of the categories makes identity unique. But, passing from one slot to another, successive integrations would make a chameleon of the self were it not for the *I*, the self's image of itself as qualitative, reproducing its quality in each integration and resting upon genes none other possesses. The genes, and behind them perhaps your God, made you and continually remake you, always wresting uniqueness from the commonalty of the herd. Those genes, though, or that God, when they speak do so enigmatically, in retreating phrases that can hardly be discerned by the mind even in a stillness of heart. A bird in song, a fox peering from his covert, a mantis waiting poised—these might help an alter reveal you to yourself. Then you might sound a trumpet and reveal yourself to others. Then you might show how you had molded what others had given. In that moment you might be, and be seen, for what you are, not merely contained in what others had thought you had done and said.

Now though, psychiatrists round off the corners, remold you into normal conformity, bring you back into the person. Opportunities for stillness have been lost in much doing. Birdsong is drowned in the clatter of a building site, the fox moves far from sight of the urban sprawl, the mantis is but an artist's thought in copper on the mantel. Smoke hides the leaping sun. The flashing silence of a forest glade has become a dream for holiday. The morning dew, a trembling aspen— these are literary conceits, remnants of another age. Nature, the womb of all our likenesses and differences, wherein we might seek our own reality, has become contained in an authorized version. Of the animals our ancestors used to watch so carefully so that they might come to know themselves, the cat and dog remain. For most of us the natural world, that counterpoint in which to perceive an idea of our selves, has moved between the covers of books: into sets of detailed ap-

pearances which hide the idea, the reality as it might be intuited. Only a few of all of us have anything but others
stamped in our likeness in which to seek our own uniqueness.
We find and know ourselves only in what others say or do to
us. Proclaiming ourselves in reflections and extensions of ourselves, we seek the potential of our social insurance numbers
in relation to a job description, a brand of soap, deodorant,
and a multitude of artifacts. The magic and mystery of life are
reduced to the prosaic. This we can handle, make judgments
about. Magic and mystery are dangerous. Allow them an
entry and who knows where the cancer would halt? Trafalgar
is a bus-stop. Because there are so many of us so briefly encountered and so rarely experienced, we are losing the habit
of penetrating to the person, let alone the self. If I do not
bother or think I have not the time to penetrate to him, why
should he be obliged to enter into me and make me more than
I was? Supposing that each of us became more and more re-
luctant to scratch the surface of another, that more and more
often we failed to find in others a response to our internal
self-questionings—How could you be you and I me without
the gift of another? And yet the European or Western cultural
instruction is to transcend the complex of given roles that
make up the person and realize our selves as individuals.

If the human is cultural, and cultures are sets of prescribed
modes of engaging preordained sets of relationships, why
should not the idea, the critique that changes the relationships—for change they do over time—also be species specific
to the human? Without the apperceptions of the self, how
could new relationships be generated? An intersection in time
and space of matter and a variety of social categories might be
distinguished as you rather than another only in the self's integration of feeling, willing, and articulate reflection on experience. To be an individual, that intersection would have to
have a critical idea and act upon it in relation to the categories
and to others. Even if the realization of the critique seems to
reach into but a small part of the idea, not one of us could be
an individual if we did not believe there was the quite un-

romantic possibility of taking the whole world into our selves. Only thereby might an effective critique be engendered.

Or, take an oblique. Encountered in a wilderness of sand dunes and light sea-spumed breezes under a roasting sun, a hermit spoke. To meet him there, this gaunt and bearded monk, not feverish or shy but alert and bright-eyed, might have been to stumble over a lonely old derelict cut off from his kind and enjoying only himself and what he called his God—buttering himself for heaven. Not a bit of it. Bringing all of himself into his thought, care, fasting, and praying for others, through belief sprung ˜from will and motive, he seemed to bring all others into his comprehension and suffering. Though alone, this was no egotist because under the discipline of his Order. A solitary on the outer edges of culture, as though unstructured in relation to others, yet he moved into life's center by affirming his being in others and otherness. Attempting to pull the world into himself sustained him, allowed him his realization of self, brought him into the ambit of being an individual—razored the cycle of thoughts which, moving from obverse to reverse and glancing at their backsides in a mirror, ask the nihilist whether nothing exists. From being as a collection of rorschach smudges brought into an order obedient to the culturally automated will of each encountered other, he brought his own order to his parts and manifested and imposed its moments upon others. Having moved aside from a given complex of roles and statuses he could perceive a truth in relation to illusion, penetrate the identities of others, participate in their beings. Standing thus, he could give and guide. Locked into truth in relation to discovered illusion, his words, reflecting truth and evinced in his being, persuaded and convinced.

Could you possibly be you if you were just one autonomous narcissus Joe, nourished by a cat walking stiff-legged into a night of enjoyment? Suppose a lone Judy posting a letter to herself—who but her alter might share in the pleasure of next morning's mail? Such a division of self—wringing a remnant of being out of nonbeing—could never be right. Nature reveals complexities of interdependence, one fate entwined with others. In cutting through the defenses of roles and statuses and entering into the beings of others we are renewed as our own being transforms them. Yet in saying just this we move from the prosaic world of social interaction into a mysterium of transformations—which are not necessarily inexplicable simply because they are presently a mysterium.

Consider the apparently solid and sensible empirical reality, the single instance, the biological organism whom we Europeans burden with individuality and living life abundantly. A body bounded in space, changing through time, slipping from one identity to another: bones, flesh and blood, a chemistry piloted by a unique constellation of genes, a bundle of sensations, mentating, interacting with an environment of rationalizations, appearances, and other similar chemistries. Successive transformations become known in relation to the only relative permanence, the body itself and, perhaps, through the mode or style of the self integrating the biology and layer upon layer of socialized parts which, when summed, make up a person: certain bearing and cast of features, characteristic attitudes and predictable modes of reacting and initiating within the given prescriptions. Sensations move, programmed by the genes maybe or, like the predestined curve of a comet, set in motion by the interlacing harmonies of the stars in their courses. Or even, by divine ordinance, freely willing in erratic leaps and pauses. Wherein lies the essence of the creature? The pulsing organism directed by the supreme presidium of the genes, the diagram of potentials given by the circling bodies of the zodiac—these are chiseled into a person by others, become an individual through the purposive and freely willing movement of the self in relation to those others because believing in the virtue of those others.

Though we stand on the threshold of duplicating the genes, and man-made planets must soon qualify our fortunes, neither gene-shaper nor star-maker can make me into you.

Suppose memory to be lost in an accident, name and ante-
cedents unknown, the face burnt off and puttied in pink, all
birthmarks gone—how do I start making the patient into me?
The you-ness in the I that was me has gone. The I that was
has been expunged. My genes remain—but is my birthdate
the same? If those around me do not help to remake me, who
will? The surviving chemistry of sensations, the new I-ness of
me, take in the world as it appears, draw order from a chaos
of impressions, rationalize from consecutive events, intuit relationship from simultaneity of experience, strive to penetrate
the unity of sense or meaning in a multiplicity of experiences.
Others speak, correct, teach, confirm, or deny an order that I
must see as merely temporary in relation to the reality of me
in myself. In time, perhaps, I may begin to think of this tran-
science as permanent and real, though my past should have
taught me differently. Press this newly-becoming back into
the womb. Whether from some fortuitous access of desire,
or more purposefully and morally ordered, the mating and
conception bring together a chancy collection of genes to pul-
lulate in movement towards a particular He or She. And from
such combinations of accident a will is born into light. Invoke
God, Nature, the divine or evolutionary purpose, or a variety
of determinisms: a will wholly free is too awesome, too wild.
Link it then to the stars.

What manner of He or She? A word-picture of physical aspect and equipment, height, girth, and musculature roughly
describe the animal. A felicitous choice of more technical
terms reveals to initiates what is distinctive about the reactive
organism or machine seeking food and, in season, a mate and
eternity. Add to this the implications of an opposable thumb,
manual dexterity, upright posture, an enlarged braincase,
stereoscopic vision, a capacity to fashion tools and put them
to use—and much else in particulars if you will. He or She
becomes a particular instance of two ways of defining the
generality of the human, the species. We may add much
more. To being as animal, and being as tool-maker and tool-
user, fill up the spaces with being as articulate thinker and

symbolizer, as dreamer, myth-maker and artist, as rule-maker distinguishing right from wrong, as lusting for power, wealth, and the infinities of sexual gratification, as questing after the truth of things, desiring harmony, order and whole-ness. . . . A few words, a shape, some colors and disputing their meaning, separate Him or Her from the rest of creation.

Elevated into definitions, the descriptions overlap: other words could be used to contain the same substance. Look at this He or She through the lens of any one of these definitions and we see what is particularly so in relation to what is gen-erally thus: an animal, participating in all that is animal—grunts, gestures, appetites, excretory functions, poses, facial expressions—like a gorilla or baboon, but denied the felicities of animal innocence. A cultural creature, able to symbol, ar-ticulate memory and inferences, associate discrete events and experiences, communicate within the limitations of conven-tional and bounded idioms, and able to arrange for the future. A moral being, aware of articulate discriminations between right and wrong, knowing the meaning of murder and mercy, necessarily involved with others, capable of reaching beyond the given into new moralities. A spiritual being, struggling in a coil of contradictions to grasp the truth of things and realize a harmony between inner and outer condi-tions. Integrating the relations between animal, cultural, moral, and spiritual components, a religious being appears, trying to order the truth and finding the truth in order. Dis-tribute the lenses to teams on the circumference and a won-drous rainbow of attributes begins to emerge at the center. In so many ways He or She is particularly so in relation to an equal number of ways in which the generality, being logically ordered, is more precisely thus.

Integration of the common and general makes anyone someone, a person, anchored in an identity where others have been but, because the self's integration is unique, swinging to the cable as none have done. Though the substance of a sepa-rate and indivisible reality is usually reserved for one's own self, one's I-ness, a presence in another which is neither com-

mon nor general can often make itself felt at once. Awareness
of such presence is usually at the level of the animal—in the
eardrums, through the skin, in the belly, the liver, the heart,
some sense beyond or beneath the articulate, and variously
identified and located in the parts of the body. Translate this
into an intuition through the self of the I-ness in another
within a perception of the generality of known you-nesses—
and it is still a peculiar integration of generality that strikes
one as singular. For as soon as we attempt to rationalize the
singularity, the given cultural categories intrude on the animal as well as the intuitive, revealing only another integration
of the common and general. Sometimes the *I* that is me, and
which makes me a little different from you, might be somewhere out there on another planet: utterly distant from the
world of empirical appearances, the categories of culture, and
people who exist, have existed, or will exist. Is there really
nothing beyond what is common—a void, a ringing nullity
muffled by the name and a collection of categories? Cling
therefore to the genes, clamors of life implementing the potential of their immanence and driving the brain become a
mind into considering the means of their integration with the
social. Yet from time to time, in moments of truth, the quality of the uniqueness in the *I* seems to reside in each one of us.
We think, we will, can realize our freedom or see our own
deaths with dread, astonishment, or equanimity.

As a quantum of energy indicated by a loss in weight at the
moment of death (Carpenter 1912: 184-86), or as genes realizing their latency in an awareness of being through orderliness,
the self is easily construed into life-stuff or soul or spirit or
image-maker. As often it is compressed by culture and the
erosive actions of others so as to seem no more than their im-
print. Yet, limp in the soil of one order, the self may flourish
in another. An intrinsic processual reality, the self is an energy
as capable of transforming its environment as it is liable to be
ground and stamped in its likeness: an imperfect but imaginative machine whose output may repeat or transfigure the in-
put. Culture presents its images and nets the responses in its

thought-tracks. If consciousness can register a different awareness, its expression and communication must needs conform to cultural moldings. An original image forming in the *I* and integrated in the self is pressed into conventionally articulate shapes—requires a gasp of astonishment and wonder, a medium looser than words and their logic to communicate its truth to itself. Then may the words give chase and try to contain it.

Take away the order or confuse it with another and the demons rush in: encapsulation, convulsions, culture-shock—some sort of insanity results. Being becomes nonbeing. Since nothing connects, no purposes and no causes are revealed, nothing can matter. Without forms of order to integrate there are simply inchoate sensations, seeking order and form. The genes are still there, images and thoughts occur. But, like an unattended radio between stations, they become counterpoints reflecting each other in an infinite regression into nothingness. When everything connects with and converges in the self, when the self attempts integration of everything, only the exceptional survive. Each kind of muddle cries madness. Identity stabilizes, is an ordered subtraction from the full force of all the categories which intersect in a human, identifies sanity. Though the self which is a bundle of integrated clichés can scarcely appreciate in another more than a reflection of itself, condemning the deviant, it is someone, one with identity. The self which is not a bundle of clichés, whose integration of the categories is uncertain, may be either more or less than someone: no one or anyone. And because less than secure in identity, and so affirming its dependence on others, such a self may reach into and revive an ailing other, briefly implanting an image which may grow. So each may nourish the other to become members one of another.

Because some selves do not wholly integrate the categories which yield an identity, and because there are selves attempting an integration of categories which do not match or whose content has not been grasped, interacting selves modify, transform, and so learn from each other. From such interac-

tion is born an awareness of the categories that clothe and
often disguise particular selves. In that interaction each self is
poised to change and reshape the categories even though the
latter are resistant and may have bonded the self, determined
the self as a bundle of clichés. Anyone becomes someone, a
person, in virtue of mutually acceptable exchanges with those
who have a defined identity. What is exchanged—a message,
an emotion, a good, a service, an idea—has a general and recognizable currency, a place within an order that the exchange
itself reaffirms and reestablishes as proper. Though the manner and style of negotiating an exchange reveal selves in interaction, they are dominated and bounded by rituals and
routines of form and procedure without which we would not
know what to do with ourselves. So selves tend to merge
themselves in the social matrix and seem invisible, imprisoned in the categories, sociological nullities. Yet as a nullity
the self is not nothing at all but as zero: that which makes a
calculus possible. In the interactional event between selves a
self which is not properly integrating the categories, or which
is attempting to integrate hitherto unsuitable categories, may
seize on what is as yet inexplicit or anomalous or strange and
move from the known and prosaic into a mysterium. In that
moment new apprehensions may root, new principles of
order may be implicitly recognized, articulated, or retreated
from in doubt: the self, not integrating in conformity, becomes a no one attempting to become a new kind of someone.

A thing produced or appearing in the mass, such as a motor
car, may be recognized and distinguished from others by the
ways in which the constitutive parts, which are general and
common, are put together, colored, and integrated. Identity
arises from the mode of integration, a statement only too easily transformed into an intuition of a particular kind of
motor-carness within. Similarly, the integrative energy of the
self tends to become the particularity of something within.
Tradition demands its tribute. Still, apart from the Christian

inheritance which identifies that something within as the soul, is there any other warrant for our attachment to the single life? Allport (1955: 35) writes: "The crying, rejecting, and anger of a young infant, as well as the negativistic behavior of the two-year-old are primitive indications of a being bent on asserting itself. All his life long this being will be attempting to reconcile two modes of becoming, the tribal and the personal: the one that makes him a mirror, the other that lights the lamp of individuality within."

If the interpretation is redolent with traditional assumptions, every ethnographer has observed the behavior and noted differing responses and interpretations. Nevertheless, at least provisionally, let Allport's words stand. A unique combination of genes, an infant is seized of its own intrinsic and independent springs of action and demands its autonomy over and against not only other organisms like itself but—and this is surely the meaning of "tribal"—also over against that set of common categories and expectations into which it is born, and which will mold the person. Particularity of being is attached to the organism *ab initio*. Other people and a set of cultural categories are the soil in which the organism will grow, develop, and become someone, a person. Later perhaps, as the critical faculties become creative, it may become an individual. The enabling energy, whether regarded as ultimately gene-given or God-given in the soul, appears as the self. When a human being is helpless and, like a vegetable, unable to say or do, it is surely this energy (and what may lie behind it) which we seek to maintain against all economic rationality. It is sacred, the fount of psychic growth and creative possibility.

In seizing on the product of this creativity, so giving to culture and the social order an objective and impersonal impetus derived from the interactions of persons, creators imprisoned in their creations, sociology outlines the rules and topography of the prison. Maintaining the prison itself, albeit suggesting different topographies and rules, becomes important. And again the product constrains the creators. Paradoxically, however, sociology was born of and participates in the tension between accepting the constraints of given categories and that ability to be free of them which will yield the apperceptions necessary for criticizing and changing the categories. Resolving the tension requires a peculiar and fruitful exercise of the imagination to widen or renew the categories, an attempt to go beyond current cultural instructions and, by means of an insight derived from the event, bring the categories into line with the self's experience rather than subordinate the latter to the former. In a word, resolving the tension requires that its moments be transcended. And Allport provides a point of departure. For the substance of his position, a peculiar expression of the European heritage, is that there exists within each human being an energy which, capable of adapting to culture, may also modify it. Further, this energy, the integrating self, seems to converge in that "coordinative condition" in which Whyte (1965) centers his description of the internal factors in biological evolution. Call it by any other name, a unique combination of genes together with a unique experience of the cultural environment must yield insights whose integration defies total social or cultural conditioning.

To transpose the idiom and put the implications more forcibly, the integrating self, one of whose aspects appears as Allport's assertion to autonomy, contains an innovative potential which, when seized with a contrary or critical perception, is capable of changing the conditioning. Moreover, this innovative potential cannot but be intimately connected with the assertion to autonomy. But if we take the assertion to autonomy to be a universal which different cultures view and deal with in their several ways, so that the logos which subsumes the latter is anchored in a universal human trait, we have to consider how it fits in with two different and opposed theories of society. For in assigning a primacy to the self and the assertion to autonomy one invokes a theory of society which regards the biological organism as the agent of truth and change; which sees society as composed of people, biological organisms with cultural proclivities and capacities; and which conceives the lineaments of the social order as the resultant of the interactions of the articulate organisms involved. A geneticist, proto-historical, evolutionary, and extensionist theory of society is evoked. The general pattern of Genesis and other myths is given expression in another idiom. The basic assumptions of the social contract theories of the enlightenment emerge in slightly different clothing. Society and social being become products of the interactions of selves and assertions to autonomy voluntarily or enforcedly relinquishing a pristine sovereignty for a variety of (social) ends.

On the other hand, it can be argued that a society or social order must be accepted as a given fact in its own right, historically and logically prior to the biological organisms which may comprise, embody, and be imprisoned by it. Society consists not of people but of categories, a complex of rights, obligations, and ideals which people may attempt to realize or subvert. Human beings are born into the categories of culture, and the hierarchy of categories—which may change over time—determines their interrelationships. Human beings are by nature social; the single instance of the species is to be derived from the categories by which members of a social order understand one another and the ordering of their interrelationships. Louis Dumont makes the point succinctly. After showing (1965b: 86-91) that in Western society the biological entity is that which is normative, empirical, and valorized, and so the normative principle, the agent or subject of institutions such as private property and the state, he goes on to suggest (p. 86) that the normative principle in India is the holistic idea of *dharma* or order in which, though particular humans are the agents of institutions, the individual as Westerners understand him is absent from all institutions save one: the sanyasi. Further, in the caste system the smallest ontological (or normative) agent is that in which order, as hierarchy, is still present: that is, when there exists a pair of higher and lower empirical agents complementary to each

other in a particular situation (p. 91). And then, since transmigration is integral to *dharma*, "the particular being acquires
a reality only by epitomizing in succession the sum of particularities found in the world; a chain of existences is the
equivalent of a single, individual, existence in the west"
(p. 91).

Nevertheless, as between taking departure from the potential inhering in biological organisms, people, which must in
evolutionary terms come before culture and its categories,
and according priority to the word, the categories and rationalizations into which the animal is born, made human,
and which predate and survive him as society, the existence
of the assertion to autonomy remains inviolate. The self,
whether thought of as constitutive and therefore containing
the assertion to autonomy, or as some sort of independent entity, mediates the tension between the proclivities of the organism and the constraints of others and the cultural categories. If those who go along with, for example, William
James (1901-2: 492) in asserting that "compared to the world
of living individualized feelings, the world of generalized objects which the intellect contemplates is without solidity or
life," find it difficult to controvert the view that the cultural
categories exist in their own right and guide us and "think us"
in all we do or say, the resolution of the contraries may be
found in the self: that which integrates the given categories
into an identity and which is also, through the assertion to autonomy, poised to change them.

When Dumont (1967: 226) writes that instead of studying
societies, anthropologists and sociologists have been projecting their own notions of the individual onto other cultures, he
touches the heart of the matter in a perhaps unintended way.
Individuality creates and also attempts to mediate and resolve
the oppositions implied in and flowing from the two views of
society. It asks not only, "What are the rationalizations, categories, and concepts that make up a society?" but also, "How
does History happen?" By adhering to extant rationalizations
in which familiar events are caught, new or strange events,

which must occur in the area of a mysterium, pass us by for ever. History is made by the new or strange event which, not or improperly rationalized and therefore unstructured, a zero, is perceived and recognized by the self, brought out of the mysterium and, captured in a new rationalization, is made to count. Without persons to realize and act them out, and without untoward events by which individuals may criticize them, rationalizations seem as unreal and—in that sense—as distasteful as Plato's *Republic*. The intellectual aspiration to the elegance of order as well as its repugnance for a disorderly mysterium and the flux of events are overcome in the perception that truth lies closer to the currently unordered than to the currently ordered.

3   PERSON AND INDIVIDUAL

Representing two quite different levels of experiencing and interpreting the social environment, "people" and "society" yet converge in or are mediated by the event. Events enable us to understand who people are and what they are doing in relation to the sociocultural categories which make up a community or society. Through events, which can only be relevant and understood or misunderstood in relation to their rationalizations, we can perceive what is happening, recognize people who do or do not fit into the identities prescribed by the categories. That which is rationalized or intellectualized or symbolized, whether the medium is painting, sculpture, music, technological device, or, most importantly because most specific, words, may be taken to be an event whether what occurs is a happening, activity, thought, or statement: the relationship between an event and its rationalization may occur at different levels, is itself relational according to the situation. Though given or traditional rationalizations may lead people into appreciating and even experiencing events, an event itself is experienced by the self and becomes an event in the awareness which, seized by the event, is moved to rationalize the concurrence.

In most social or cultural ambiences the repertoire of recurring events and rationalizations becomes familiar and well known. Without new events which need new rationalizations, traditional or given rationalizations tend to a certain rigidity, are or seem to be in keeping with the truths of experience. And it can be said of such situations, or of societies in which such situations are general, that events are generally subservient to their rationalizations ($E < R$): new events are either not perceived or smothered in traditional rationalizations; possible new relevances to familiar events fail to make themselves known. Conversely, it can be said of situations or societies where there is a readiness to rerationalize, or in which rationalizations vary or change in relation to the same sorts of events, that the event is more important than the rationalization ($E > R$). And, as will be seen from examples in later chapters, such proclivities arise from features of the social organization. For the present, however, it suffices that reiterating the given or traditional relationship between event and rationalization points to the person. For the person, a traditionalist firmly locked into the formal properties of his community, given rationalizations are more important than the event: new events and new relevances to familiar events are thrust aside. On the other hand, engaging a dialectic between a traditional rationalization and the relevances perceived in a new event or the hitherto unperceived facets of a familiar event is peculiar to the individual and individuality, and evokes a movement into new understandings and fresh rationalizations: new truths become immanent.

The event and its rationalization are crucial: the relationship discriminates between a reproduction of the given order or structure on the one hand, and the critical attempt to define a new and emergent or possible structure more in keeping with a perception of the truth of things on the other. Assertions to autonomy, working against the processes of socialization which create the person, are opposed to and negate a given moral order. They incubate the individual, but they also give rise to mere nonconformities, arrogance, the criminal, or the insane. What distinguishes the individual from his likenesses manqué is a stand on a truth revealed or perceived in the event; positive moral concern springing from a grasp of the truth of things; the transformation of gross negation into moral relevance—something on behalf of others, possible only through participating in their beings. From these comes the negation of a given moral order so as to realize another more in keeping with the perceived truth of things, rationalizing new events and rerationalizing familiar events so as to bind the moralities firmly to the truth.

Consider briefly puberty and adolescence, linked as they are to marriage, birth, and death: a cycle describing the elementary bounds of physical and moral being, modeling the moments of all our renewals. Hedged about with ritual activities and axioms and assumptions about their significance, birth, puberty, and death are alterations in animal or biological condition heralding moral changes or transformations. They are focused in marriage, a moral event in which sexual access, reproduction, the division of labor, cultural continuities, and the more general relations between men and women are brought together. The sociocultural activities and procedures attending each of these events emphasize traditional categories of understanding, and seek to ensure moral stability and the continuities. Puberty and adolescence reflect physical birth as moral rebirth; and death, never simply an animal finis, reverberates in inescapable truths, immortalities, rebirths, and moral opportunity. Marriage is a new status for two, is itself a moral rebirth, affirms responsibility, produces legitimate births to continue life's cycle into puberty, adolescence, marriage, and death. Yet if biological evolution is any guide, it is precisely at these moments when alterations in animal condition and proclivities are being processed into the traditional continuities that moral changes and transformations may occur.

A human babe is born into the world like an animal, yet is seized of a unique constellation of genes, some sort of selfhood (and/or soul), and at least the germ of an impulse to assert its autonomy. Socialization begins at once: in contact of body skin, in fondling, cuddling, and feeding. As the assertion to autonomy develops, socialization becomes the more explicit through punishment, rewards, example, and exhortation. But throughout, present in a myriad events, the effective socializer is love, all but caught in as many rationalizations. If there is no love in the first days and weeks of skin contact and handling, the assertion to autonomy is likely to run wild, to come under control only through coercion. With love, the assertion to autonomy is invited to realize itself through others. Exercising the cultural faculties, capacities to communicate, memorize, and symbol articulately are led into the prescribed moralities. Events are experienced, and experience is explained by reference to the cultural categories, or by reference to life in nature which is given point and relevance by the cultural categories. Given a name, kinsfolk, and membership of particular groups and associations, identity is established through an intersection of common or general categories. This identity (or identities), integrated by the self which is the only authentic continuity, changes and develops as the child matures, becomes accustomed to stepping out of one role or status into another, puts on the person, and eventually marries and accepts the responsibilities of parenthood and community affairs.

At puberty, signaling a radical change in animal condition, the assertion to autonomy is expressed in a variety of forms of self-willedness. Yet this last is only partly due to the release of animal energies. For apart from controlling and suppressing these energies through some sort of *rite de passage* which usually includes physical ordeals, mutilation, and a traumatic educative process, few cultures know what to do with this perhaps prolonged and potentially productive liminal period of adolescence. The shortest route to a formal bestowal of moral responsibility followed by marriage—thus presuming adequate socialization, making youth or maiden responsible and legitimating retributive action—is the commonest solution. Then all those discriminations between right and wrong, into which others and the categories of the social order have led the apprehending cultural faculties, begin to make their real impact. Nonconformities tend to elicit unpleasant reactions from others, bring trouble, pain, loneliness, suffering, punishments, and even death: not simply physical death but the termination of varieties of social or cultural—principally moral—being. On the other hand, those who conform earn prestige, wealth, honor, and respect.

For many, moving from one given status to another and filling out the sum of the conformities made available by the culture constitutes the good life, the realization of wisdom. With a little luck, the benevolence of the gods, and a better than average share of health, guile, cunning, foresight, and the capacity and opportunity to work, happiness might be added to wisdom. For a few a further maturation is possible. Exploring their animal nature in the light of the associative faculties which culture affords them, becoming wholly aware of their animal being, they may be able so to fuse their animal being with their awareness of the cultural possibilities that, transcending the normative moralities while in conformity with them, they may achieve that harmony of inner and outer conditions which indicates the spiritual. Thus the person, wholesome and admirable. The individual, like the person, attempts to fulfill the available categories but should subject them and the moralities to the criticism of perceived truths, test their correspondence with the real. And the conflict entailed in the critique tends to preclude a harmony of inner and outer conditions even though precisely this is being sought.

To most Westerners, conception, like birth, is an animal event. But it is neither clearly observable nor regular, predictable, ordered. Inferences and assumptions about its occurrence and significance in relation to the social order form a rich matrix of science, dogma, and mystical lore. Biological and cultural continuities are involved. Why am I here, why should I be here? If by design, whose design, and what am I supposed to do with this gift of life? If by accident—implying design elsewhere—or simply existentially, what can be done with life? Most people look to the cultural categories for their answers. And since for the vast majority the answers have been supplied before the questions are put, they accept and conform with them. Puberty is within the personal experience of each adult, who can draw upon the experiences of other adults, observe it taking place in the young, talk with them, and reflect on the nature and significance of what happens. For most, however, the pubertal experience of being born into adulthood, new cultural vistas, and wider moralities is the only cultural rebirth ever experienced. *That* experience, freeze-dried and becoming less and less adequate as time rolls on, more or less suffices them to the end of their days. Others continually reexperience the pubertal transformation in a spiral of deepening and broader awarenesses, developing in themselves what culture has to offer. An individual may do no less, but questions what is available and asks for better. The conflict may result in confusion, madness, criminality, withdrawal, or a sacrifice on behalf of others.

If the experience of birth could be recalled, astrologers might be in even greater demand. As it is, the time and date of an appearance recruit a pattern of stars to plot a course through the interstices of an intuited image of society's spaces, shoals, refuges, and treasure grounds. And even though accumulated observations of pregnancies and births related to the experience of cultural rebirths can provide an imaginative inkling of what physical birth is possibly like—even pressing back through time to the moment of conception—the mystery remains. Parents provide the genes—but why that constellation, why then and not under some other star? So tales are told, webs of belief and conjecture spun. Without them culture would be sparse indeed. If we could remember and know how and why we put on flesh there would be little need to know much else. As it is, even to say that there are no reasons why anyone should be born is in itself a conjecture, a theory or tale of sorts: each fate demands its ordering at both personal and collective levels. For though creation and life may be a steady and continuing process, they are experienced as a beginning, a developing, and ending. If the human begins and ends as spirit, he or she is experienced as a dream or image, and then as an animal whose developing awareness discovers morality and may reach into the spiritual. With an awareness of self and other, quickly reversible into other and self, reciprocity, morality is born then amplified and extended in the process of socialization. At puberty the accumulated oppressions of culture and socialization reach a climax: the self's autonomy must be asserted as truth—only to be swiftly resocialized in the presentation of rewards and pains. Between truth and its experience, culture, both obstacle and vehicle of truth, interposes its systems of roles and statuses, its prescriptions and rituals which selves become persons seek to honor in spite of events and impinging realities. What has created them, they in loyalty recreate. An individual is aware of self and the selves of others. Alert to events which seem to negate the given order as good, he seeks to revise and redraw the cultural program so as to make it more vehicle than obstacle.

The restructuring of animal condition which is entailed in animal transformations is accompanied by quite different perceptions of the environment: additional or different animal capacities make the environment other than it was. And in ordering these transformations culture tricks them out with relevances that have to make some sort of sense in relation to lives that will have to be lived. Reflections on the miracles of conception and birth tour the circuit of extant rationalizations in wonder and return to given procedures. The bubbling images and energies of puberty are expended in apparently pointless escapade, then focused on marriage, work, and the advance in relative status. Death brings a pause—cut short by rituals in which claiming and maintaining status become paramount. The arrow of human potential wobbles in the wind of morality, the pressures to conform are strong. Sharing the given relevances of the events brings satisfactions, warmth, and contentment. Nevertheless, because the events herald a beginning as the end and vice versa, the hesitancies and ambiguity of transition—smoothed over by cultural procedures and the moralities—present the opportunity for an awareness that can perceive the given moralities as diverging from, running parallel to, or bent around the truth of things.

The features of human animality and the cultural faculties have remained remarkably stable over historical time. Indeed, since particular spiritual conditions seem to be accompanied by much the same physiological states, just these stabilities may account for the transcultural homogeneities of spiritual and ecstatic experiences. But that exploration and awareness of the possibilities in human animality which, when leagued with the cultural faculties, may transform the animal into spirit, is only for a few: they realize the self by harmonizing their animal and cultural awarenesses within the given moralities. The energies of the assertion to autonomy are mastered, channeled into the stillest of lakes. The moralities, on the other hand, are the least stable of the components of being, and subject to change. And particularly has this been so in the European or Western experience. Yet vehicle for the reach into the spiritual though the moralities are, they can also obstruct. Their burden of eternal truths is light, the litter of illusion considerable. Small wonder that the individual, reliving the pubertal experience on a further plane of maturity, is so concerned for them. His the plunge into truth, the revitalizing of the religious impulse from which the moralities take their departure.

Centered as they are in marriage and political life, however, on the maintenance of roles and statuses, the moralities remain all but immune to the dreams and imaginative dramas that would change them. Trimmed to the contingencies of political power, the allocation of rights and duties, the conduct of exchanges, commerce, and industry, the regulation of sexual activity, the routines of raising new generations, the protection of life and property, the moralities bring pattern and order to what otherwise might be chaos. It is an order negotiated and mediated to be sure. But it carries the impress of those with power in positions which tradition has established. Organizing the cultural faculties, the moralities make life regular and predictable, offer the opportunity for righteous indignation and self-justification. They are the referents for most of our thinking and doing, they restrain and recapture the imaginative impulse that would go beyond them. If, for most, maintaining the normative moralities seems reason

enough for their existence, for the individual the same moralities exist to be improved, changed, or transcended. Drawing
on the experience of events which have transformed him, he
wishes to transform in his turn. Hence that concern with
moral problems which others might shrug off with an epithet
or night of carousal. Hence, too, the concern for rearranging
and transforming the roles and statuses which make up the
political order. In Plato's footsteps, the individual seeks an
ideal morality, one in closest conformity with what is perceived as real and true.

Birth, puberty and adolescence, marriage and death form a
life-giving cycle in which the person, moving into given roles
and statuses, is emphasized. Nevertheless, the events of the
cycle allow an individual to criticize and rerationalize. Paradigmatically, however, a set of roles and statuses is indicated
by the referents *someone*, *no one*, where anyone and everyone
either mediate or are inclusive. And the critique of the logic of
a set of given roles and statuses, arising from the experience of
events in relation to particular roles and statuses, must involve a no one opposed to someone, a relationship which, it
has already been implied, is included in the relationship between individual and person.

"My name is Noman!" Odysseus' response to Polyphemus
echoes down the centuries. And Borges reiterates a theme
familiar in Western thought when he suggests that in Shakespeare there was no one. So, he intimates, the playwright was
able to participate in and articulate the beings of scores of
others. To become someone he had to become an ordinary
person of day-to-day experience—"a retired impresario who
has made his fortune . . . interested in making loans, in law-
suits, and in petty usury" (Borges 1967: 115-17).

Taking departure from certain assumptions and general relations which become grounded in sets of dyadic relations,
community life demands that the person be realized in terms
of the dyads in which he or she is involved. Formally, each
position or role contained in a dyad is realized in virtue of the

other: each is the means to the realization of the other, and the
ends of each are realized in the legitimate ends of the other.
Thus, for example, full realization of husband within the
dyad husband-wife can only be achieved if the interaction between them results in the full realization of wife. If the birth
of a child makes this more difficult, such is the burden of
community life: husband and wife must also interact within
the dyad "self and other parent-of-my-child." A person is
someone: a precise intersection of the common and general
categories prescribing the series of dyads, a combination or
permutation of category clichés. These yield an identity
which, readily identifiable in terms of the clichés, is also
unique in virtue of the integrating self. Possessed of a unique
constellation of genes, sensations, and experiences, the self
puts its stamp on the clichés but, because of the clichés, remains someone, a person. While singularity of being may be
found in a known and structured detachment from the dyads,
in a status insulated from the interacting roles and statuses of
the moral community, a no one is unstructured, does not fit
into the dyads, cannot be pinned to the given roles and statuses of the interacting community, is an imprecise intersection of the categories, acts variably, can have no certain identity. Being no one is, paradoxically, to be both many and
singular. Borges (1967: 117) imagines Shakespeare face to face
with God, asking why he could not be himself alone. "From
out of a whirlwind the voice of God replies: *I am not, either. I
dreamed the world the way you dreamed your work, my Shakespeare: One of the forms of my dream was you, who, like me, are
many and no one*" (original italics).

An individual is not anyone, though anyone may become
an individual. The person, someone, may strip himself of
given roles and statuses, distance himself from the dyads—
thus losing identity—and, in moving into the unstructuredness of no one, may become an individual by extracting an
order from it. This indeed is the gist of William James's "Individuality is founded in feeling: and the recesses of feeling,
the darker, blinder strata of character, are the only places in

the world where we catch real fact in the making, and directly perceive how events happen, and how work is actually done" (1901-2: 492). From this area of the unstructured, where events happen and facts are made, person and individual, respectively precise and imprecise intersections of the common and general categories, enter an antithetical dialectical relationship arguing the truth to be reflected in the moralities. An individual thus both defines and is defined by the person with an identity (role and status, dyads) within a context set by what is conceptualized as someone and no one. Hamlet's soliloquy on being and nonbeing reveals the developing position. Neither someone nor no one nor everyone nor anyone, he poses the moral dilemma as one of conscience, and searches for the event whose relevance will impel the will to action, create being out of nonbeing, and put the self in command of the moralities rather than being subject to them or emasculated by them.

If there seems to be an implicit nobility in individuality, the ascription is subjective and selective. To the person an individual can be a misfit on a continuum from the inane through the criminal to the insane: a warped human being projecting his or her own disabilities onto society. But there is no reason why new moralities should not emerge from such disabilities. If the individual is likely to emerge from contexts where the moralities are at issue, the individual creates the issues which allow him to emerge. The many empirical expressions of the individual can be discerned in the light of the abstract but specific relations involved. Discovered in a movement toward the unstructured no one, an individual extracts order from the unordered by participating in the beings of many or everyone: the self and/or the assertion to autonomy bury themselves in the beings and interests of many or all. And this may be done by withdrawing from the scene to think through a dilemma specifically on behalf of others from some Archimedean point, or by directly participating in the beings of others through interacting with them. While the perception of a truth which casts its light only upon own being may develop the self, it invites a total and autistic withdrawal and so a denial of individuality. Lacking participation in some form, the individual drifts into insanity.

Individuality so transforms the person that, being more or less than someone but not someone, he or she becomes merged with no one, many, or everyone. The self in relation to the perceived event so permeates the person or social being as to achieve a distinctiveness which, being immersed in moral issues, is relevant both to persons within the community and to the apperception which seeks to understand that relevance. It may be supposed that, within the European or Western environment, it is within the potential of each person to enter into this distinctive structure of relations and become a "proper" individual. Indeed, our own day-to-day experience is well enough stocked with examples of ordinary persons who, either fleetingly or more habitually, stand on an event, proclaim its relevance and truth in relation to acknowledged sources of truth—a vision, revelation, biblical text, or "proven scientific fact"—reveal several faces, interact with others, criticize the social categories, and actively involve themselves in moral issues. But finding this structure in other cultures requires a model that is both abstract and down to earth: the former in order to effect some kind of transferability, the latter to retain concreteness and perspective.

The moments of the model, moreover, should be determined not so much by characteristics of personality as by specific and manifest relations. And this may be effected by considering the Hero. Odysseus, for example, was and is both concrete and abstract. As hero, he takes position as Hero. On the other hand, the heroine has become so much a mere adjunct to the hero (small case) that when, in ordinary discourse, a woman fulfills the necessary conditions we generally refer to her as Hero. Joan of Arc was no heroine but, like Odysseus, a Hero. Positionally, the Hero is he or she or that to which members of the community look. A Hero is a center of interest, a magnet in whose being others participate

or would like to participate, see themselves or would like to
see themselves. A standard by which persons measure themselves, the Hero is a means by which an aggregation of persons becomes a community, members one of another. Conversely, to maintain the position, a Hero must demonstrate
acceptable universals of being and thus become assimilated to
the beings of many or everyone. Moving toward the notion
of no one, if the Hero demonstrates that which is wholly beyond even the vicarious realization of members of the community, then surely the Hero must be truly no one.

No one is also intelligible in the Hero as symbol: a number
of disparate notions caught up and cohering in some kind of
concrete entity. Further, no one is again intelligible in the
human stripped of all rights and duties: a self only. Or in
those claims to extraordinary capacities and rights or privileges which make him or her a nonperson: monarch, lunatic,
or prophet, for example. Still, all these senses of no one may
be subsumed in the Hero. Though singular in the sense of
being one and not common, a Hero is the reverse of independent. The Hero exists and retains position in virtue of
what others perceive, accept, and value in the demonstration
of being. As a symbol a Hero should communicate the continuities; embody, reveal, and be perceived as overcoming
moral conflict; and contain latencies, the invitation to realize
that which is not yet explicit in the culture. As an event the
Hero is subject to rationalization, and to understand the Hero
is to understand the complexity of the social relations which
make up a community, as well as to gain an insight into the
possibilities of its future direction.

Although the structural relations between the Hero and
members of the community tend to remain constant, they can
change, and in any case their expressions are interactional,
governed by feedback and subject to change. Primarily a
figure of myth and legend, the Hero is an elusive reality out of
which varying moral discriminations may be woven. And
when moralized the Hero may become an ideal or embody an
ethic. Under a variety of names and in numerous guises He or

She or It draws boundaries between truth and illusion and becomes the instrument of their resolution. If the social categories and mores are often portrayed as illusions opposed to the realities of inspiration, dream life, perception, and physiological condition, the dangers of gainsaying the moralities are made evident. Discoveries of the heart, instinct and impulse are indicated as treacherous. Nevertheless, they may be superior to what mind and intellect can provide. The conscience which is slave to the given moralities is juxtaposed with the folly of that command over conscience through which a finer morality or truth may emerge. Conformist and innovator, it is intimated, exist in virtue of each other. The gifts of culture can only be renewed because preserved; new gifts come only when the old have been properly appreciated; the new is always dangerous. Power exists to be used to the fullest extent. But doing so destroys. Constraining power within the strictures of morality preserves the chaff as well as the wheat. Being different kinds of animals, man and woman have differing if complementary kinds of social being. Neither is solely privy to the truth of things; a man participates in femaleness and a woman in maleness. Apparent success in the given environment spells ultimate failure, and only in failure is truth perceived.

Such riddles the Hero, an ambivalent event, may resolve by being the fulcrum of the competing rationalizations of members of community, persons. A Hero encapsulates not the goody-goody but the many faces of being which, in the eyes of a beholder, can shock with cunning, outrage with ruthlessness, confound with simplicity, and appall with truth.

More familiar positions, which are contained within the figure of the Hero, may be recognized in partial analogues. Saint, hero, heroine, diviner, one with charismatic qualities, and leader may be added to monarch and prophet. These participate in, approximate to, indicate, and are measured by, the Hero. In greater or lesser degree they are expected to show forth at least some of the lineaments of the Hero, and, if they fail in this, activities are mounted to remove the pretender or usurper. Like the Hero, the analogues are distinguished and stand apart from the ordinary person in virtue of their ambivalences of being, their tasks of reconciling competing, divergent, and disparate principles and interests, and in the margin of innovatory and even currently nonmoral behavior that is allowed to them. On a lesser level perhaps, we may add to the list the mediator or arbitrator. Not given the same margin of deviance from a norm, the position still involves active and positive participation in different kinds of being and the reconciliation of competing interests. Unlike the Hero, whose existence is usually if not always at the level of the mythic or ideal, the analogues are embodied by living human beings who find their focus in social life when moral issues are in question. They must grasp the ambiguities and turn them into certainties.

Oracles, auguries, computers and such are apt to take on lives of their own, become decision-makers and thus relieve humans of the burden of their privilege. But the Hero, standing outside the moralities, nonetheless enforces a moral decision. Cutting through idolatry, the Hero demands that men and women decide for themselves, enter their crucial humanity and take the moral risk. Which is just what saints, prophets, and political ideologues feel called upon to do even though, so often, they lose direction, become confused, and cause confusion. Yet if heroes and the lunatic and mad are often counterpoints of aspiration to the Hero, a hero takes departure from the Hero, and the lunatic and mad are what they are because their indications of the Hero are inappropriate or ridiculous: the links between their cultural faculties and the given moral discriminations seem disorganized and random, do not cohere and synthesize but break and scatter in apparent chaos. The Hero's riddles, properly a framework for entering the unstructured mysterium and being transformed in understanding, become either a babel of despair or a comedian's quarry. The would-be individual who fails or declines the moments of the Hero often becomes a clown: an unstructured comic whose apperceptions reveal our pomposities and might-have-beens in a situation prescribed as safe.

Paradigmatically, the formal and overt structure of a society becomes evident in the activities and rationalizations of persons as they mediate and manifest their interrelationships in relation to criteria which measure what is right and proper. The opposed, complementary, and cooperative interests attached to identities or roles and statuses provide the generally cyclic dynamic. The latencies in the structure, the interplay between what is and might or will be become evident in the individual. To become an individual a person should abandon self-realization through the fulfillment of dyadic relations, cease to be the means and ends of the self-realization of those who reiterate the given structure, lose identity and, dissolving roles and statuses in the self, interact with all in ways that indicate that each is contained in all and all in each. Becoming thus an imprecise intersection of the general categories, the metamorphosed person is poised to enter into the moments of the Hero: singular and authoritative, yet enigmatic, a symbol manifesting and reconciling contraries and also latent with the promise of a new realization. But at this point, though the concern with morality is often heroic, the individual has to step aside from the Hero, stand on the event and pluck certainty out of disorderly ambiguity. The proper individual centers the components of being in life and the life-giving, seizes and is seized by the event, perceives the truth of things and, bringing the truth to order, steers the self and others into those new moralities—new modes of mediating and manifesting the right and proper in social relationships—which most clearly reflect the truth of things.

Such a statement about an ideal individual does not, however, comprise a set of purely autonomous activities. Without persons and the given or traditional categories and truths they manifest, the individual and individuality could not exist. Both the reiterations of the person and the reformulations of the individual are dependent on the continuities of memory which conserve those activities, events, and rationalizations of the past which exist in the present. And these memories, fixed in technological devices, or in stone, steel, wood, picture, or story provide intentionality, comprise the fulcrum upon which the otherwise existential becomes relevant, purposeful, in keeping with truth. For the person, traditional or given rationalizations contain and secrete truths which challenge the self's integrative and developmental capacities. For the individual the same rationalizations screen the truth: the properties of culture and the natural world interact with the self to produce fresh perceptions of truth; and fate, immanent in the event, must be reflected in new kinds of moralities between the self and other. Safe harbors and arrivals for the person, given roles and statuses become the individual's departures. Life's continuing unfolding flows with causation. And these kinds of causation, going to what are perceived as ultimate truths beyond those to be found in purely physical and mechanical domains, require assumptions grounded in faith and belief: some sort of essentially religious stance. Which, indeed, is the proper context of our European or Western notions of the individual. They were born of and developed in faith and belief joined to love and a reverence for life, the life-giving, and creative processes: the idiom of religion.

Criticizing the view that religions are simply defense mechanisms, Allport (1955: 96) identifies religious belief as the positive force "in the core and center and substance of the developing ego itself." And elsewhere (Allport 1960: 142) he writes that, "A man's religion is the audacious bid he makes to bind himself to creation and to the Creator. It is his ultimate attempt to enlarge and complete his own personality by finding the supreme context in which he rightfully belongs." They are good words. For where categories such as "domestic" or "political" or "economic" confine and exclude, the idiom of religion gathers together, is integrative or unitive, involves an effort to realize the whole of being. A religious act

or occasion brings together and integrates or unites into the
one situation or experience, at the private as well as at the collective level, all or most of the differing contexts of experience
in which the relevances of the interactions between the animal, cultural, moral, and spiritual components are to be
found. Integrating selves, using or caught by the cultural
faculties of memory, thought, reflection, and given modes of
communication, confront—in order to mediate or overcome—the oppositions between the animal and moral, the
moral and spiritual, and the animal and spiritual (cf. Burridge
1973b). What is thought about, communicated, integrated, or
united, how the oppositions are mediated or resolved, is to be
found in social relationships and their rationalizations, in *"the
redemptive process indicated by the activities, moral rules, and assumptions about power which, pertinent to the moral order and taken
on faith, not only enable a people to perceive the truth of things, but
guarantee that they are indeed perceiving the truth of things"* (Burridge 1969a: 6).

An established religion, comprised mainly of persons, is
discoverable through the moralities, those consensual discriminations between what is "good" or "proper" and "bad"
or "evil" which, explicit or implicit, are to be found in the
systemics of social relationships within an ordered environment of events, experiences, and their representation in symbols, rationalizations, and intellectualizations. The authentic
religious impulse or stance is that which, engaging all the
components of being, moves toward a perception of the truth
of things in order to verify or question extant rationalizations.
More crucially—and here again the difference between person
and individual is touched—the creative truths and realizable
developmental potential of a religion, established or otherwise, are to be found in the spiritual life, in the latencies of
symbols and the moralities, in the spaces between experiences
of events and perceptions of truth on the one hand, and the
roles and statuses, rituals and rationalizations concretized by
socioreligious institutions on the other. A properly religious
statement is discovered in the rationalization which realizes

spiritual or psychic growth: the transformation that stems from temporarily reconciling contradictions in the categories of the social order, particularly those within the oppositions between the animal and moral, moral and spiritual, and animal and spiritual. Since, however, articulation of the truth of things requires a communicatory idiom, and a coherent and intelligible idiom assumes a pattern of moral discrimination, given truths (or assumptions) are reflected in the moralities and, if they are to be realized at the level of the collective, truths that are newly perceived must be formulated as new moralities. But the last cannot be done without first entering a mysterium of events and experiences distinct from the expectations predicated by the formal properties of a given social order.

Yet this is precisely what, in our terms, an individual properly does. He or she formulates, or is the agent for the formulation of, new rationalizations and new moralities. That is, to explore the constitutive relations of the individual is to come to grips with moral innovation. And this, inevitably in extreme cases, must lead into an examination of charisma and the charismatic: the individual participates in and may demonstrate charismatic leadership. But to get started on the road to moral innovation there has to be some kind of alienation, incipient or well developed, from the current categories; and expressions of this alienation arise from the assertion to autonomy. In turn, if alienation and the assertion to autonomy are not to result in negativisms, in isolation, egotism, selfishness, and varieties of deviance, nonconformity, and eccentricity, the self must seize or be seized by the event, perceive and be moved to articulate or rationalize the truth of things in the determination to persuade and share with others that what has been perceived does indeed represent the truth of things.

The truth of things is that which is perceived or thought of as governing being. Given a particular time and place, the cultural ambience prescribes the relationships and activities which, appropriate to the context, purport to realize or approximate governance of being. An outside observer, how-

ever, or one who reflects on the situation and its cultural prescriptions, may qualify, criticize, or even transform the given
with some such statement as, "The *real* truth of the matter is.
. . ." Allowing that where there is a variety of roles and
statuses involved there will be differing emphases, most
people, persons, take the criteria of truth to lie in the axioms
embedded in the cultural categories which guarantee the truth
of things. But for those who enter a critique of the cultural
categories, the truth or governance of being must lie
elsewhere. And the issue becomes how far the existing cultural categories do or do not correspond with the demands of
truth. And whether truth or its sources are represented as Deity, an intellectual construct, the promptings of the inner self,
or the urgings of spirits or ghosts, what is demanded of the
individual is that he or she respond to the pricks of truth,
question the given categories and look through and beyond
them to those other modes which will in fact guarantee the
truth of things. This is the sense in which an individual is or
becomes an agent of truth. Taking departure from the experience of the event, the self reintegrates the components of
human being in relation to traditional and new categories.

Given their sources or perceptions of truth, individuals
strive to change or restructure the environment of social relations. And where change and restructuring are in fact occurring—a situation implying varieties of alienation and perhaps
anomie as well—persons are more and more led into becoming individuals, only to collapse back into the person as the
situation stabilizes. In perceiving truth an individual becomes
aware of being experienced by reality. Truth and reality en-
velop him, invade his being. But this can hardly occur unless
given social roles and statuses are sloughed off, leaving the
self naked to the event. Rationalizing and communicating the
experience, however, is bound to reclothe the self in familiar
cultural forms. On the one hand the direct experience of the
event reveals the categories as illusory, on the other hand a
failure to communicate the experience in terms of itself points
to the given categories as authentic guardians of truth. Still,

standing in the truth itself is surely what matters—even though when we feel and are aware of doing so, perceive it, and then try to articulate it, platitudes pour out. Words, linked to and drawing meaning from familiar contexts, constrict and imprison us. The formal modes at our disposal become masters not servants. The event runs loose, the truth we had felt seems lost, perception runs aimless. All we can do is recombine the platitudes, analogize, choose fresh situations for illustration, attempt to qualify the formal modes. A new start is made. Once again images and words seem to reflect each other and we try to stop them from flying apart. The truth draws us and we pursue it. But we only discover it when it comes to us, forces itself upon us—while shaving, in ecstasy, in boredom, when composing ourselves for sleep. Nor, gloomily viewing the apparent cost in the hedonisms of happiness and contentment, is it always welcome. But we cannot in the end avoid it.

4 HISTORICAL PHASES

In summary fashion: failing to distinguish person and individual as opposed categories of thought and action centered on the assertion to autonomy and the integrating self, and the imbalance and often confusion between the experience of people on the one hand and of society on the other, may be returned to the sacral nature, in the Western tradition, of the human biological organism. And this, which we may contain in the formula, *mouth = soul*, indicates the union of flesh and word: an expression at once of Christian participatory values and the conjunction of an anomie with intellectual orderliness. Separating them in relation to the native experience of people and social relations, transforming that into the wider and more objective categories contained in an explicit intellectual construct or logos, and then moving over into another culture and epistemology to give that logos a more universal relevance, seems to have entailed a serial distancing in which the constituent parts of the living organism are lost to become, in Dumont's words, "essentially a norm of modern thought rather than a fact of experience" (1967: 230). Whether the dilemma is more apparent than real, discovering its moments requires some brief consideration of a few historical phases in the European or Western tradition.

In particular aspects, Greek drama and Greek life reveal a familiar opposition. On the one hand were those who, presented in a variety of guises but always constrained by their own reproductions of principles of character, qualities, and situation, were thereby subject to the processual logic of the interplay of their reproductions. Today, as step by inevitable step a Greek tragedy moves towards its conclusion, we feel a

fascinated estrangement. More accustomed to the expectation, hope, or fear that one of the characters will resolve the
situation by a startling initiative, we are nonetheless touched
by the appreciation that nobody will or can. The Fates command. We are presented with a representation of those who
are subjectively deluded into thinking they can modify or influence the conditions under which they live, who struggle
futilely in the grip of impersonal socioeconomic, evolutionary, or biopsychological forces much greater than they.
On the other hand there is the rough and tumble mêlée of
Greek life, of ambition, motives, envy, jealousy, and adultery; of plot and counterplot, initiatives seizing the event, taking risks, and riding or striving against the consequences. Reverse the terms with the orgiastic performances and the same
opposition is emphasized. In the platonic synthesis the villain,
the assertion to autonomy, is subjugated, harmony achieved,
anxiety excised. All except one—and he has absolute power—
are to be persons constrained within the dictates of a narrow
morality which, because of the inner logic of its harmony,
well known and understood by the one with power, yet has a
potential for improving itself.

If the more general Greek emphasis on the exterior constraints laid on human beings swung between satire, reconciliation with fate, and ideal, as it comes down to us through
Plato mathematical or logical harmonies and the possibilities
of harmony in social or human relationships converge in a
strictly policed and ironclad social order. Obedience and conformity yielded peace and harmony. In contrast Christianity,
born into rigid and punctilious Jewish and Roman forms of
law or order, was centered in that love of others which must
set at nought all those roles, statuses, and exclusivisms with
which forms of order clothe the self and fashion an identity.
The self (or soul) at one with other selves in spite of differentiating roles and statuses—this was the essence. And the living dilemma of effecting this was resolved in Pentecost: transcendence of the given law to realize that ideal state in which
either there were no laws or where all laws were in harmony

with loving participation. At bottom Christianity is antistructural, antiorganizational: it demands the transcendence of given moral orders; no one is a true Christian who is not resolved to transcend a given moral order; no social structure or organization is specifically Christian. But what is (and was) difficult enough to grasp when the social order is imposed from without becomes (as it became) much more difficult when the Christian community itself attains (as in history it frequently has) the power to impose its own order. In this conjunction and contradiction has always lain the corruption. Christians tend to define themselves less in reference to the transcendence of a moral order and more in relation to conformities—their identities and the maintenance of the coherences of the categories of the given order which define roles and statuses. The way out of the dilemma—to use free will, transcend the given, work towards a social order in which the mystical body is more nearly replicated—becomes the more dangerous as power grows more absolute and corrupt.

The medieval *societas* can be seen as a platonic adaptation: each single instance an integral part of the whole, a participant member of society, under the authority of a given office or body. But if some of the platonic movement towards a more perfect moral order or form of society was contained in the relationship between authority and the social order, the greater part was much more certainly and importantly contained in the soul (or self), free will, transcendence, and the mystical body. The errant biological organism with a soul was both beginning and end. Each human being, each mouth, was a potentially whole being, a universal, given the opportunity for self-realization in the Godhead (which encompassed all being) through a loving partnership with others. Plato's mathematical harmonies were translated into the harmony of love. In whatever manner traditional or extant social and political constraints might impinge, each soul was held responsible to the Godhead and was set the task of seizing the truth in an event and overcoming the disabling effects of particular and contingent rules and categories. While the institutionalized Church provided a ladder to political power, it was also a haven for those whose intellectual capacities and imaginations sought a transcendence of the conditions into which they had been born.

Whether in manual labor, the crafts, clerking, study, contemplation, or in pursuits such as law, medicine, teaching, research, and politics, entry into that part of the Church distinguished from the general laity enabled the gifted and ambitious to move out of the sets of restrictions imposed by politico-economic orders and the circumstances of birth and seek a future within a much wider range of opportunities. And, as the frequent millenarianisms indicate, where the organized Church was inadequate, local populations sought their own modes of transcendence. Since the ideal form of society was the Christian community, the mystical body with which the soul should be at one in love, social orders as they happened to exist were imperfect imitations which each soul, in a proper or improper relationship with the Godhead, and subject to revealed knowledge and dogma, could improve, ruin, or change. Still, the provision by the Church of worldly as well as spiritual opportunities, and the growing worldliness of the Church itself, were surely not unconnected. Certainly this combination, aided by the series of plagues which struck Europe both before and during the renaissance, decimating communities and bringing large-scale population movements in their train, completed the destruction of the medieval *societas*.

Following the plagues, the new learning, the advance of the renaissance, and its own growing worldliness, the Church found itself trying to preside over a very different Europe. Relatively closed local communities, classes, and associations opened themselves to each other. The ordered and compartmented medieval world, characterized by kin, group, and local memberships which determined position, work, and service, became a relatively open and competitive world in which the former conventions and rules governing the internal and external interrelations of particular segments and strata of society no longer held, and in which the enforcement of conventions and rules by particular authorities became less and less sure, more and more arbitrary. At a time of social and technological change, and of populations redistributing themselves, whether single instances put their trust in their stars or themselves, the securities of an identity which would bear them on life's journey hardly presented themselves. Whatever the "spirit of history" may have had in mind, people succeeded or failed to muddle through in virtue of contingent events and circumstances and their judgment of the motives and capacities of others. Such as it was, society offered no certain framework for action. Persons were forced into the likeness of individuals.

With the development of the reformation and counter-reformation authority and the guardians of morality were strengthened, rules became enforceable, the securities of an acknowledged identity were once more available. Yet it was still Christianity in its constituent and institutionalized denominations which provided the widest range of controlled opportunities for transcending the given for those without the preset advantages of birth and wealth. Nevertheless, though the power of the universal Church had been broken, and the narrower and stricter rules and moralities of the denominations substituted for it, conscience had been, at least overtly, freed from the constraints of the *societas*. The single instance as a sovereign entity beholden only to God had been loosed on the European world. One result was the proliferation of reformative or protestant sects. Another was the development of the idea of the single instance as essentially a loner who, for the certain benefits of association into communities, sacrificed parts of the primeval sovereignty that was his or her heritage. The medieval stress on sociality, on single instances realizing themselves in love within the community of Christians, the mystical body, had been an integral part of being beholden to God. These twins had now been separated. On the one axis the rationalizations of the renaissance and reformation began to cohere into new rigidities and dogmatics. Local and associational communities drew the boundaries of conformity more and more tightly—thus generating from their very stringencies the dissenters and deserters who either associated together to form new sects or became loners. On another axis, continuing change and instability generated would-be renaissance men, commercial as well as moral and intellectual adventurers, who sought their opportunities and prizes in the empty spaces overseas. There, whether as loners or as members of closely controlled denominational communities, they could be free from the interferences and restrictions of more powerful sects, churches, and political interests.

As social orders were established overseas, varieties of renaissance men could always move further into the peripheries and there find the freedoms of action in which they reveled. Others, reliving the biblical heritage, could go out into the wilderness to find the promised lands in which to build their model communities. Empty lands combined with an absence of kin and other continuities linking them to home became the substitute for those social spaces which renaissance man had made and in which he had found his opportunity. With the dawn of the enlightenment, among intellectuals rather than among ordinary folk, reason and rationality, epitomized in the ways of life and social relationships of the upper classes, became sources of truth, the bases of an immanent rather than transcendent faith. Where the medieval scholar had seen the rational as contained in the Godhead, in the enlightenment rationality became God. Yet it was not only the poor and dispossessed who took the further options of clinging to local mores and established religion, or moving out into varieties of millenarianisms or enthusiasms.

Just as established religion depends on continuities of social relationships, so the continuities of social relationships among most of the upper and educated classes of the enlightenment ensured for a while the adherence to rationality. Yet this faith in rationality was forced to accommodate universes of discourse which, during the renaissance, had already begun to individuate themselves. Moreover, beneath the crust of rationality and outside the ambiences of continuing rural communities, population movements and increases, coupled to events, were giving rise to new kinds of encounters which, in turn, entailed shifting and changing social relationships. Experiments and innovations in technology, new productive processes, and the growing demand for mineral resources brought together into communities people with diverse cultural backgrounds. They had to rerationalize their new and emergent social relationships in terms which would reflect the truth of things as they perceived them to be. Charismatic or millenarian movements were plentiful, symptomatic at once of the rejection of rationalizations inadequate to social relationships as they existed and of the attempt to discover new and ideal moralities which would be adequate not only to experience but to notions of the ideal community.

Though the intellectual construction of ideal social orders ran back in an established tradition through More, Bacon, St. Augustine, and Plato, a consensual reconciliation of the conceptual and operational problems involved was difficult. Conceptually, the liberty of the single instance and his equality with others ran in opposite directions; and different universes of discourse engaged from different viewpoints and strata of society gave rise to conflicting solutions. Intellectual, moral, and political continuities could only be opposed to schemes for drastic reform. Reconciling the stabilities of order with the creative possibilities in anomie, freedom with the oppressions of discipline, altruism with natural tendencies to egoism, and the ideal of at-oneness with the experience of alienation were, and are, hardy and continuing dilemmas. Lacking sophisticated political techniques, ideals and operational difficulties have usually demanded charismatic revelation and leadership: the attempt to resolve at a stroke both operational difficulties and the paradoxical ideals of being as gods, equal and free, yet subject to discipline and order in social and moral relationships.

In the Christian idiom such sorts of transcendence have traditionally required the inspiration of the Holy Spirit or its simulacrum. At the same time the social commentaries which have accompanied—and sometimes inspired—these kinds of direct action, have also sought to resolve the paradox at an intellectual level. More or less capable of being translated into courses of action, intellectualizations—in the shape of ideological tracts, discourses on human nature and the body politic, satires, imaginative utopian tales, and early science fiction—of both current conditions and those to be sought as an ideal, attempted soberly, and often bitterly or enthusiastically, to unravel and repattern the paradox rather than resolve it at a stroke. Whether hand in hand or in mutual distrust and suspicion, action and intellectualization have accompanied each other, are in their peculiar intertwining a part of the paradox contained within the Christian heritage: the attempt to reconcile the Incarnation, Resurrection, and Pentecostal experience on the one hand with the ordered logos of the Greeks on the other.

To transcend the shibboleths of a given man-made law, to affirm life, love, and the truth and then to act accordingly, either under inspiration and/or because it seems necessary in truth to do so, and at the same time attempt to see oneself, others, and that action and its implications not from an ego-centered viewpoint but, as God might—in an objective way in the light of a particular logos or intellectual construct—is written into the European heritage. Through Locke, Hobbes, Rousseau, and others, theories of the social contract attempted to intellectualize the contemporary situation in historical or proto-historical vein, seek the ills and disadvantages of the present, and then point to a hypothesized state of affairs which would (in effect) penetrate to the truth in events and satisfy the assertion to autonomy on the one hand and the need for ordered social relations on the other. The emphases were political and legal. What kinds of laws, enforced by what means and distributions of power in institutionalized forms, would enable the human being to realize the impulse to autonomy consistently with the reciprocal rights of others to do the same? Since human beings are political animals, and the political ambience at whatever level engaged is necessarily competitive—what kinds of political ordering would permit liberty to the single instance without injuring others? Within the general assumption that human beings were not naturally social but loners or independent entities who had entered into association only for their mutual benefit—what kinds of least damaging sacrifices would have to be enjoined on the single instance in order that the majority might reap the advantages of living in society? Much turned on the distinction between "society," which tended to be identified with hierarchy and a political order based on force and coercion, and the "association" or "partnership" which implied the surrender of autonomy and abiding by agreed rules and conventions.

De Tocqueville provided an intellectual polarization of extant solutions with his "individualism": "a novel expression, to which a novel idea has given birth" (1840:III: 202-203). And "individualism" was thereafter to become the homing point of quite distinct and even conflicting unit ideas (cf. Lukes 1973). In the generally hierarchically ordered European communities the values of the *societas* as well as the renaissance persisted: the former in the continuities of family, hierarchy, and denomination, the latter in political and mercantile opportunity. The individual as distinct from the person was recognized in spirituality, in the qualities displayed and brought to particular tasks, positions, and offices within the hierarchy, and in entrepreneurial success. But the special attributes of the individual were grounded in the person, went to particularities of interaction with kin, neighbors, friends, associates, rivals, and master or employer in relation to current and traditional categories. Though renaissance man might be admired, an individuality not quarried out of interactions with those whom, like it or not, interactions were obligatory, was only half won. In de Tocqueville's America on the other hand, a mobile, relatively scattered, and loosely controlled population dispersed over vast spaces made it possible—often incumbent—to live by oneself or choose one's friends and neighbors. As de Tocqueville had it (1840:III: 202-203) American individualism "disposes each member of the community to sever himself from the mass of his fellow creatures: and to draw apart with his family and friends; so that, after he has thus formed a little circle of his own, he willingly leaves society at large to itself. . . ."

In contrasting Aristocracy (in Europe) and Democracy (in America), de Tocqueville (Lively 1962: 71-93) uses continuity/discontinuity as his main axis. In Aristocratic conditions there are fixed hierarchies, continuity of families, social groups, and relations. Those who form the groups are necessary to each other, and the groups themselves, often competitive, are complementary and mutually interdependent. Chains of relations exist both through space and time. People see themselves as links in particular kinds of continuities, owe service and allegiance to their exclusive classes and groups, and regard mankind as a dim abstraction outside the range of significant comprehensions and effective interaction. In Democracies, on the other hand, the fixed hierarchies are absent, as are the continuities they imply. Service, loyalty, and allegiance are mobile, shifting with changes in circumstance and interest. Families spring up and die, the tracks of generations past become effaced. Though affections are extended further than in Aristocratic conditions, they are more relaxed, less imperative, and might in time wither away or cease to matter. Since each is free to follow his own bent, particular and selfish interests rather than inherited loyalties and allegiances to others become the guiding maxims.

Folding the contrast into the present theme and idiom, let us say that as between the impulse of autonomy and the claims of others, or the assertion of self and loving interaction with others, the single instance of universal value realizes itself as an individual in a variety of possible arenas determined on the one hand by the stable continuities of group memberships and fixed authorities, and on the other by the mobilities and discontinuities occasioned by a multiplicity of

interests, diffused initiatives, and changing sources of authority. On either hand, however, the lineage goes back through
the renaissance and the medieval *societas* to the Graeco-
Christian synthesis. Moving towards the achievement of a
more perfect and universal order through a transcendence of
the given, the pattern repeats itself in a developmental spiral.
It may be discerned in the tensions between the early Christian communities and the outer Roman world, in the contrasts between the relatively ordered modes of medieval
Europe and the more boisterous conditions of the renaissance,
in each millenarian, revivalist, fundamentalist, or revolutionary movement in European history. Shifting from person
to individual, the agent of criticism and change, the single instance is impelled to transcend the given and take advantage
of events to realize a new moral order. When that order is
achieved the single instances who have been individuals revert
to the person—and new individuals come forward to continue the process.

Those living in a tightly organized social order tend to see
that order as definitive and determinitive, something *sui
generis* which, conceptualized as "society," becomes something separate, more than the sum of its parts, even as though
deity. When in such a situation a single instance as an individual enters a critique, seeking to bring about change, to say
that he or she is the agent of change is much like saying that
he or she is being activated by "society." Which is to give
"society" an autonomous and mystical consciousness distinct
from the processual logic of its properties. Accepting that the
latter may require individuals to announce and initiate
changes—as European or Western culture does—the responsibility for doing so still rests on the single instance who risks
contumely and obloquy as much as admiration and respect.
An individual's critique arises from an unsatisfactory integration, consequent alienation from the forms of order as given,
and the positing of an alternative which will provide the opportunity for a more satisfactory integration. Single instances

both create and are created by the machine they serve. Conversely, those living within a loosely organized social order tend to stress the overriding importance of the single instance and the responsibility laid on him or her to maintain satisfactory relations with others. In this situation, the critique, arising as it does from unsatisfactory relations with particular people, comes as it were naturally—though of course the same circumstances render the critique less than readily acceptable to others. Still, instead of people's attention being directed to the machine, people are addressed directly. Echoing the native circumstances, European sociology has been characteristically sociocentric, emphasizing the experience of society, and American sociology has been characteristically egocentric, emphasizing the experience of people. Now, however, as North America has become more crowded, necessitating tighter organizations, the tendency is towards the sociocentric. But the tension between people and society exists and has existed on both sides.

For arrivistes and the established—whether high or low— the situational circumstances making up society tend to be not only rational but also the locus of life's mystique and sacra. For the mobile and struggling, the mystique and sacra of life tend to be located in people, in the anomie of events and the caprice of others. In a time of unrest, civil wars, and religious quarrels, Hobbes concluded (in effect) that the strength of the assertion to autonomy inevitably rendered man egocentric, self-centered, and prone to treat others as temporary means rather than permanent ends, and that man was, therefore, antagonistic to ordered society. Yet it is difficult to think how there could ever be a time of rest and tranquillity in a civilization founded on a union between the intellectual rationality of a platonic republic and the anomie of Pentecost. The Kantian solution, reaching to society, was still addressed to people: if people changed, society would change. Ironically, the clear moral and intellectual solution to the operationally most complex reciprocities underlying all human association could only attempt to realize itself in breakaway religious communities which emigrated to the spaces of the Americas.

Given the pattern-making and purpose-seeking nature of man wedded to the Christian notion of a gradual unfolding of the divine purpose, it was perhaps expectable that human caprice and apparently random events should also be perceived as epiphenomena indicating a developmental design. Working not from human weakness to the pretensions of contractual relations, but from the abstract idea to the empirical example, men and women and their social orders began to be seen as prisoners of the dialectical processes inherent in history. Yet not prisoners wholly. For though people were borne on events, it was demonstrable that history was spun from the significance perceived in some events at some times and not in other events at other times. Nailing this process to a materialist dialectic made sense. By his own efforts man might master the random and capricious and build a new earth if not a new heaven. Yet in denying that society and the single instance were mutually opposed, Marx was turning to at least a part of the model of the medieval *societas*. It was only in terms of society, his social being, that man could realize himself as an "individual" (quotation marks supplied as Marx, like most others, used the word as synonymous with "single instance" or person). Social being bestowed the virtues, graces, and faults which one thought of as distinguishing the human from the beast; changing society would change the man. Consequently, turning Kant on his head, what was needed was a transformation of those economic conditions which, in encouraging egoism and selfishness in some and oppressing most, alienated so many from what should be their most appropriate environment: participation by all in the whole for the benefit of each.

In thus equating the individual with the person with the further objective of constructing a society in which all were persons, Marx was echoing Plato. But, as Plato had made clear, achieving this required someone or some body or institution correctly labeled "tyrant." Exploring rather than ideologizing, Durkheim's separation of social representations (making up society) from people, and his emphasis on the systemic and normative nature of social representations, brought him the grief of most successful modes of analysis or exploration: its transformation into ideology. Such was the inherent ambiguity of "individual" that he was thought by many to be subordinating the single instance to the political order or state—so often identified with that much looser and more abstract hierarchy of categories understood as "society." And for this he was much criticized. He wrote, after all, in the heyday of bourgeois individualism. Yet (see Lukes 1969) in the maelstrom of argument that accompanied the Dreyfus case, Durkheim came out clearly to the contrary. The "individual," a relationship between society and the single instance, was sacred. To suborn or attack the individual (single instance) was sacrilege: an act leading to anomie and the destruction of the social order—which reveals Durkheim as less a scientist, who might otherwise have grasped that his civilization was one founded partly on anomie, than an ideologue desirous of order. If it has often been thought that Durkheim seemed to identify society with God, he, like Dostoyevsky (1871/1971: 257), seems not to have thought of himself as reducing God to society but as raising man to God. "Just as each of us embodies something of humanity," he wrote (Lukes 1969: 26), "so each individual mind has within it something of the divine, and thereby finds itself marked by a characteristic which renders it sacred and inviolable to others."

In his use of "divine" Durkheim must in spite of himself have meant something very like the soul. And his separation of actual living beings (people) from the ordering of their social relationships made evident in social representations (society) corresponds with his implied separation of the "divine" from the single instance as a person. Nor is either set of relationships one in which one term is necessarily subordinate to the other. Yet if there has always been some confusion on the point, the ambiguity seems in part at least to stem from the identification of "individual" with the single human organism, and in the failure to separate the "single instance" from the "special attributes." Individuality can be assumed, but not taken for granted. If, given the assertion to autonomy, the human organism and society are antithetical, becoming a person represents a reconciliation. Not unreconciled to society as such, the individual is targeted to a different kind of society, a new moral order. When that new moral order is realized or approximated, the individual reverts to the person and other individuals commence their critique. An individual thrives in that anomie, temporary or incipient, which is indicative of a moral order not in tune with the truth of things. He or she is authentic to a tradition based on a marriage between order and anomie.

Consider now Kierkegaard (1846/1955: 30-50). He isolated and identified: the "individual" (quotations supplied); the "individual" who was *extra ordinem, extraordinarius*, or, as it may be rendered here, the "special individual"; and the "man of movement" (quotation marks supplied). Kierkegaard's "individual" fairly corresponds with what is here called the person. The "individual" reproduces in his life the established order of things, is normal, regular, displaying in his existence the life of the universal. The established order is the basis of his education and development. But this does not mean that the "individual" is necessarily insipid or spiritless: such is simply the accusation of those who are evil-minded. On the contrary, the "individual" is free and independent *because* he reproduces the established order and displays the universal. And this he can only do by participating in the being of others, identifying himself with established ideals and social representations. To be such an "individual," continues Kierkegaard, is the highest qualitatively significant task assigned to every man. And if much seems to go begging with that "reproduction of the established order"—for it was precisely this, in Marx's view, that was stifling the realization of *his* individual—it is surely also implied that Kierkegaard's "indi-

vidual" is held open to change, development, and transcendence in the assertion that he (or she) displays (or should
display) the life of the universal. That is, lives according to the
truth of things. Which makes Kierkegaard's "individual"
rather larger than our person, impliedly including some
movement toward our individual. Still, if Kierkegaard is here
a little less clear than he might have been—and if he could
have been clear about the inherently ambiguous he would
either have been wrong or have destroyed the dynamic contained in the inherently ambiguous—his second and third
categories ease the matter.

He who is *extra ordinem, extraordinarius*, a "special individual," is one who reflects on the fundamental presuppositions
of the established order, refuses to follow the *impressa vestigia*
(*sic*, Kierkegaard 1846/1955: 35) or traditionally fixed forms of
the social order, and no longer reproductively renews in himself the life of that order. Instead, he stands apart, and out of
the bosom of his reflections and relationship to God he introduces new points of departure. Occupied with his relationship to God (the source of truth), classifying himself as im-
mediately under God, he refashions the moral order. He is
quiet in character, running deep, willing to make sacrifices
both for his own sake and the sake of the universal. He looks
for opposition, for pain and trial. But he is certain of his
stance, ethically unconfused. In the moment of refashioning
tradition he is excluded from the universal, stands alone upon
an Archimedean point outside the world, must conquer and
face judgment. Yet this judgment refers not so much to the
consequences of his thoughts and activities in human terms,
but is, rather, wholly concerned with the relationship to God.
Being one who makes his own discriminations without the
aid of others or society in general, he may take his extraordi-
nariness in vain, regard it as a glittering distinction, become
narcissistically obsessed with himself and so cause incompa-
rable confusion. On the other hand, through sacrifice, by his
own immolation, he reconciles himself with the universal.

So far as he (or she) stands alone, apart, and makes his (or her) discriminations without the aid of others, the "special individual" would seem to be a loner, nonparticipatory, and would not appear on the surface to enter into significant, particularly loving, relationships with others. Yet it could be argued that one who sacrifices himself must surely be lovingly interactional in the highest degree. And, as though protecting himself against the ambiguity, Kierkegaard takes pains to warn us that neglecting others is dangerous, something which leads to a pole quite opposite from that held to be desirable. Still, taking the point at face value, it seems useful to distinguish two general modes of engaging relations with others: positive and involved interaction; withdrawal combined with sacrifice. Let us add, for clarity's sake, sacrifice on behalf of others.

Kierkegaard's "special individual" clearly evokes the Old Testament prophets, obvious and prototypical individuals. He also reminds us of Max Weber's charismatic figure—one who is set apart from ordinary men and treated as endowed with supernatural, superhuman, or at least specifically exceptional powers or qualities which make him a leader and initiator of changes in the social order. On the other hand, Weber's charismatic qualities and powers could also be ascribed to Kierkegaard's third category, his "man of movement." This is the charlatan, the spurious "special individual," one who acts as though he were a "special individual" but who in fact has no real and lasting conviction, whose course is altogether temporal, in no way springing from a relationship with God or truth. That he triumphs—as he often does—convinces the "man of movement" that he was and is right. He is politically oriented, looks for supporters, is ever prepared to compromise such ethical principles as he may possess in order to gain support. That is, he shows himself to be ethically cynical or muddled. His problem is how to triumph and gain the victory. His means are referred to the criteria of success or failure. Such as it is, his ethic only acquires definition or certainty when he is either victorious or in custody. Perhaps, Kierkegaard suggests (1846/1955: 45), the "man of movement" might better be called a "stirring stick" or "muddler." It is characteristic of "men of movement" that they are confused, find their best ambience in confusion, are moved by worldly ambition. If all "men of movement" do not overtly claim to be head of a movement, few do not seek to become so.

Both Kierkegaard's "individual and "man of movement" are categories clearly recognizable as fitting particular men and women of our historical and own experience. The former is an ordinary person, an establishment figure attempting to realize to the full the categories which society has made available. In many small ways too, such a person usually also makes those further efforts which traditional Christianity asks of him or her as a proper individual: some small change in local moralities, some easement or betterment of the situation. The "man of movement" may be found in almost any European or Western community. Ranging from, say, renaissance-man and the leaders of political or social movements to small-town political hucksters, noisy clergy busy with social works, the firm's squeaky wheel, and even the habitual moaner, he or she is the "special individual" manqué, ambitious, embittered, and frustrated perhaps, greedy for power but, nonetheless, etching the moments of the individual as determined here. Kierkegaard's "special individual," familiar in the history of Western civilization as an ideal, is only rarely encountered in person. Each of us, maybe, knows someone who is quietly and perhaps obscurely "special" in this sense: an artist, a writer, a singer—someone whose imagination and thrust into the truth of things commands respect and induces a certain humility. But to communicate the lineaments of such an individual we have to turn to the heroic, to Old Testament prophets, the Christ figure, St. Peter, St. Paul, St. Francis, St. Joan of Arc, Martin Luther—men and women of religion, men and women dedicated to the truth of things.

Which is squarely to the point. The most important criterion of the "special individual" is the relationship with God, source of truth. And if this seems a relationship which an anthropologist cannot verify empirically, the problem is just as slippery in relation to alternative sources of truth. All that can be done is infer or approximate the nature of the relationship by examining the quality and direction of what was done and said in relation to what the source of truth is considered to embody, contain, or require. There is plenty of room for differences of opinion. Nevertheless, the category stands. There is sufficient that is plain and explicit; it provides a measure for considering degrees of success or failure in realizing individuality both in ourselves and in others. And although the overt expressions of individuality either within or outside the European or Western environment must differ with language, period, dialect, polity, region, locality, class, and profession, the difficulties inherent in such variety are overcome by going to particular modes of engaging the religious impulse: the continuing process of negating particular cultural categories and converting or transforming perceptions of the simple or more tangled truth of things into those ordered new moralities which invest being with new cause and purpose.

The foregoing brief and cursory foray has been entered simply to give the present essay a placement by putting an idiosyncratic twist on familiar landmarks in the topic. Most of the literature since the eighteenth century seems to contain a confusion between the "single instance of the species" or biological organism on the one hand, and the individual as a specific social category or set of relations on the other. As an "-ism" (see Lukes 1973), the idea (individualism) has done duty for anyone who has wished to enshrine or sacralize each human life, deplore the self-centeredness and selfishness of capitalism, recommend the virtues of socialism, or redress a perceived imbalance between the institutions of society and the rights, duties, and opportunities of each of its members toward one another. An ideal in this way for some, individualism has been the reverse in another way for others. For the main part the debate has centered on the moral implications of the egoism, egotism, and selfishness inherent in a sovereign

entity, and that loving concern for others which is neither
selfish nor interfering. Ideas and political movements have
generated themselves in response to motives which themselves only become explicit and self-conscious when the ideas
are analyzed and returned to their social contexts of origin and
development.

Following Hayek (1946: 7) and others, the individual as a
social category never was or could be a wholly sovereign
agent—though epiphenomenal and contingent expressions
might lead some to suppose that sovereignty indeed exhausted the relations. William James's (1920: 294) criteria of
"novelty" (seeking the new) and "progress" (in the moral
sense) hit the mark more closely. If Kierkegaard's "special individual" is to be found in withdrawal, this is specifically on
behalf of others and entails a sacrifice. As exemplified in the
medieval *societas*, traditional Christianity conceptualized (as it
still does) the human being as essentially social and interactional, affirming the world and those inhabiting it. The ideal
is that balance between the demands of society and the needs
of others which will enable each self, each human being, to
realize his or her potential within a given morality. But, since
the given is imperfect, realizing the ideal requires continuing
movements into new moralities more in keeping with the
truth of things. Despite bureaucracies, the impersonal relationships that go along with social mobilities, economic
selfishness, the decay of the soul, and a myriad pseudosci-
ences—which tend to make of human beings that which they
are not, biological organisms wrapped in more or less useful
job categories—it is still not easy for a European or Westerner
to maintain quite the same respect for a single instance who is
not positively prepared to act in the interests of a new morality acknowledged to be more consistent with the truth of an
event. Ethically confused though most of us are, we still value
the assurance that we are not.

The memories that still adhere to the word "individual"
and the political ideologies and moral orders that have
stemmed from contingently differing notions of how the rela-

tions entailed in being an individual should or might be expressed or realized in concrete activities—how, prescriptively, to engage the levels or components of being and the redemptive process—make up the central thread of our European or Western continuities of being. With each generation something is added, something is forgotten. We even go to the trouble of rediscovering and bringing back into our consciousness that which had seemed to have been forgotten. Accustomed to frequent changes in our social or moral orders, continually initiating and pushing developmental processes into new and different kinds of morality and categories of understanding, creating new heavens and new earths is a constant demand on our energies. Within the European cultural heritage the individual, always moving towards the falsification of given and accepted truths and the discovery of new ones, is the most immediate and ultimate agent of truth.

Because the social or moral orders of the European experience have not only differed among themselves but have been clearly transient in their particulars to their bearers, in themselves they could only embody and reveal temporary truths. More permanent standards of truth, whether conceived as God, Love, Law, Rationality, Science, Evolution, the Spirit of History, Coercive Differential or whatever, have had to be derived from the self in relation to others on the one hand, and, in moving from generally accepted truths, the perception and realization of new truths immanent in the event related to conceptions of absolute truth on the other. And it is of course that continual overleaping of the given but contingent categories of the moral or social order through a recourse to a source of absolute truth, perceived in the event, that has enabled Europeans to conceive of new moral orders. Howsoever impersonally and existentially one social order may be said to have yielded place to another, incipient change has been recognized by individuals, welcomed, persuasively articulated and rationalized. But the old categories and images necessarily keep impressing themselves on the new situation, perpetually transforming perceived truths into paradox and appearance. Through a variety of situational devices, poets, novelists, dramatists, and scholars have restated the paradox in a host of refractions. It is one of those fundamental ambiguities that pour their life and power into a dynamic dialectic between the self and cultural being which, transformed by the effort to articulate an understanding of it, becomes a dialectic between present being and the possibilities of new being.

If the individual coincided with or was simply an enlargement of the person there would be no paradox. Every culture may be presumed to offer opportunities for realizing the self: an integrative transcending or reconciling of the opposition between the behests of the cultural categories and the natural or biological proclivities. An individual is one who has experienced and been experienced by that event—physical, psychic, intellectual, or spiritual—which reveals the current cultural categories—and so the person—as false, illusory, not in conformity with the real truth of things. Attempting to articulate the experience indicates a movement from the person to the individual, a movement from apprehension to comprehension. In the European and Western tradition this movement is generalized and institutionalized. It is habitual, normal and, usually, followed by a return to the person:

$$person \rightleftharpoons individual \rightarrow individuality$$

Rooted in the religious impulse, the quest for ontological truths to be made manifest in the moralities, the moments of the individual may be summed up as:

$$(self/others) + (self/moralities) + (self/truth) \rightarrow individual$$

Even if truth and reality were nothing if not that which words and other idioms of rationalization reaffirmed as order or structure, the revelation of what that structure might or should be is articulated by one whom we call an individual. Given a source of truth, the individual is poised to transcend the cultural categories, defeat evil, and transform thought and the world.

From our own particular standpoint in time we can appreciate that much of the discussion about individuality has centered on how far what might be an expression of individuality is not simply an assertion to autonomy. This, indeed, is the built-in risk and danger in realizing the individual. And it often results in Kierkegaard's "men of movement" and their henchmen crowding the stage. The "special individual" tends to be lost in the tumult. And, since "men of movement" are ethically confused, when power is won it is not long before the exigencies of retaining power lead to treating people as though they were things, the means to and of power, mere tools. Neither Stalin nor Hitler nor Mussolini rose from the void. They were typical examples of Kierkegaard's "man of movement." They rose to power and eminence within a context of social confusion and heated intellectual discussion on the nature of the relationship between society and the single instance: people continually lost ground to society. Sociology and social or cultural anthropology, properly understood as born of the apperception of oneself and others as social beings (Dumont 1965a: 16), are or can be, to be sure, bridges of understanding and communication between one culture and another. Located in the platonic tradition as it is, however, sociology tends towards absolutisms, strangles itself in mechanical intellectual automaticisms, usually fails to apperceive the nature of the soul or spirit in the human, often becomes the ready-made blueprint for ambitious "men of movement." Our latter-day tyrants were brought down by people, men and women—mainly in the image of Kierkegaard's squarish plain "individual"—who responded to another, deeper, and more fundamental component of the European heritage.

In the end Dumont's stricture (1967: 226) that sociologists have been less concerned with describing societies than with projecting a sociology of the individual through the medium of other cultures turns out to be a paradox with more virtue than vice. Individuality provides the apperceptions which make sociology possible; sociology transforms individuals into persons, events into categories, and the chancy vicissitudes of real life into a logical order. In turn, because ideology cannot abide disorder, a discovered orderliness or its mode of discovery becomes ideology. Then, completing and restarting the cycle, the self as the locus of truth-perception in individuality challenges the ideology. Constantly moving from the person to the individual and back again to the person, the self is positioned both to idealize and criticize. Even if we are still trying to construct the logos or Archimedean point that will truly comprehend the individual, without individuality there could have been no ongoing and systematic study of other cultures, nor could there have been an intercommunicatory logos. There could only have been epistemological confrontations and, therefore, conflicting social sciences. As it is, because individuality involves a dialectic between what is and what might be, it carries the potential of realizing a general and universal ontology.

PART II
SOCIAL ORDERS
AND OCCASIONS

5 PRIMARY ORDERS

THE GENERAL CONTEXT

What has now to be explored is how far different kinds of social order produce situations which allow, encourage, or inhibit the moments of individuality as they have been discussed in the foregoing pages. The question whether social conditions produce the individual or vice versa is a false problem. For if the individual is as creative in the event as we suppose him to be, then he creates the conditions which allow him his opportunity. As a surface observation an individual is one who articulates new moralities even though no new conditions may result, and those that do may not correspond to the articulation. Whether the initiative orginates from within the self, is due to a particular interaction between the self and social conditions, or is a making evident of that which was latent or inherent in a particular bio-socio-cultural condition, is, since hard data are lacking, a matter of faith and doctrine. It suffices for present purposes that if initiatives, interactions, or responses are such as to make the moments of individuality possible or evident, they may be taken to constitute attempts to apperceive the lineaments of the social order and stand in and recognize the truth of things. At the least we have to identify relationships in which, through an apperception of current conditions, a criticism of the social order—invoking the relationship *person* $\rightleftharpoons$ *individual*—is capable of being carried forward to generate and implement a new moral order.

Within our own European or Western commonsense experience the daily encounter with differing situations and social contexts leads us into finding a certain individuality in all.

The pressing obligation to restructure our social relations as we get promoted, change residence, engage in new activities, and incur fresh responsibilities gives an impression of persons continually becoming something very like individuals. Behavior, attitudes, and responses have to vary with the situation, must be restructured if the situation is to develop in amity. And we know that in a social order such as our own, in which change and multiplex and diverse ego-centered social relationships are given continua, this habitual restructuring would have to occur whether or not there were those positive accesses to sources of truth which could reveal one as standing in and recognizing the truth of things. Under such conditions, where individuality is institutionalized and generalized, permitted to and even incumbent on each, whether truth was located in the transcendent or in the differentials of power in given roles and statuses would make no objective difference. Either all involved would seem to possess a source of truth, or the truth of things was impressing itself upon them. If there were no means by which to order and so moralize the continuing readaptations and restructuring, how could anyone survive?

The incidence of violence, murder, suicide, mental illness, drug-taking, withdrawal and so on indicates that many do not survive. Either they had no source of truth, it failed them, they failed it, or, objectively, truth has become so variously located and recognized that its differing guises appear as competitive and, therefore, confusing. Or, having a source of truth is a figment, a subjective and convenient but wholly deceptive encapsulation of a large variety of extremely complex factors which, acting in concert, have been engendering change, multiplex and differing relationships, and so individuality. Not that a given source of truth and the existence of all those contributory impersonal and objective factors making for change and complexity of relationships are necessarily incompatible. Both may exist together. And though none may deny another his source of truth, each may contest the validity and usefulness in the circumstances of particular sources of truth. So that, where other cultures are concerned, if a viable initiative is phrased as having originated with a recognized source of truth, such as an ancestor, a ghost or a spirit, or a dream or vision, then the instrument of that initiative has to be considered as at least temporarily standing on the truth of things.

Since, however, each organized human aggregation or congregation is different in some particulars from all others, locating individuality or its semblances in other cultures requires some mode of subsuming relations that seem irrelevant to the context and emphasizing others that seem significant. Identifying populations as, broadly, Hunter-gatherers, Subsistence cultivators, Pastoral nomads, Peasant cultivators, Townsfolk, City dwellers, and the Connurbation is not always wholly satisfactory. Still, the labels are well established and, regarded as primary orders, they provide a familiar format in which to organize and present significant kinds of relations. They yield an evolutionary perspective, indicate modes of production or exploitation of resources, and conveniently bring together rough limits of population size in relation to the politically organized group and the development of a relatively complete and interdependent set of cultural categories within terms of which activities are conducted and rationalized. In this sense it becomes possible to use a shorthand and speak of "complete" societies—though of course no society is actually ever such. Nevertheless, the categories suggested enable us to see whether the individual can or does exist in quite different conditions, and what, if any, qualifications have to be made. Generally, what provision is made in other cultures for the emergence of the individual in roughly the sense determined so far?

HUNTER-GATHERERS

The generality of Hunter-gatherers, a broad category which includes peoples as diverse as the original Australians, the

Inuit or Eskimo, the Congo pygmies, and the Indians of the
northwest coast of North America, are regarded as the smallest and most elementary groups to have developed a more or
less complete range of categories within which to conduct and
rationalize their activities. Exploiting the resources of flora,
fauna, and materials to be obtained from, variously, sea, rivers, tropical forests, temperate forests, savannah, deserts,
mountains, and downland, life's meaning and purport were
embedded in rhythms of aggregation, dispersal, and reaggre-
gation tied to seasonal changes and the availability of resources in relation to the requirements of social and ritual or
ceremonial occasions. Total populations speaking the same
dialect or language varied considerably, and constituent political or quasi-political groups which worked over mutually
recognized estates and properties could comprise from
twenty or thirty men, women, and children in sparse country
to some three hundred or more in more bountiful areas.
While some of these peoples were settled in villages or permanent camps for a good half of the year, and others moved
from camp to camp throughout the year, the range of continuous interactions would have averaged in the largest communities much the same as our own, about forty to fifty
others,* and in the smaller communities rather less. But even
in communities with differentiated ranking orders—such as
among the Indians of the northwest coast—the variety of
roles and identities encountered was limited, well known, and
formalized, contained in the dyadic relations of about twenty
primary kinship categories.

Marriages between the members of different groups speaking the same language or dialect was frequently if not always
enjoined, and because the relationships devolving from marriage were also exchange, trading, and property relationships,
marriages also took place between those who did not speak
the same language. The unknown stranger was rare, could in

*Mary Douglas (1970: 62) hazards fifty for such a group, maybe leading up
to one hundred if postmen, milkmen, and other occasional but regular encounters are included.

any case be made to fit into familiar categories, and was only unusually the bearer of information that was in principle unknown. Most of the knowledge available was generated from within the group and not unambiguously conserved in myths, rituals, and artifacts. The source of knowledge was experience of both inner and outer conditions. The adept interpretation of dreams and knowing how and where to hunt or gather a wild harvest went together. If tradition and memories of the past guided experience, the latter was not an invariable constant through the generations. Bits and pieces of the available knowledge were forgotten and relearned in cycles. Longer and shorter cycles of climatic change; animal population increases, decreases, and movements; and variations in the availability of vegetable resources together with the not so constant activities, ambitions, and desires of neighboring groups—all contributed to one generation's experience being rather different from that preceding and yet, perhaps, not so different from that of two or three generations ago. In such circumstances, with old and forgotten knowledge being revivified by a common experience separated by several generations, ancestors could indeed become authentic sources of truth.

The basic productive unit was the family centered on a husband, his wife or wives, their children, and perhaps one or two aging dependents. Among some peoples, two or three such units might form cooperative groups in virtue of specific kin relationships between the spouses. A family, or cooperative group of families, shared most of their production from day to day. But if a large beast was killed, or the wild harvest rich, much—sometimes the whole beast or harvest—would be donated to other families and cooperative groups in the sure expectation, under obligation, of a return donation in the future. This sharing was usually competitive and related to status, embodying an ethic derived from a regular production requirement in relation to varying amounts and qualities of resources. While major properties, such as land or estates or fishing grounds, were vested in the cult or social group, most artifacts—weapons, clothing, decorative paraphernalia, domestic utensils—were personal property. Some artifacts, usually those of sacred or symbolic value to the group as a whole, were vested in those groups. If for the adult time was one's own, this was countered by the necessity to produce food and artifacts, and the obligations to aid family production and make repayments of past donations from others. Over and above this were the duties entailed in managerial roles, maintaining the political order, and in carrying through a variety of ritual tasks.

The relations between men and women were interdependent and complementary. Hunting, the swiftly changing situations of the chase, fostered initiative and innovations in ways that gathering berries, corms, roots, leaves, and fruits—women's work—does not appear to have done. Particularly among the Plains Indians, where each male had to find his own guardian spirit, or source of truth, but also generally, it was thought desirable that at some time before marriage, usually during the period of pubertal treatment, a young male should go out into the wilderness by himself, test himself, and there find not simply his metier but what for him would constitute his particular ground of being. Tried in this and other ways, men were overtly and explicitly entrusted with the management of community affairs. If the influence of women was by no means insignificant, it was covert. Men were held responsible. Yet in most instances by far the greater bulk of the food supply was found and processed by women. Hunting took time, was hard, and except in regions where game was plentiful, was morally rather than economically rewarding, achieved status rather than wealth (cf. Lee 1968: 42-48).

Some Hunter-gatherers had extremely rigid and highly intellectualized or sociocentric social systems which were apparently "external" to what might be thought to be the "natural" or economic needs of the people. The Australians, for example, were organized into cult or totemic groups, marriage classes or section and subsection systems, matrimoieties and patrimoieties, avoidance or interactional relationships, which were specified and prescribed. From puberty onwards males went through a series of initiations which conferred further group memberships as degrees of formal knowledge (contained in myths and their exegesis) were attained. Interactions were in terms of group memberships; each member of community shared interests and relationships with others. By contrast, Eskimo or Inuit organizations were based on cognation producing localized kindreds, entailing each member of a community having unique interests and a range of interactional relationships shared by no others. Where, faced with the event, Australians conformed to traditional and relatively rigidly intellectualized and sociocentric sets of rules and rationalizations related to group-determined relationships ($E <$ R), Inuit society was egocentered: events evoked a stock of alternative rationalizations depending on who was there, what interests were involved. And situations were temporarily resolved by a tacit understanding of the interplay of the varied interests being brought to bear on the matter ($E > R$). Other Hunter-gatherers and, indeed, all forms of organization, could be placed on a scale between these polarities.

Nevertheless, if any member of an Inuit band could, occasionally, reach into individuality, on the whole men and women of Hunter-gathering cultures were what they were, or became themselves, in virtue of their realization of the given cultural categories. They were persons, identities determined by intersections of the dyads in the general categories. Although the formal proportions of personal to corporate properties were not much different from our own, exchange obligations prevented those peculiar accumulations of wealth which might have provided a springboard for individuality. If some of the dyads were nonreciprocal (parent-child, senior-junior), the remainder were generally governed by some form of reciprocity. The Plains Indians excepted, war—a seedbed of individuality—was not for Hunter-gatherers. Certainly they had their fights, their feuds, their abductions, their revenge killings. But their military skills were undeveloped. They were more often prey than raiders, were too few in numbers to mount any considerable affray, each life was too valuable to be put at risk without dire need. Not lacking in courage, in general they did not—again excepting the Plains Indians—invite occasions for the test and display of initiatives where death might be the price.

Though there is little to suggest that Hunter-gatherers were wholly unable to seize the event, transcend the normative values, and realize individuality, life's exigencies and the weight of tradition made it a temporary affair and would-be individuals were returned to the person, their initiative forgotten, perhaps to be rearticulated and forgotten again at a later date. Yet if a chief in the sense of one set apart and vested with initiating authority was rare, in every community there was at least one diviner or shaman, singletons alone who could step aside from the dyads and be as though no one. Expertly responsive to dreams and encounters with spirits on the one hand, and to those who sought help or advice on the other, shaman or diviner mediated the moralities through given sources of truth. Though normally maintaining the continuities, they might apperceive, could become the fulcrum for potentially new ways. Because women were not usually held responsible for the management of community affairs, they could and did act and talk in ways which kept the men on their mettle and obliged them to use their initiatives. And if taking advantage of such opportunities was more difficult for an Australian than for an Eskimo, at least the germ of individuality seems imminent in the demand that a youth find himself by himself, in the emergencies of the chase, in technological challenges, in the problems encountered in managerial and political life.

Hunter-gatherers represent elementary groups both in a proto-historical and evolutionary sense. Though the ranges of continuous interactions between people were only slightly smaller than our own, the totality of experience involved lacked the variety of the strange or different. Life's potential was developed in terms of the given categories, experience was shared, each in a lifetime had much the same experience of another of the same sex. The strange or untoward event or experience was returned and absorbed into the given categories. Togetherness had its price. From our own standpoint the way of life of Hunter-gatherers seems to have had an innocent and pristine quality. Despite the discomfort and pain, the stable range of interactions seems to have fostered a peculiar reliance on, attachment to, and intuitively easy understanding of others which Hunter-gatherers themselves find it difficult to forego, and which we, grappling with differences and the unstable, tend to idealize. We forget they were nomads, that much of the bite of inevitable envies and malice was absorbed into being forced to part company for a while. We tend to forget, too, that were it not for their initiatives, their adept interpretation of dreams and handling of encounters with spirits or ghosts, their perceptions of something new or strange happening, humanity would have remained Hunter-gatherers.

SUBSISTENCE CULTIVATORS

Following the evolutionary idiom, Hunter-gatherers were succeeded by Subsistence cultivators—though there are historical instances where such cultivators, after a natural cataclysm or disastrous war, have become Hunter-gatherers (cf. White 1922). Still, the general supposal is that the care and nurture of wildstuffs developed into positive cultivation, and that the relatively unrewarding economics of hunting gave place to the more rewarding domestication of livestock. And the record of prehistory supports the hypothesis. Yet the historical experience over the last two centuries amply demonstrates the extreme reluctance of Hunter-gatherers to take to cultivation and the domestication of livestock. Force and physical coercion have been found necessary—though they may indeed have been counterproductive through reaction. Still, there is no doubt that Hunter-gatherers find the settled life—attachments to property, becoming the virtual slaves of crops and animals, and continuing unavoidable interactions with others—entirely repugnant. Hunting and the rhythms of concentration and dispersal of nomadic life seem to have provided a neat balance between the participatory values and privacy and the assertion to autonomy. If the transition to cultivating took place slowly, it was surely individuals with, perhaps, charismatic qualities who articulated the steps, made others aware of a new way of life.

Aggregations of Subsistence cultivators might be as small as twenty people and, averaging between one hundred and fifty to four hundred, might be as large as twenty-five hundred, though the total of colinguals might reach several thousands. While the number of people involved in an interactional range would be about the same as in the larger Hunter-gatherer groups, it could shift within the limits imposed by the numbers of the aggregation. But again, the totality of experience involved was and is limited to relatively few interactional categories. As in the small towns and villages of our own experience, Subsistence cultivators live a closely knitted life: neighborly love, care, and attention are inextricably mixed with inquisitiveness, envy, interference, criticism, and judgment. Competing interests, personal incompatibilities, feuds and quarrels are kept under close control, can erupt into the open very suddenly, and in any case are carefully sheathed in ritualized demeanors and procedures. Life in such relatively closed communities entails participating in the beings of enemies, rivals, and competitors if only on a formal level, and is and was as necessary as enjoying the company friends and cooperators. As with Hunter-gatherers, but lacking the nomadic opportunities for privacy, all were kin, by descent or affinally, and all interactions were contained in the categories of the kinship and friendship idioms.

The basic unit of production is still the family centered on a man, his wife or wives, their children and aging dependents. But this family is now much more firmly agglutinated into a cooperative group which might or might not be a corporate descent group. Social relationships are still determined by a series of given dyads, and virtually all roles and identities appropriate to the sex could be experienced in a lifetime. Though keeping domesticated livestock and engaging in the cultivation of root or cereal crops—which mode requires a continuing reliance on trusted cooperators, those whose cooperation is axiomatic—Subsistence cultivators generally supplement the domesticated food supply with aboriculture, a wild harvest, fishing, and hunting. Not always economically worthwhile, these activities nevertheless provide opportunities for withdrawal and privacy. And if success in these activities is often highly prestigious, being too private and withdrawing too often earns suspicion. Feud, war, and killing are, or were, one might say, well integrated into the pattern of life: interior tensions become transferred onto exterior enemies. Given a preexisting notion of the individual, feud and war might well have evoked the individual. In fact, they much more certainly elicited loyalty to the group, dramatizing and confirming the person. In general, sociocentric images of social relationships determined the pattern of life, communicated to men and women what they should be and what they should do. And this was so even where a dispersed population implied a greater degree of ego-centered initiatives and responsibilities.

Internalization of the image was effected in pubertal rites, and these usually entailed a traumatic transformation. From the generally free and easy, permissive ways of childhood, youths—and sometimes maidens—were forced into the lines of the image. Even so the rites would normally include, either through exhortation or setting the neophytes a series of situational tests, some introduction to the loneliness of having to make a responsible decision for and by oneself. Contained in the relationship between senior and junior, such rites of initiation modeled the process of entering into moral responsibility through the reconciliation of the opposition between the assertion to autonomy and self-willedness on the one hand and self-restraint and acceptance of the given moralities on the

other. Senior cajoled, threatened, instructed, and forcibly in-
ducted a recalcitrant, wayward, and self-willed junior into
acceptance—as though it were known that the most enduring
initiatives could only come from one with imagination who
had learned obedience. Further, precisely these moments
were crucially reexperienced in the relationship between elder
and younger sibling, husband and wife, and men and women
generally. The participatory values and the self-willedness inherent in the assertion to autonomy were tautly opposed and
in tension; the more responsible senior was opposed by the
less responsible initiatives of a junior; those in parity had to
maintain the parity.

As with Hunter-gatherers, major forms of property were
vested in the corporate group determined by descent and/or
neighborhood. Personal property was much more definitively attached to particular persons. Communities might be
stratified into ranks or statuses open to any who could achieve
them; divided into two or more hierarchically organized
classes, membership of which was determined by birth; or
organized within an egalitarian ethic. There might be a
"slave" category, prisoners of war or permanent debtors, or
there might be "rubbish men," poor, lazy, or incompetent
men and women who did not or could not participate in activities in the accepted mode. Mutual sharing and exchanges
of the fruits of production were obligatory, competitive, and
related to status selection and moral standing. One who did
not or could not honor his exchange obligations abdicated
moral status and, being in that sense less than human, was so
treated. The industrious and acute who could produce more
donated to a wider field of recipients, found dependants and
allies, and so gained in relative power and status. Donations
were the equivalents of investments.

Confined within usually rigid sociocentric moralities, the
generally competitive ethic was and is associated with witchcrafts, sorceries, and the like. Though comfort and security
could be found in the bosom of the group, in the automaticisms of conformity, each in such systems is drawn to the

powers apparent in successful self-assertion by, for example, shifting alliances or making changes in an interactional range. For the ambitious as well as the lazy, the slippery-tongued, the envious, the wily, the self-righteous—and each must participate in such qualities at some time during a life span—the given moralities, though strictly enforced, were constantly at issue. The interpretation of dreams, auguries, oracles, and encounters with spirits, ghosts, and familiars—accepted as sources of truth—mediated the moralities either directly or through a diviner. To be successful the ambitious had to initiate, take risks, finesse the given moralities, even go beyond or outside them. To remain successful there had to be responsibility—keeping within the moralities—and a demonstrated capacity for transcending the rules in a crisis.

In the formal opposition between "male" and "female" men and women were generally in complementary relationships. Yet even when, as frequently occurred, the title to major properties was vested in women, women were generally subservient to men and had much less scope for independent action than among Hunter-gatherers. They were tied to children, the home, livestock, field and garden, and to a host of supportive tasks such as food processing, cleaning, knitting, weaving, pottery and the like. In general they did not overtly participate in, or were debarred from, the political activities in which the major bulk of the tensions generated were subsumed. These difficulties men had to resolve. They took their reward in success, faced the consequences in failure. Yet if the general pattern of social relationships called for the pooling of common interests, cooperation, and grouping together in relation to categories of sameness, such solidarities might at any time be vitiated by the competitive advantages dormant in the categories of differentiation. Conformists were faced with expressions of assertions to autonomy. While most centered themselves on the person, insisting on the stabilities and continuities of the given categories, a few, whose desires and ambitions maintained the edginess, momentum, and dynamic of social life, were forced by the situation to those peripheries where the presently nonmoral or immoral might well become tomorrow's moralities. And from such a position it would have been at least possible to apperceive the total situation and become, in some part if only for a short while, something like an individual.

SUBSISTENCE AND COMPLEX

Whether ego-centered or sociocentric, the mode of exploiting resources of itself provided Hunter-gatherers with regular occasions for privacy and withdrawal from the guidelines and prescriptions in which a culture imprisons its members. That these opportunities for reflection and critique were at times grasped cannot be doubted. Otherwise there would have been no change, no other social orders. While it is possible that kinds of charismatic activity, epitomes of individuality attempting to realize itself, brought about some of the shifts into the cultivating mode, orders of Subsistence cultivators reveal an accent on conformity which, nonetheless, engenders its own reaction of positive criticism as well as mere nonconformity. Where among Hunter-gatherers during periods of dispersal assertions to autonomy are permitted and, indeed, are necessary to survival, among Subsistence cultivators the same assertions to autonomy, no less necessary, are largely absorbed in the competition for status and prestige. In both sorts of order, however, tradition, technology, resources, the participatory values, and mode of exploitation generally seem to have sufficed to prevent the incipient individual from becoming wholly so. Or, to subsume the last sentence, both Hunter-gatherers and Subsistence cultivators live or lived within the terms of a Subsistence economy or community as distinct from a Complex.

As used here Subsistence and Complex (capitalized initial letters) refer to mutually exclusive sets of social relations. Subsistence economy is not necessarily the same as the more general "subsistence economy." For while the latter usually refers to generally poor resources, a primitive technology, and a lack of adequate storage facilities, the former refers to a pattern of social relationships which may fill out a whole culture, or characterize a subculture or sector of a Complex economy.

Subsistence economy refers to the situation where all in the community participate in the same range of subsistence activities, organized within terms of a simple division of labor based upon age and sex. Each adult member of the community may command some specialist activity or skill—medical, magical, technological, social, artistic, military—but these are additional to the common and general participation in subsistence activities. There is no separate full-time specialization. Performance in the subsistence activities provides the basic measure of relative status and prestige. Though specialist skills certainly add to a person's prestige and status, productive capacities—skill and industry in forest, bush, desert, field, garden, rivers, and sea—combined with a certain acuity in distributing the fruits of production to kin, friends, associates, and others remain the basic measures. Apart from those particular prescribed positions to be considered shortly (pp. 116-43) which are generally insulated from the general status system, honoring exchange obligations, having status, engaging in the competition for relative status, are requirements for membership in the moral community. Gaining possession temporarily or more permanently of particular valuables, or making well managed and large exchanges of produce, mark those with higher relative prestige and status.

Since in the circumstances, however, production must be limited, not all who have expectations can always be satisfied. Thus, though reciprocity and an equivalence in exchange are the rule, choosing who shall be more, or less, satisfied in particular circumstances becomes the basic determinant of tensions, rivalries, and political ability. Exchanges are prescribed both as to products involved and as between persons in particular social relationships. They are also continuing and ongoing: *A* gives to *B, B* returns to *A, A* again gives to *B*

($A \leqq B$). The process is completed either when both parties express themselves satisfied, or when one becomes the permanent debtor of the other and so the latter's retainer. Basically and in principle the moral determinant of Subsistence economy is the equivalence of giving and receiving (*giving* ≈ *receiving*). While industry, skill, and qualities of character in the common and general tasks measure both men and women, and specialist skills add to stature, managerial capacities—ultimately dependent on extending the range and number of exchanges—are required to fill out the whole man.

The primary and focal institution of the Subsistence economy is the feast which combines religious, social, and ceremonial features with exchanges of produce, status sorting, and the settlement of disputes. Celebrating births, deaths, betrothals, marriages, initiations, and other significant occasions or their anniversaries, feasts entail the exchange and consumption of large amounts of produce. And the amounts and ranges of exchanges that are made indicate relative status and prestige. Shows—such as dancing, theater, the ceremonial enactment of appropriate myths, a variety of rituals—are staged. All in the community involve themselves, but the initiatives for organizing the production and bringing together of the produce, the rituals, dances, and entertainment, are in the hands of the leading men, those with acknowledged prestige and status, or those laying claim to such status.

A large or important feast usually requires the presence of some thing, animal, or foodstuff that is very clearly at risk, difficult to obtain. For example, a Naga man has to provide *mithan* cattle for slaughter. But these beasts, though domesticated, are ranged in the forests, continually prey to tigers and leopards. Yap islanders have to bring to the feast large stone discs up to six or seven feet in diameter. But these have to be quarried and carved overseas, and then brought home on a seaborne journey of some days on a raft built upon flimsy dugout canoes. Many Melanesians require particular kinds of yams, where these yams are delicate and subject to blight.

Where failure to provide the stuffs at risk marks the loser, continuing success in resolving problems centered in risk reveals that effectiveness which, not wholly explained by known and acceptable measures of skill, cunning, care, and foresight, seems or is taken to indicate qualities of being in rapport with benign divinities and able to defeat the malign. The amounts of produce distributed demonstrate industry, organizing ability, and effective cooperation and direction. The modes of distribution involve qualities of demeanor, dignity, and address. The ordering of distributions and amounts of particular donations indicate relative status.

Subsistence economies are consumption economies in which notions of cyclical rather than linear time predominate or are decisive. The seasons, crop cycles, social relationships, being born, learning the tasks appropriate to one's sex, marrying, reproducing, working, feasting, exchanging, engaging in rituals, and gaining status repeat themselves through the generations. Apart from some articles of stone or shell, which are regarded as valuables and of symbolic value, all the products of work are consumed within a generation. Food is eaten, artifacts wear out or break, houses rot and fall down. The standard of living oscillates about a mean, may fall, but because wealth cannot be conserved is incapable of ongoing improvement. Yet this does not mean that Subsistence economies are poor either in culture or materially. Naga tribesmen, for example, are healthier, better fed and clothed than their neighbors in the plains who participate in a Complex economy. And the latter may be characterized as a "conservation" economy. Having money, a store of wealth which can outlast a particular life or lives, the possibility exists for raising or improving the standard of living. Wealth, in money, can accumulate and command labor, services, and goods not available in a Subsistence enonomy. Whereas in a Subsistence economy exchanges are continuing ($A \leftrightarrows B$), prescriptive, and within the kin or friendship idioms, thus enforcing narrow and traditional moralities, transactions with money may cut the relationship with a single *do ut des* ($A \rightleftharpoons B$), make free markets possible, open relationships to choice and preference, convert the moralities into allowable options.

Without free markets or money, bound and restricted to exchanges within specified categories of relationship, the prestige and status systems of Subsistence economies are necessarily based in the common engagement in subsistence activities. As a common medium of exchange and measure of value and worth, money frees the exchange of products, goods, and services, differentiates the division of labor, makes possible full-time specialization, and yields a basic measure of prestige and status such that unlike occupations and activities can be scaled against each other. On the other hand, with money the products of labor can be alienated and appropriated. Money diminishes the value of labor as a productive activity and transfers that value to a quite different skill: the manipulation of money itself. And money tends to absorb the human qualities, transforming them into quantities. People can be bought, become mere "hands," tools. Factorial, the concrete expression of abstract mathematical relations which have an explicit consent through the authority which mints it, money makes possible and habitual an idea of unity which is not necessarily qualitative and thus ultimately dyadic. Working against the narrow and rigorous moral discriminations typical of Subsistence communities—where love cannot be developed as a value in itself though its semblances are enforced—money vitiates strict reciprocities and differentiates given roles and statuses so as to provide options impossible in situations where *giving* $\approx$ *receiving*. Money opens the moralities to shades of meaning, making them susceptible to qualification and change and, paradoxically perhaps, allows for the development of love as a value in itself. Handling money, thinking about and "being thought" and constrained by it, vitiates firm dyadic relationships and makes possible the perception of oneself as a unitary being ranged against other unitary beings. The opportunity is presented to become and be singular.

The distinction between Complex and Subsistence economies hinges on money. Money gives rise to factorial thinking, corrupts reciprocities and dyadic relations, makes possible full-time specialization and so differentiated criteria of
status. Forms of so-called "primitive money" are nonfacto-
rial, subject to variable and independent judgments of quality,
and locked into systems of dyads. It is possible to identify sec-
tors or subcultures within a Complex economy in which the
characteristic features of a Subsistence economy are present.
Money works against them. The bonded securities and values
of a coparticipant community as well as networks of inescapable obligations are at hazard, varied stocks of options become available. Sets of definitive dyads may dissolve and
wither away as some seek more advantageous relationships
outside the group. Rigorous moral discriminations, in the
light of which each person enjoys the security of knowing
precisely where he or she stands in relation to others, are open
to the kinds of qualification that breed uncertainty, anxiety,
and insecurity. Basically and in principle, *giving* ≠ *receiving*.
The values and determinants of the Complex economy, indicating the "open" society, stand opposed to the patterns of
social relationships to be found in the "closed" society or
Subsistence economy. Nevertheless, just as Hunter-gatherer
values have persisted into our own society, but can be appreciated most clearly and pristinely in the kind of total society that a Hunter-gatherer group represents, so Subsistence
economy values can exist within the open society but are appreciated more clearly among Subsistence cultivators.

Where both are found together within the same total society, the difficulties and insecurities, anxieties and loneliness of
the Complex economy continually generate movements and
organizations which seek to reestablish the securities, human
worths, and participations in the beings of others associated
with a Subsistence economy. Conversely, the conformities
and moral rigors of a Subsistence economy provide a seedbed
of criticism and assertions to autonomy which, in turn, ener-
gize aspirations to the relative freedoms of the open society

and Complex economy. Clans and other group organizations and allegiances hold persons together for a while, but money tends to erode the sociocentricities and builds up a lonely and selfish ego-centeredness. Charismatic activities, which seek a new balance between the sociocentric and egocentric, are often the result.

Individuality is not impossible in a Subsistence economy. It is latent in hunting activities, in pubertal rites, in the relations between the sexes, in the nomadic rhythms of concentration and dispersal, in organizations based on the kindred, in the diviner or shaman, in those who attempt to push their ambitions beyond the normative moralities. But again, the basic formula *giving* ⇌ *receiving* constrains nonreciprocal behavior and assertions to autonomy, returns initiatives to the traditional person. On the other hand, where the basic formula is *giving* ≠ *receiving*, nonreciprocal behavior becomes permissive, and the differentiating functions of money invite assertions to autonomy. A generalized individuality becomes probable. But the critical situation is where the tensions between *giving* ⇌ *receiving* and *giving* ≠ *receiving* occur within the same aggregation. For in this situation, informed as it also is with contrasts in the variety of roles and identities to be encountered within approximately the same interactional range, the person is continually presented with opportunities for moral choice, critique, and innovation.

PASTORAL NOMADS

The absolute numbers of colingual or quasi-politically organized aggregations of Pastoral nomads, which may vary between some hundreds in northern Eurasia and several thousands in central Asia, the middle east, and parts of Africa, seems to be of small relevance in the present context. It is more significant that while some Pastoral nomads reveal the characteristics of a Subsistence economy, others, particularly in central Asia and the middle east where they are and have been in contact with Towns and Cities and Peasant communities, participate in a Complex economy. They use money, the division of labor is differentiated beyond sex and age, there are full-time specialists, and though the interactional range is much the same as that of Subsistence cultivators—there is a limit to the number of interactions a single human being can deal with on a continuing basis—shifts are less frequent but the range itself can contain a greater variety of roles and identities. With the exception of the reindeer peoples of northern Eurasia, rhythms of trading and raiding mix with the nomadic rhythms of aggregation and dispersal, and feud and war are, or were, part of the pattern of life.

On an evolutionary scale Pastoral nomads can be derived from Subsistence cultivators. Since domestication of crops and animals seem to have taken place at about the same time, it may be supposed that those who herded animals gradually wandered further away to seek fodder and grazing. In time, these herders would develop a life of their own, and a distinct ethic. That they would never be completely independent of the cultivation base is supported by the historical experience. There are (and have been) few Pastoral nomad groups who have not had home bases where crops are cultivated. On the other hand, the evolutionary transition can also be supposed to have derived from Hunter-gathering. Preying upon herd animals, following the herds as they concentrated for mating or in response to seasonal variations and then split up into sections to graze in particular valleys, capturing and domesticating the animals (where they were susceptible to domestication) would have appeared as an ideal solution to the problem of regular needs and a variable supply. But there is no need to choose between the two kinds of transition. The one is more likely in some parts of the world, the other in other parts. In either case the values and opportunities offered by the nomadic rhythms of concentration and dispersal remain.

By and large the family—husband and wife or wives, children, and dependents—may still be picked out as the basic unit. But the efficient management of herds requires some basis of sure cooperation. Where, as among the peoples of northern Eurasia, it can be reasonably surmised that the transition to Pastoral nomadism was from Hunter-gathering, the bases of cooperation are sure enough but not always rigorously prescribed or structured. Among other peoples the family merges into and becomes part of a corporate descent group, and these groups themselves form segments of still larger groups based upon ideals of matrilineal or patrilineal or agnatic descent—an emphasis on group feeling, membership, and solidarity which, emphasized by Ibn Khaldun (1958) in the fourteenth century in contrast to the ego-centeredness and selfishness of city life, appears to contradict the description of Pastoral nomads in travel books and anthropological monographs as "superb individuals" or "having great individuality" and the like. Still, accepting that much of the hyperbole has flowed from romanticized projections of European individuality, there remains a hard core of truth. If the nomadic rhythms of concentration and dispersal do not wholly resolve the tensions between self-assertion and participation in the being of others, it is not easy to imagine a more efficient mechanical aid to the emotional and moral problems involved. The comforts, securities, and annoyances of participatory group life seem balanced by the hardships, self-reliance, risk-taking, initiative, and rough comradeship demanded of life on the grasslands. Yet self-reliance and independence of mind do not necessarily entail the moral reach of individuality.

Pastoral nomads are usually intensely religious, iconoclastic, morally concerned, and often monotheistic. Herding animals accents the quantities and encourages—as indeed does monotheism also—the notion of the "one" opposed to the "many" at the expense of the dyads. But care and protection of the herds foster a regard for the qualities in the beasts as well as in man, and human virtues usually carry the day against money. Group loyalties and Subsistence economy values win out. Proud, stiff-necked, and swift to take offense, most Pastoral nomads are as solicitous of the group as of their own personal honor and standing. Indeed, both go together.

So much so that habitual feud and war might well have been disastrous had it not been for the very particular person—holy man, saint, mullah, or shaman who, as though no one or everyone, stands between the mutually opposed segments which might otherwise destroy each other, and symbolizes their essential surrender to a common morality. He mediates between them, makes their common interest in the selfsame moralities explicit, negotiates the truce and peace, and *maintains* traditional moral continuities. This, together with the group loyalties and interests of members of the community, inhibits reaches into individuality on their part. Still, weighing the moralities in the light of a source of truth and interaction with others and the cultural categories, the mediator himself might, if usually he did not, realize individuality.

Among feuding and warlike Pastoral nomads, cultivators are generally regarded as inferior beings. Herding animals is for men; cultivation at the home bases is for old men, "incomplete" or poor men who do not own beasts or cannot make it on the grasslands, and who stand to the herders in a relationship of inferiority, often commoner to noble. Women, who are childbearers, domestics, and work-horses, are in much the same effective relationship to men. Certainly they have their rights, but many more duties. They have security and protection of a sort but, virtually the property of their men, their roles are subservient and supportive. They may not emasculate their men with nagging demands on their time, care, attention, and tenderness. If a spirited woman might have and reveal emotions of her own, and make use of her mind and tongue in the privacy of the home, in public that mind and tongue were efficiently stoppered. Yet to crush the woman in this way is to emphasize tradition and smother the spark of individuality. Adultery is regarded as heinous among such peoples, but common: it gives men the opportunity to reveal their manhood. Women bear the consequences in pain and suffering and so, inadvertently perhaps, maintain an image of male dominance.

Among other sorts of Pastoral nomad, particularly and for

example among the reindeer peoples of northern Eurasia, male dominance is not as manic. Women may speak their minds, become shamans, are regarded as positively essential as men in maintaining the ethic. Feud and war are avoided rather than welcomed or actively sought as test and proof of manhood. The idea of a proper man is not contained within a highly structured and exterior image of maleness, but is allowed to emerge from the routines and exigencies of daily life, work efficiently done, cooperation, and the handling of relationships linked to tasks which, when appropriately executed, mean more than mere survival. Women make and develop the characters of their men within a variety of complementary and personal relationships, and so provide opportunities for perceptions which are not at once placed against the rigid and sociocentric image of what a man should be. Domestic relations, instead of being dependent on political relations, become the soil in which political relations become manifest.

Whether warlike or peaceful, however, the general conditions of Pastoral nomads demand tried and mutually acceptable modes of cooperation. Participatory and group values tied to tradition require that one with different perceptions enter prescribed positions—such as mullah, shaman, diviner, and the like—where their perceptions can be disciplined and rigorously controlled. Unless conditions are abnormal, the singleton alone with his vision cannot survive long enough to make his vision relevant. And, as the historical record shows, when conditions were abnormal, one with different perceptions certainly could, at least for a while, alter the moralities and semantic environment and so give to life a new impetus and meaning.

PEASANT CULTIVATORS

The cultures and social organizations of Peasant cultivators vary considerably. Still, there are certain significant uniform features. They use money, think factorially, have full-time specialists, participate in a Complex economy, and are culturally dependent on Town or City, requiring the latter's resources in technology, learning, and literacy if they are to realize the full range of possibilities open to them. Aggregations may vary from thirty to about five thousand people, but interactional ranges include a significant variety of roles and identities: each is aware of a totality of experience beyond his or her present reach.

Whether the idiom is historical or evolutionary, Peasants may be derived from Subsistence cultivators, Pastoral nomads, or Town or City. Caught between the cultural wealth, social diversities, and economic opportunities of the monied Town or City on the one hand, and the relative wealths and cultural integrities associated with Pastoral nomads and the closed communities of Subsistence cultivators on the other, Peasants are generally poor, culturally and economically deprived, unorganized to defend themselves, the prey of all others. Peaceable and lacking in military skills and virtues, their periodic revolts have boomeranged in disaster. Exploited, taxed, despoiled, impressed into others' armies, Peasant lives are punctuated by famine, pestilence, and wars not of their making or to their advantage. But doggedly they return to their hoes and plows, their chickens, cats, dogs, pigs, and cows. Life has to go on.

Resuming the continuities after each interruption, Peasants are accustomed to the derision and rough handling of those to whom they are prey. Meeting natural and mad-made disasters with an imploring faith in the gods who seldom smile, generations of hardships suffered at the hands of their fellow men have taught them cunning and a reliance on traditional modes of cultivation and animal husbandry. The rewards for their skill and labor they hide and hoard lest they be taken from them. And almost invariably they are. Notoriously attached to the land, Peasants are addicted to working it. But title to their lands is rarely their own, their labor and its fruits are usually appropriated by others. Though regular community festivals encourage the participatory values, these are more than countered by mutual suspicions, hostility, and the prime value of self-interest. For if often, but certainly not always, the family or basic household unit is organized within a descent group or extended family, these groups and units are mutually opposed, competitive, and vulnerable to the blandishments of outsiders from the City. Each relationship in the basic set of dyadic relations is continually at risk.

Though Peasants are well aware that many of their misfortunes flow from weakly developed participatory values, fate and chance in the shape of the ambitions of wealthier and more powerful outsiders play such parts in their lives that it is difficult for them (or an observer) to believe that developed participatory values would be an adequate defense. When calamity calls, each must take his own counsel. The peasant is always looking for levers that will enforce loyalty, cooperation, alliance, trust, and confidence. Yet the participatory values being continually at risk is a condition of his life, part of the definition of Peasant. Held by the features of a Complex economy, but distanced from the generating center of events, Peasants are swift to recognize seeming opportunities that come out of a clear blue sky. But they also know that those who would grasp them are most often left maimed and wounded. Aside from benign authorities in the City—and this, in the nature of things, can only be temporary—there is no way Peasants can defend themselves and be more certain than uncertain about it. With fate and potential disaster hiding behind every corner, every cloud must surely have a silver lining.

Few of our folk wisdoms do not derive from the contrariness and anxieties of Peasant life. Dreams, astrologies, auguries, oracles and portents, continually derided as superstitious nonsense, are yet necessary supports for both strong and weak: knowledge and experience of the regularities and caprices of nature are forever being set at nought by the greed, ambitions, and good intentions of others. If perceptions of human virtues are well developed, understanding the full range of vices is more useful and decisive. Money values predominate. Because money retains its value, is transportable, convertible, and easy to hide, money spells the surest security. Yet few Peasant proverbs do not mock this foolishness. Occupying decisive positions of power within the household or extended family, women goad their men into activities they would not otherwise have undertaken, and restrain them when a rare enthusiasm urges them on.

The ambiguities of Peasant life make individuality more probable than possible. Though Peasants are more addicted to rites and rituals than wont to reach into a spiritual grasp, sources of truth abound in the stars and portents as well as in the established modes received from City or Town. New ways and moralities continually offer themselves. Chaplains and priests and school teachers, in more or less protected positions, advise, mediate the moralities, resolve conflicts and quarrels. They also communicate horizons of awareness and desire whose realization is only for a few. For others a resignation—surly or envious or wrought into wisdom—has to be accepted. Other kinds of intermediaries arrange marriages and business deals both within the community and outside it, convey the needs, interests, and values of the City or Town to the village and vice versa, and also attempt to mediate and resolve differences. But they, too, open avenues whose further reaches are blocked. There seem to be plenty of opportunities to transcend the locally given set of cultural categories and move into a new key. Nor is there any lack of attempts to do so. But the vulnerability of the native participatory values, weak, at risk, susceptible to competitive assertions to autonomy and self-interest, render any particular set of new moralities difficult to establish. The only alternative is a return to traditional ways. Those who can do so move out.

Peasant communities are stocked with eccentrics, wiseacres and character parts generated by the conflicting claims of Complex and Subsistence values, the tensions between *giving* ≃ *receiving* and *giving* ≠ *receiving*, the dilemmas of money combined with prescribed exchange. As a consequence, the problems involved have often given rise to charismatic activities which have sought to resolve them. But since the basic dilemma, Complex versus Subsistence, *giving* ≠ *receiving* versus *giving* ≈ *receiving*, can only be resolved by adopting the one and eschewing the other, and the given conditions make this impossible, as soon as the charismatic activities have exhausted themselves the moments of the dilemma reassert themselves. The individual and individuality continually emerge, then are snuffed out. Singletons and families move to Town or City, others migrate to wildernesses to found the communities they think they want.

CITY AND TOWN

The City, its ancillary the Town and its derivative the Connurbation are, for present purposes, centers of learning and bureaucratic control which comprise collections and combinations of subcultures, communities, and associations brought together into a relatively confined space. Possessing their own mores and institutions of self-regulation, the constituent groups have varied criteria of membership: ethnicity, interest, neighborhood, profession, class, financial status, birth, caste, work, and recreation are some. Relations between the groups and their members are ordered by informal conventions and rules, by formal and explicit principles of interrelationship such as the Hindu caste system, and by overarching prescriptions managed, maintained, and enforced by a bureaucracy and its subordinate branches. Money, the pivot of the Complex economy, the open society, tends to corrupt community boundaries, encourages the creation of a multiplicity of unique networks of ego-centered relationships, may be used to circumvent the bureaucracy, and begets its own reactions: a strengthening of the bureaucracy, movements toward the formation of relatively exclusive participatory groups. Ego-centered relationships, assertions to autonomy and self-interest are brought into an acute oppositional tension with the qualitative and moral imperatives inherent in the participatory values of group and community allegiance. Where there is no money, as was the case among the ancient Incas, or where money has come wholly under the control of the bureaucracy, relations between the constituent communities are, and have to be, carefully prescribed and policed.

In relation to the aggregations already considered, City, Town, and Connurbation represent a quite distinct and discontinuous numerical order. If the population must be sufficiently large and energetic to support the defining or characteristic institutions, the maximum may be regarded as virtually infinity. Though continuities are to be found in the size of the constituent communities or groups—rarely much larger than those of Subsistence or Peasant cultivators—and in interactional ranges, the variety of roles and identities encountered and the totality of experiences involved are, again, of a quite different order. The composition of interactional ranges changes over time, usually includes people with different moralities, and is often centered on an Ego rather than the family or descent group. But it would be a mistake to think that this by no means universal feature of urban conditions, even when combined with a notion of egalitarianism (cf. Chang 1971: 14-15), necessarily gives rise to individuality. On the contrary, faced with diversity, most draw back into an assured identity. The person is emphasized. Further, in realizing that variety and convergence of spiritual, intellectual, moral, technological, and coercive skills which distinguish a City, however small, from a population aggregation, however large, human beings came face to face with their worst fears and vices as they fulfilled their best hopes, virtues, and less coherent strivings. In particular, and although movement in either direction provides role, identity, and membership of a subculture, these relations as well as those with other communities are ultimately mediated and determined by bureaucracies.

In this sense bureaucracies tend to appropriate that burden of moral choice which is the prerogative of the human, and either transform the person into an automaton or force him into the anonymity of random or haphazard contacts and relationships. Under rural conditions most of the exchanges of goods and services which mediate and express social relationships are mutually engaged and within the competence of virtually all participants. Moral critique springs from commonly held values, acknowledgment of the work and activities to be pursued, the mutual obligations involved. Under urban conditions—the more so when industrialized—the number and variety of exchanges increases, commonly held competences decrease. Varieties of participatory options—whether of work or in social or religious or service or charitable or sporting clubs and societies—are offered. And each self may grasp and integrate a particular selection: participatory bases vary. Acquaintances, friends, and colleagues, each of whom have their own sets of interests and obligations, and who therefore may not be able to implement exchanges or obligations contingently expected of them, occupy most of that social ambience which, in rural or Subsistence conditions, is taken up by kinsfolk and neighbors from whom aid and comfort are regarded as axiomatic. The lack of a general and common participatory base certainly ensures a tolerance unknown in the rural or Subsistence environment. Each is allowed his peculiar form of deviance. Indeed, to describe the aggregation as comprised of varieties of deviants inhabiting demimondes of nonconformity is not inaccurate. The stranger becomes not so much the compelling if suspect source of new information as another face in the crowd. When the situation is appreciated as random, disorder and amorality are evoked. The order that exists arises from a complex of structures revealed by and subject to work routines and the procedures, rules, and rituals which, authorized by constituent bureaucracies, first usurp and then become the effective moralities.

Under such conditions the self develops and integrates the person. In turn, the person yields a sense of self which, different from other selves, may well bemoan the lack of community and cry loneliness. Autonomy may be claimed but is more surely a chimera produced by the variegated memberships and role categories inherent in the range of options available. Routines and procedures absorb the attempt to realize a morality that might go beyond a limited participatory base. Integrity in identity, the peculiar integration of what all hold in common and acknowledge, becomes an anonymity stamped with the identities of different bureaucracies. The epitome and summit of self-realization are contained in a knowledge of the rule book, the perfect bureaucrat or committee member. Conversely, particularly in the European or Western ambience, eccentricities and evasions of the rules—expressions of the random—become frequent. Defrauding bureaucracies becomes popularly permissive. Lacking the common and cohesive participatory audience, the warped individual—Kierkegaard's "man of movement"—becomes a continually recurring phenomenon. But because they are ethically and morally confused these "men of movement" can rarely succeed in doing more than add to the procedural rules. Bureaucracy becomes magnified, the moralities are buried even deeper in the interstices of procedure.

The tensions generated by the opposition between *giving* ⇌ *receiving* and *giving* ≠ *receiving* are not exclusive to social relationships in the City or Town. But when joined with the opposition between the provision of a wide—and often appreciated as random—variety of social contacts, cultural amenities, and opportunities on the one hand, and the constraints of official procedures and daily work and social routines on the other, social relationships become informed with an almost unreconcilable opposition between the random or undisciplined and the tightly constrained. This means opting for, or alternating between, the one or the other. Personal integrity, if it exists, is difficult to perceive in another. Individuality is then left with three main avenues of realization: charismatic activity and the formation of a moral community in those physical or social spaces which will not engage the spoiling attentions of bureaucracies; fulfilling the moral task within an existing but restricted social ambience, from which the greater community might take example; or by withdrawal, in which case, if the attention of the greater community is not held, the would-be individual and his perceptions tend to be lost in obscurity.

REFLECTIONS

Brief though this survey has been it suggests that while individuality or its semblances can be said to be—indeed must be—everywhere possible, there are certain conditions, occasions, relationships, and forms of organization which either inhibit or encourage creative apperceptions. The social organizations of the Australians and the Inuit or Eskimos demonstrate the polarities. While persons in particular roles and statuses governed by the given expectations and reciprocities of dyadic relationships are common to both, the former evokes prescriptions of order, the latter ranges of permissiveness. Marriage classes, clans, corporate descent groups, associations, cult or property holding groups, bureaucracies and the like recall the group memberships, shared interests, and sociocentricities of the Australians: events are held in relatively rigid, traditional, and given rationalizations of them; rerationalizations tend to be referred to tradition and found wanting $(E < R)$. Where on the other hand an organizational form, such as the Inuit kindred based on cognation, provides each with a unique set of interests and interactions, events become subject to alternative and, therefore, possible new rationalizations $(E > R)$.

The rhythms of nomadic life certainly seem to encourage self-reliance and independence of mind: putatively an excellent basis for individuality. What is found in fact, however, is either, as with some Pastoral nomads, a rigorously prescriptive ethic and morality which effectively inhibits or prohibits moral innovation, or physical conditions of life which return the would-be moral innovator to accepted modes of dealing with them. Nevertheless, the opportunity seems to be there even though, when grasped, it cannot be fully realized. And, echoing Kierkegaard, the rhythms of concentration and dispersal may be subsumed in relationships of involvement/withdrawal; such rhythms and their analogues or correspondences in other orders and circumstances are usefully abstracted as possibly conducive to the emergence of an individual. Puberty and initiation, and the relations between senior and junior, men and women, elder sibling and younger sibling appear as occasions and relationships capable of energizing fresh rationalizations. They reveal various kinds of responsibility and/or accountability pitted against sorts of non-responsibility which move from the not yet responsible through impulsiveness to the fickle and irresponsible. On the one hand there are the obligation and burden of commitment to tradition and loyalty to the consensual group, on the other a critique and no such burden. Subsumed in relationships of responsibility/impulsiveness, the fresh rationalization may be taken to emerge from the interaction. It is not necessarily perceived or articulated by the original critical impulse. Transformations of each other, involvement/withdrawal and responsibility/impulsiveness indicate differing aspects of the constitutive conditions of the individual.

Of itself population density seems irrelevant to the emergence of an individual. And it is instructive to note that the size of an interactional range does not alter very much. What is significant is the totality of experience and varieties of moral stretch inhering in the roles and statuses which comprise the interactional range. For while status, the having of an acknowledged position and identity within a known and acceptable system of roles and statuses, is essential to every coherent social order—and must present a stony face to new moralities which would imply a different status system and threaten those in power—the experience of variegated systems of roles and statuses implies choice and critique. And urban conditions, offering the encounter with other moralities and varieties of experience of other statuses, seem on the surface conducive to realizing the individual. But unless there is a community of interacting and mutually participatory selves which is prepared to accept a new status system and not penalize the movement from someone to no one, the movement that might have led into individuality is more likely to lead into mere eccentricity. Yet money may resolve the situation in a series of ambiguities which, again, spell out relationships of involvement/withdrawal. By bringing variegated roles and statuses into relationship and mutual involvement, money demands contractual or quasi-contractual exchanges, "prescriptions of order." It also, however, loosens the prescriptive dyads, relaxes sociocentrically intellectualized rationalizations, images, and ethics, brings the sexes into ambiguous relationships, and engenders ego-centered relations, "ranges of permissiveness." Which is to reiterate in another way the dilemma of Peasant conditions. But while *giving* $\approx$ *receiving* inhibits new moralities, and *giving* $\neq$ *receiving* presents opportunities for moral innovation, under urban conditions money goes along with bureaucracies which seek and obtain more and more control over the money which is their lives' blood. And though bureaucracies offer involvement, their procedures take the place of personal moralities, tend to become the model for morality, and so become almost as prescriptive and restrictive as, for example, Australian marriage classes and section or subsection systems. Individuality is throttled and constrained into the person. And if varieties of corruption in relation to the procedures become the only escape from the system, we have surely to question not the corruption but the procedures, and then ask why anyone should try to elude the grip of what, for most, is a reasonably comfortable berth.

The institutionalized and generalized individuality of European or Western society is apt to be taken for granted. Though each may become and remain an individual, most are persons most of the time, realizing individuality by moving into the individual for a while and returning again to the person. This indeed is what generalized and institutionalized in-

dividuality means. At best we realize very restricted universals, living very much inside the potential of the categories,
let alone fulfilling or hurdling them. We feed on and are fat-
tened by the categories. We die for them, they kill us, we
allow them to become truth, as God. Only a few stout souls
with spirit fight them and survive. Nevertheless, generalized
and institutionalized individuality is distinctive of European
or Western civilization in contrast to other cultures. In spite of
varieties of inhibitory social conditions as they may exist at
any chosen time, the basic and imperative axiom and instruction is that each should at some time become an individual.
Having done so, a return to the person is mostly but not always inevitable.

   This imperative appears as a quantum leap in relation to
other cultures in which individuality or its semblances,
though not always necessarily proscribed, is either contingent
and occasional, or reserved to particular people in prescribed
positions—leader, mediator, diviner, shaman and the like:
situations which evoke an opposition between those imprisoned in the normative moralities or cultural categories and
those others who, expected to resolve moral conflicts, are
placed to mediate the moralities and, by so doing, may initiate new ones. For ourselves, however, if we tend always to
individualize and individuate, this is because the idea of the
individual permeates our civilization. Our modes of production require obedience and cooperation, team work and
group loyalty, just as in any other social or cultural environment. Nevertheless, individualities are continually generated.
Except perhaps for a brief period in the nineteenth century,
collective ownership, whether in the shape of family groups
or corporate bodies or governmental institutions, has always
dominated personal ownership or rights over property. Still,
individuality is habitually realized. Indeed, the more property
a single person has in relation to others the less involved and
the more isolated in thought and activity that person tends to
become. And the eccentric is not necessarily an individual.
Even where a single person comes to exercise a tyrannous

control over property the result is usually not individuality but just tyranny.

Mary Douglas (1970: 102) has argued that the difference between our own society and small-scale primitive societies is that in the latter persons can continually interact with and modify their constraints, while we cannot argue with the system but are held prisoner by the constraints of industrialized society. The sociocentric and exteriorized ethics and images of the Australians and some Pastoral nomads are surely just as restrictive. Douglas also points out (1970: 40) that withdrawal from society, denying the potential of the social organization, results in a poverty of developmental scope. Yet, again recognizing Kierkegaard, a withdrawal may be necessary. Individuality is the refusal to surrender to things as they are or as particular traditional intellectualizations or bureaucracies want them to be. Individual and person are opposed. The latter is product of conditions, the former exists in spite of them. Bureaucratic procedures create the person, emasculate individuality. Nevertheless, the person is both end and purpose of individuality. For in the moment that an individual successfully persuades others of new moralities—implying new rules and a new arrangement of roles and statuses together with own identification with them—*that* particular individuality dissolves into an identity. The scene is set for a fresh transcending.

If individuality arose from material conditions solely, bureaucracies would long ago surely have expunged it. And to argue that the material conditions themselves make possible the reactions to them is but to remove material conditions from the equation altogether. The correspondence between material conditions, social relationships, and thought processes or intellectualizations points to the person. The intuition or perception which, hinging on the event, results in a new intellectualization, a new view of the relevances of existing sociomaterial conditions, points to the individual who, in creating new conditions, makes a new person possible. The question whether one must first change oneself before changing the world or first change the world so that one might be transformed and free could only arise out of and seems to be resolved in the individual as here determined. In most societies individuality and its semblances are reserved to prescribed and identifiable positions within the social order. This is because individuality is fundamentally opposed to tradition and creates disorder. As we shall see, generalized individuality, the idea that each has the right—even obligation—to become an individual and, moreover—a qualification that can sometimes amount to a contradiction—move from person to individual and back again to the person, has very particular roots. Now, however, illustrating the moments of individuality as a universal, we turn to examine individuals or their likenesses in prescribed positions.

6 PRESCRIBED POSITIONS

Because individuality has been characterized as a movement between person and individual (*person* ⇌ *individual* → *individuality*), it may seem confusing to consider some examples in which individuals or their likenesses are forced to occupy prescribed roles and positions within the community, and may not be individuals or like individuals outside those positions. Yet if one remembers that the characterization of individuality has been drawn from the European experience, and that the movement between person and individual is not necessarily restricted as to frequency or duration, much of the confusion disappears. What is important is to appreciate the ways in which something like the individual or individuality with which we are familiar occurs in other cultures. It then becomes possible to recognize individuality as a thematic fact of culture with varying expressions. Starting with the Shaman, we consider in turn the Nuer Leopard-skin chief, the Melanesian manager and/or Sorcerer, the Australian Man of High Degree, and the Hindu Sanyasi.

THE SHAMAN

Under a variety of local vernacular terms, specialisms and differentiations which point either to a common origin or to a common human trait, the Shaman is to be found among most of the indigenous peoples of Asia and the Americas, and may be discerned in at least some aspects among many other peoples (see Eliade 1964). For present purposes it is the pristine and undifferentiated Shaman of the small Hunter-gathering group who is important. In larger groups this possibly prototypical individual becomes differentiated into a host of more specialized roles—prophet, priest, king, saint, diviner, seer, charlatan, doctor, spirit medium, confessor, psychiatrist, judge, and mediator are some examples. But, as with the other examples to be considered presently, interest in the Shaman is here confined to ways in which he or she illustrates the moments of the individual.

The proportion of Shamans to others in small Hunter-gatherer groups is generally high: between one to three in some areas of northern Asia to about one to thirty or forty in more heavily populated areas. All of a Shaman's considerable powers are seen as gifts from the gods or spirits: not derived from other men or women or from his or her position in society—though learning how to cope with these powers is a matter of tutelage. And although becoming a Shaman is very often hereditary, it is not open to any one who might want to do so to become a Shaman. The Shaman is called into being; becoming a Shaman is truly vocational. Afflicted in the first instance by sickness, dizziness, fits, and mental disorders which are seen as the results of spirit activity, he or she who would become a Shaman should attain self-knowledge through an effective interpretation of dream life and must master the spirit or spirits causing the afflictions. In more prosaic terms, the unsocialized elements within the person, those warring impulses and perceptions rooted in the animal and in the psyche or soul, are not to be suppressed but mastered and utilized. Indeed, this mastery of dream life and the spirits (and so of those impulses and perceptions within the self) is the defining characteristic of the Shaman. Achieving such mastery is a long and tiring ordeal entailing a continuing struggle against the temptation to give up and become someone else's sick dependent. And it requires being apprenticed to an acknowledged master-Shaman.

The apprenticeship completed, the neophyte is initiated. This takes the form of a symbolic death and dismemberment followed by renewal and resurrection. That is, he or she dies

to the society of persons and becomes as no one before entering into the Hero who can survive a death and become as
everyone. Separated from the mutually engaged community
of persons, with the distinctive powers which accrue from or
go together with the mastery of spirit life, the Shaman is also
differently clothed. Shaggy-haired, dirty, wearing long gar-
ments hung with shreds, streamers, and pendants of iron
talismans, he or she is distinctive at the level of eye-glance.
An ecstatic, this transformation in physiological or animal
condition is taken to indicate the Shaman's ability to commune with animals (movement from moral and cultural to
animal) as well as with spirits (movement from moral and
cultural to the putatively spiritual). Yet since it is required
that the ecstasy be controlled within a limited repertoire of
expressions and manifestations, cultural and moral capacities
must also be employed. Allowing, then, that the ecstasy is of
itself some kind of spiritual experience, it combines the realization of cultural and moral potential with entry into the
being of animal. Whether that harmony of inner and outer
conditions which defines the spiritual condition is always
achieved, only a Shaman could tell us. Presumably not. But
once or twice in a lifetime would be sufficient.

A Shaman's ecstasy is also described as a "magical flight"
(Eliade 1964: 477ff.) outside society—to commune with and
manipulate the spirits or a particular spirit. For although a
Shaman's powers come from "outside," are derived from the
gods or spirits, a Shaman is not possessed by the spirits or
spirit but possesses them. That is what *mastery* is about. A cultural being but not a person, a Shaman stands aside from the
interacting community from initiation on, and the magical
flight develops this separation to secure a viewpoint outside
the social order: a correspondence with Kierkegaard's Archimedean point in relation to the "special individual."

Among the Shaman's many roles and functions, within or
outside the context of ecstasy, he or she is a doctor. But if
some part of a Shaman's expertise is directed to the diagnosis
and cure of physical lesion with medicines, the greater part is

devoted to healing the soul or psyche: the cure of moral or spiritual lesion. And to succeed in this the Shaman must be able to enter into the being, the selves, of those who seek his or her ministrations. He or she has to experience—and in the vocational trauma has indeed acutely experienced—what others are experiencing or have experienced and become as everyone, knowing the possibilities of being in all. As a diviner the Shaman resolves or rather delineates moral problems, reveals them, suggests solutions, and in so doing reiterates the normative moralities. Yet the process contains at least the seeds of qualifying, developing, or even transcending current moralities. In this way a Shaman may become at least the instigator of moral innovation even if there is no direct and explicit innovation on his or her part.

A male Shaman is able to cross the sexual barrier and become as a woman; and though it is reputedly a much more difficult feat, a female Shaman can become as a man. If the exchange of primary sexual characteristics must be very rare, exchanges of voice, demeanor, being, and moral perspective are certainly not as rare. A Shaman is said to be able to penetrate to the underworld as well as the heavens, is supposedly the master of fire and air, and can travel in magical flight both into the future and into the past. In thus crossing the boundaries between, and transcending at least in a symbolic sense the polarities typical of the human condition—heaven/earth, underworld/surface world, gods or spirits/man, spirit/matter, man/animal, past/present, present/future, male/female, life/death, hidden being/overt being—the Shaman is a transformational agent, revealing transformation, and clearly a symbol: both reiterating and reconciling the contraries involved. But since other sorts of symbols might do these same things, what seems important is the Shaman's ability to reveal the process involved in being a whole human being. The cultural faculties are used to confront, move between and overcome the divides between the animal and moral, and the moral and the spiritual, thus demonstrating the difference between the person's experience and what is actually there to be experienced, and revealing the continuities and interrelatedness of all things and experience over against the distinctions and discriminations of current cultural categories.

As encountered among Hunter-gatherers, who seem to have retained much the same social orders over many centuries, the Shaman, it is clear, does not necessarily initiate new material orders. And the fact that Shamans of virtually the same kind are to be found among Pastoral nomads and Subsistence cultivators, as well as within the ambience of a Complex economy, indicates their virtual independence of particular cultural and material conditions: individuality receives a certain shape. Removed from the interacting community of persons, yet necessarily in specific relations with the community as a whole as well as in a variety of relationships with each of its members, the neophyte's struggle to become and then remain a Shaman reveals a sacrifice on behalf of others. Because a Shaman is usually also a spouse, a hunter or gatherer and maker of artifacts—plays a part in the general subsistence activities of the community—he or she at least participates in the person. Specifically separated from persons at initiation, a Shaman's career suggests a series of movements between a structured someone and an unstructured no one, anyone, or everyone. Unstructured, the Shaman is in command of acknowledged sources of truth. Moving thence to someone, the moralities are mediated. What is appropriate to social relationships is made manifest, and, in particular circumstances, what *should now* be proper—hurdling extant categories to realize new moralities—may also be at least suggested.*

THE NUER LEOPARD-SKIN CHIEF

Evans-Pritchard has described the Nuer in great wealth of detail (1940; 1951; 1956). Cattle-keeping Pastoral nomads who

*Basic material on the Shaman taken from Eliade's masterpiece (1964).

live in the savannah lands of the southern Sudan, the Nuer might easily be described as "individualistic." By which is meant, roughly, that Nuer men are proud, self-reliant, egalitarian, have their own opinions, are independent-minded, do not take kindly to personal criticism or rebuffs, are jealous of their pride, honor, and integrity as men, think of themselves as hardy and brave, give knock for knock, feel themselves everyone else's equal or superior. In somewhat lower key and register, Nuer women follow their men. In general, their lives are subject to determinations and disposi-tions made by men. Nevertheless, some women of independ-ent character may become as men, marry a wife (paying the necessary bridewealth), and become the father of children through a man retained as a begetter.

Organized in segmentary agnatic lineages, Nuer frequently fight among themselves. Sometimes large segments of op-posed lineages are involved, sometimes smaller segments. In one affray a couple of men might be allies, in another on different sides. With strong group allegiances, Nuer are brave and determined, quick to take offense, contemptuous of ask-ing for quarter. But if the logistics of the situation prevent large groups from confronting each other and fighting to a finish, and values developed through marriage counteract those attaching to the agnatic group and provide the basis of a peaceful settlement, the instrument of truce and peace is the Leopard-skin chief.

Though most of those who become Leopard-skin chiefs are agnatically related to each other, many are not, and, in con-trast to ordinary Nuer who are agnatically related, they do not form a solidary group. They live apart from each other, as strangers attached to other clans and lineages. The proportion of Leopard-skin chiefs to other Nuer is not accurately known, but may be one to several hundreds. Leopard-skin chiefs are of and within, yet also outside of or aside from the commu-nity of mutually engaged persons. Like a Shaman, a Leopard-skin chief is distinctively clothed, with a leopard skin over his shoulder. He is dirty and shaggy-haired, in many respects the antithesis of what ordinary Nuer would regard as a model of manhood. Though Leopard-skin chiefs have powers of cursing and blessing, are in a sacred association with the earth underfoot, have certain ritual powers in relation to the earth, and are rainmakers, ordinary Nuer, Nuer persons, do not regard these powers with more than ordinary respect. This is reserved for the prophets, those seized by the divine spirits. Nonetheless, Leopard-skin chiefs are regarded as sacred, not to be lightly treated or gainsaid.

When Nuer are about to fight, a Leopard-skin chief may dart between the lines of combatants, digging up clods of earth. The fighting must cease. When segments of the community come into conflict in obedience to the same moral code, the Leopard-skin chief draws the disputants into making peace, mediates the moralities, settles the amounts of compensation to be paid. He gives sanctuary to homicides, negotiates a settlement, and supervises the rehabilitation of the killer. Owing to the broad scope of Nuer incest rules, the incidence of incestuous sexual relationships, unwittingly or otherwise, is relatively frequent. A Leopard-skin chief cleanses the parties to an incestuous relationship, officiates at the sacrifice which brings them back into the community. He negotiates the compensation consequent on an adultery. Homicide, incest, adultery, and quarrels over women and cattle are the principal occasions on which Nuer take to their spears and clubs. In each case the Leopard-skin chief makes peace, negotiates a settlement, and officiates at the sacrifice which resolves the moral conflict by finding unity in the spirit.

In thus presiding over situations that can be briefly defined by the oppositions, life/death, animal/moral, moral/nonmoral, moral/spiritual, the Leopard-skin chief emerges as being mainly concerned with maintaining and mediating the moralities. Though he may have gifts of the spirit, the powers and functions of a Leopard-skin chief derive not from his personal qualities, knowledge, insights, and compulsion to know and speak out the truth of things, but from the position or office. As a peacemaker and negotiator, the Leopard-skin chief fulfills the cultural categories. But he is restrained from going beyond current moralities in order to initiate a new morality: the strong group allegiances and interests of ordinary Nuer hold him to what is given. Yet individuality is there in embryo if not fully fledged. Separation from the engaged community enables the man to interact with others and the given moralities in ways which need not always be predefined. Sacrifice is entailed in the hard life that he is forced to live: dependent, outcast, on the peripheries of community. His existence and being are on behalf of others, not for himself. Associated with the above, the air, the sky, and also, particularly, with the earth, he officiates at sacrifices which invoke spirit, and reconciles the conflict between men-in-community by referring to spirit or the spiritual.

A symbol of the possibilities and continuities which the cultural prescriptions and normative moralities must both acknowledge and reject, the Leopard-skin chief stands on the outer frame within which the body of the culture is contained. Moving thence to persons in community imprisoned in the cultural categories, he is enabled to mediate and resolve moral conflicts, affirm and make clear what is proper to the issues in question.

The Shaman and Leopard-skin chief do what they do in terms of quite distinct cultural representations. But they are on common ground in having being apart from the mutually engaged community of persons, in their access to spirit or the spiritual, and in their use of the cultural faculties to confront and overcome pertinent oppositions. Each stands in and symbolizes a body of truths larger than and distinct from but apparently necessary to the given cultural prescriptions and moral discriminations of persons in community; each expresses a relation between the definitively structured and the relatively unstructured or unknown or uncontrollable. The Leopard-skin chief presents himself to mutually opposed segments to uphold and reaffirm given moralities, resorting

to the spiritual to do so. But he is bound to his office. Whatever his discoveries about the self, and however he himself
realizes the self, he is restricted in communicating his discoveries and realizations. And in mediating the moralities he
is held to the normative modes. Still, he reveals some of the
shape of the individual and the circumstances in which that
shape can be found.

The Shaman, overcome by emotional or psychological
trauma, has an initial problem between the self and the cultural categories to deal with. The teacher-pupil relationship
helps him or her to overcome the trauma and integrate differing orders of truth into the self. Later, though restricted in
repertoire of expressions, there are opportunities to transcend
the normative moralities and communicate discoveries and
realizations whether they relate to the nature of the Shaman's
own self or to the nature of the human. That there have been
Shamans who have left a lasting impression on the audiences
of the nature of the human self cannot be doubted. Nor is
there any doubt that there have been Shamans who have been
able to translate their insights into the human self, soul or
psyche into acceptable new moral categories. And so far as a
Shaman does find new moral categories that are acceptable to
others, so far does he or she realize individuality. Even the
evil Shaman, the Shaman who works for his or her own
selfish ends, who exacerbates conflicts and trades on fears,
does this in a perverse way—a way that is scarcely open to the
Leopard-skin chief, who is bound to the terms of his office.

THE MELANESIAN MANAGER
AND / OR SORCERER

In contrast to the set-apartness of the Shaman and the
Leopard-skin chief, the next example, abstracted from the
New Guinea scene, illustrates something very similar to generalized individuality: the individual about to emerge from
the community of mutually engaged persons.

The basic configuration may be discussed in terms of four main categories: the manager, the sorcerer, ordinary persons, and the "rubbish" (Pidgin *rabis* = rubbish, trash) man. Within a generally competitive and egalitarian ambience grounded in the reciprocal and roughly equivalent exchange of foodstuffs, where each significant exchange is criticized in relation to equivalence and the egalitarian ethic, a manager is one who, through his industry and managerial ability, gains for himself a wider range of exchange obligations than most others. In disbursing more foodstuffs to more others than most, he gains in relative prestige and status, creates a larger circle of people who become obliged to him, becomes a political boss or leader. Some in this circle of exchange relationships are other managers, while most are ordinary persons at a variety of stages in realizing their own ambitions to become managers and politically relevant. The bulk of the community consists of these ordinary persons, who are mutually engaged to one another and to managers in complexes of exchange relationships. Those who, for a variety of reasons, cannot or choose not to engage in the competitive ambience of exchanges, are the "rubbish" men. They forgo significant relative status in the community, virtually abdicate moral status, but may be politically useful in that they can be relied on to transmit injurious gossip and tittle-tattle which the originator can disclaim with impunity. If some maintain a narrow circle of exchange obligations with close kin, others opt out almost entirely, working only to maintain themselves and their immediate families. In a community of, say, forty or fifty households, there may be as many as six fully fledged managers, one or two "rubbish" men maintaining only themselves and their families, and perhaps four or five maintaining minimal exchange relationships.

The category "sorcerer" is, generally, a label looking for a man. Some men are "known" as sorcerers, a few may even rejoice in being known as such. Still, despite a wide range of connotations, most people do not like sorcerers. A sorcerer is a nonconformist of evil intent who is prepared to resort to mystical, unfair, and underhand methods to realize his ambitions or desires. He may induce sickness in others, thus reducing their productive potential. He may kill, directly or by mystical means. He is an adulterer. Because sorcerers are dangerous, willful, and self-motivated, ordinary persons fear them, are circumspect in their presence, take care not to offend them. Ideally, managers are expected and enjoined to act openly and fairly. This does not mean that they have to be transparently honest, revealing their stratagems and plans. In the most brief and summary sense it means that a manager should not be a sorcerer. Still, because there comes a time when a manager, reaching the limits of his productive capacity to cope with a widening circle of exchange relationships, must tap the reservoirs of confidence he has built up over the years in obligations actually met, and has to use personal qualities of persuasion to obtain credit, the temptation to resort to sorcery is almost irresistible. The label sorcerer begins to hover very close. Few managers are not thought of as sorcererlike, few "known" sorcerers are not also managers. As "gangster," "political boss," and "entrepreneurial tycoon" are ideally separate categories which may nonetheless cohere in one person in the Western world, so is it with sorcerer and manager.

Becoming a manager and maintaining the status requires not only industry in the productive process, but a sure sense of social situation. This entails acute and shrewd perceptions into the natures, motives, capacities, and ambitions of others seen against the inherent possibilities and probabilities of their maintained ambiences of social relationships. It also entails— in relation to sources of truth which may be found in dreams, encounters with ghosts or spirits, or an encapsulation of mythological lore in relation to the observational experience of what people actually do in particular circumstances—an effective knowledge of oneself in relation to others. Manipulating ambiguous or ambivalent social relationships, a manager is continually called upon to finesse situations when his cards are weak, and extract the maximum advantage when his hand is strong. Testing himself and being tested by others against a complete fulfillment of the available cultural categories, a manager is frequently forced into going beyond the normative moralities, must rise above principle. If, however, he is discovered going beyond the divide he falls into amorality or immorality and becomes much like a sorcerer. Then, if he has not the necessary resources of character, disaster follows. On the other hand, if his managerial capacities are exceptional he may create a quite distinct and publicly acceptable ambience of morality for himself and his activities (cf. Watson 1971). Or, by manipulating the colonial administrative apparatus, he may even impose a new morality on the whole community (cf. Hogbin 1951: 151-63). In both cases cited, as well as in others, the assertion of control was demonstrated by committing adultery at will with impunity. That is, supermanager had become as though supersorcerer.

In such a system the "rubbish" man may realize the self in those ways which he feels are open to him. But he is not tested against the full range of activities afforded him by his culture. In particular, if it so happens that he is aware of a moral problem and crisis, and not simply lazy, he cannot effectively test his solutions in the deed: he becomes a mere drop-out. He creates a style of his own, to be sure, but it is a style held in contempt by others. Rather than interact and so experience the extent and force of the given moralities and then transcend them, he ignores the challenge and wraps himself in a cocoon of his own being. In other cultures this kind of disengagement may be thought so exemplary and appropriate that a special niche is provided. But in New Guinea, and Melanesia generally, where participatory interactions through exchanges of specie are moral imperatives, the "rubbish" man is regarded as something less than a person.

In their several ways manager, sorcerer, ordinary person, and "rubbish" man realize the self, integrate their contexts of being. But the manager who breasts the full range of given moralities and can transcend them moves into the individual. The sorcerer, on the other hand, appears as an individual manqué. Instead of realizing the individual by transcending moralities, he either ignores them, breaches them, or uses other peoples' adherence to them to engender hatreds and fears to gain his own selfish ends. Yet whether it is to exemplify the good successfully, or work evil effectively, both manager and sorcerer must enjoy fruitful relations with their sources of truth, their dreams, tutelary ghosts, and spirits. And, since interpreting dreams and encounters with ghosts or spirits can be shown to be encounters with the covert self or subconscious in an ambience of given moralities framed by larger truths and possibilities (cf. Burridge 1969b: 434-36), it becomes clear that managers as well as sorcerers should not only know themselves in their entireties but be acutely aware of themselves in relation to others, the normative moralities, and life's further possibilities. And precisely this awareness of the relations between the given structure and truths which are presently unstructured, anomic, accounts for their success and effectiveness. Yet a manager who moves too obviously too far into the presently unstructured, who embraces too closely perceptions of truth unknown to others, becomes thought of as a sorcerer and is either undone or forced back into the accepted managerial role. In manipulating an imposed but quite different system such as the colonial apparatus, a manager defies rather than transcends commonly held moralities. And in time this defiance becomes his undoing. Though manager and sorcerer, each, demonstrate some of the moments of the individual, individuality is more clearly revealed in the movement between manager and sorcerer, in the temptation to forgo or defy morality and yield to arrogance. For it is surely in the hesitations of such temptation that a sorcerer's defiance can become distinguishable from the manager's command over conscience—from which new moralities may be generated.

Managers and sorcerers do not stand apart from the community. On the contrary, they are engaged in more interactions than most more intensely; they are heavily involved.

Nevertheless, they become singled out, they focus the gaze of others, reveal contradictions and oppositions, and attempt to impose their resolutions. The manager fulfills most of the conditions of the Hero. The sorcerer is villain certainly, but also Hero manqué. For although in the empirical situation few sorcerers are not managers, and few managers are not also sorcerers in some ways, the sorcerer is explicitly an adversary set over and against the moral community while, ideally, the manager participates in and attempts to fulfill the beings and desires of those who look to him. More than anyone else a manager bears the burdens and responsibilities of managing community affairs. His are the initiatives which count for most. Himself subject to the active criticism of others, and compelled to overcome these by a constructive handling of the ways in which others do or do not honor their exchange obligations, a manager's pressures sharpen the edges of the moralities, make their structure evident, and may even overflow into new moralities.

Manager, sorcerer, Shaman, and Leopard-skin chief have one important feature in common: when they act or intervene in community affairs they do so at moments of danger, conflict, ambiguity, and at least incipient disorder or anomie. As a result of their activities a traditional order is reimposed or a new order created. Their activities make the ordering or structuring of social relationships sensible, felt, evident. Unlike the Leopard-skin chief, who is constrained by his office, the Manager may become a sorcerer and the Shaman may use his powers for evil. But while the Shaman and Leopard-skin chief realize themselves and reveal their parts from protected and privileged positions, sacrosanct to the community at large, a Melanesian manager is as vulnerable as any other—more so if anything—and has only his own resources of character and will in relation to perceptions of truth on which to base his thrusts and build his defenses to defy the assaults of others. In many respects merely a "man of movement," seeking his own advantage irrespective of the moralities and often provoking the situations he is asked to resolve, he, in relation to the constituent parts of a sorcerer, shows forth what it is like to be an individual.

THE AUSTRALIAN "MAN OF HIGH DEGREE"

In their classic condition nomadic Hunter-gatherers, Australian communities had in their traditional Law a well-defined and articulated body of knowledge and rules of conduct which was inculcated in males through a series of initiatory rituals and ordeals from puberty through middle to late middle age. Women, under the direct control of fathers or brothers or husbands, did not have to suffer these procedures. Unstructured in relation to their men who had to abide by the Law, women were a main source of the dynamic in social relationships. Promised in marriage in infancy, when a girl reached marriageable age she might object, arrange to be abducted, run away. Such events caused quarrels, fights and, perhaps, rearrangements of the relationships among the men. And the whims, vagaries, or initiatives of married women could give rise to much the same results. But if the men's reactions to such apparent caprice was firm, the resolution of the situation was in accordance with the demands of the Law as, in more serious cases, interpreted by the elders in council.

Both points of departure for, and the ideal realization of, community activities, the Law was meticulously articulated in prescriptive rules which applied to all dyads, rituals, ceremonies, exploitative and cult rights in relation to game, land, topographical features, the spirits, ancestral beings and other noncorporeal beings associated with them. Categories of kinship, marriage class or section or subsection, and totemic or cult affiliation (of which there could be several), determined identities. Members of community addressed each other not by personal names but by the categories appropriate to the situation. The Law and its ordering of social relationships formed a tight, sociocentrically defined defensive ring which could be qualified by consent after significant interaction with other groups, but could only be breached or shattered by overwhelming events such as starvation or the inroads and activities of European settlers. Even then, despite the absence of sustaining networks of active social relationships, survivors have clung to what they have thought was their Law, given to them in the ancient dreamtime. The Law made them human, worthwhile. Without the Law they were as nothings.

Australians had their wrongdoers, transgressors, and their sorcerers: men who used the knowledge given them by the Law to evade and counter it for their own selfish ends. They had also their "men of high degree" (Elkin 1944), specific exemplars of extraordinary achievement within the Law. And it is possible that there were times when these men became individuals, explicitly made new law, new moralities, and so transformed the Law (cf. Elkin 1944, Eliade 1973). But it could not have been frequent. Initiation, too, provided individuality with its opportunity. But one may fairly doubt whether much advantage was taken: the Law as it stood invited fulfillment, prestige, and influence. A death, on the other hand, left a small loophole in the normative modes. A blank on the social map had to be filled. Outstanding debts and obligations had to be honored by kinsfolk and successors. Persons had to rearrange themselves in relation to one another in terms of the enduring categories and the Law. But before the Law closed in and pulled members of community into line, there was a brief period of something like anomie: interrelationships within the community were uncertain. Then, in the midst of complex discussions and disputed decisions in relation to the funeral arrangements and the rights and obligations of others in relation to the dead man and his estate in personal property, ritual rights, privileges, and dependents, a man of outstanding character and ability, a Man of High Degree, might use his initiative, transcend current moralities and responsibly impose his will on the situation. But how regularly this was done remains in doubt.

Australians found their symbols in meteorological phenomena, celestial bodies, material artifacts, the ancestral beings, topographical features, flora and fauna which they made into refractions of themselves and their thoughts about themselves. Rich mythologies welded the ambiguities of culture into a sustaining and integrated whole. Realizing the self through a complete understanding and integration of the various complex aspects of the traditional Law was fulfillment enough: Kierkegaard's "individual," the realization of a (local) universal. On the other hand, becoming an individual in the sense determined here was necessarily restricted. People were persons. Each was someone, an identity which, when fully realized, reiterated that mastery over conflict and opposition leading into a harmony of inner and outer condition contained in a correct interpretation of the Law.

The Australian case suggests that having achieved a particular kind of sociocentrically organized steady state, individuality or its semblances become unnecessary, even undesirable. On the other hand, while individuality or something like it seems to be required if thought and culture are to change, grow, and develop, the former does not always predicate the latter. The steady state of traditional Arctic cultures was based on frequent expressions of at least the semblances of individuality. And while a sophisticated computerization of the variables involved might tell us whether Australian organizational forms could survive in arctic conditions and vice versa, on the face of it the variability of Australian physical environments in relation to the homogeneity of organizational forms, and a comparison between the resources, hardships, and exigencies provided by arctic and Australian conditions, leave us little on which to ground an accounting for the differences.

When Europeans first encountered them, the Australians seem to have made a near perfect adaptation to exterior conditions, and their intellectualizations of their experience were as complete in the circumstances as human imagination could take them. The initial impact of European settlers shattered the Law among those communities with whom they came in contact. The survivors, and those out of reach of the new-comers, seem then to have held to their Law more rigidly than they perhaps might have done. They had the choice of remaining themselves by holding to the Law and rejecting European ways, or becoming something other than they had been. And this the majority disdained.

Often tiresome, usually with a viability that long outlasts their attachments to former conditions of life, the moralities constitute the large bulk of all that human communities have and must hold if they are to survive and demonstrate their humanity. Moral rules are the guide to spirituality as well as the obstacle to spirituality, determine the dialectics of explo-ration and self-conscious knowledge, and, when appropri-ately confronted, indicate the differences between the human and other kinds of life. In particular and in relation to our theme, artificial though they may have become in other re-spects, moral rules provide identity. They provide the person with placement in relation to others in the community, dis-tinguish one kind of community from another. And only the individual, who is prepared to forgo a present identity and enter a limbo of nonidentity, seems to possess what is neces-sary to bring about a change in the rules and forge new kinds of identity. He or she creates new being, explores and enters a field of inestimable value to the sum of human potential.

Until fairly recently, echoing the imperatives of ages past, the Australians have clung to their Law, realizing themselves within it. If there were, here and there, some who in fact be-came individuals, it was that great artist, Albert Namatjira, who marked the beginning of a new pattern. Without the words on his tongue, he put his individuality into paint. And what he put into paint, others are now discovering and ex-pressing in other ways. Unable to retreat any further, ines-capably becoming a part of the European or Western heritage, but still determined to retain a separate identity, individuals are springing up to change the traditional Law (cf. Berndt 1962; Pilling and Waterman 1970). Though for many years the Australians were thought to be a dying race, the fact that

their populations are now increasing and coming to terms
with the changed environment is due in no small measure to
their development of individuality: it has survival value in any
environment, particularly so in one that is unstable, and no
environment that includes man can remain perfectly stable for
long. In their centuries of isolation from the rest of humanity,
Australians seem to have virtually achieved in their social orders and rationalizations that wholeness and completeness
which allowed a person to realize the self in a harmony of
inner and outer conditions. Events, social relationships, and
their rationalizations—the ingredients of a community—were
an almost perfectly interconsistent harmony. That is, in and
by themselves they had more or less fulfilled the human quest
and potential. When placed side by side with other cultures,
however, the Australian achievement forces us to accept the
fact that wholeness has different levels of fulfillment depending on the range of the total social ambience. Opposed to the
given local universal, the generalized individuality of European or Western civilization seeks wholeness, and so its own
destruction, in terms of that ideal morality which, rooted in
love, incorporates all peoples everywhere. What the Australians had achieved locally is an analogue of what European
civilization might be said to be searching for on a universal
basis.

THE HINDU SANYASI

From the days of Alexander, when Westerners first encountered him, the Hindu Sanyasi has fascinated Europeans, excit-
ing wonderment, doubt, and half-formulated fears. Admired
and respected for his control of the animal condition, his mastery of the spiritual, his single-minded pursuit of truth, his
desire to unite himself wholly with the divine, his austerities
and aloofness have seemed repugnant. Early temptations to
adopt some form of *sanyasan* were rejected. Suspicious of
lonely austerities, Christianity has preferred varieties of

iconoclasm and puritanism. Demanding interaction and full expression of the participatory values in community life, Christianity affirms the world, focuses on moral life, holds each soul to be redeemable in the eyes of God here and now, and traditionally has insisted on the prime value of salvation and redemption through the sacraments within the body and community of the Church. Clearly not unconnected with maintaining the authority of bishops and popes, elders and leaders, the hermit has always been obnoxious, an anomaly in an organized Church which has always stressed the participatory values. Only rarely and in very special circumstances is a Catholic religious permitted to become a hermit. Even then he remains subject to his Order. Set over against the explicit preference for community life, religious or secular, the hermit, like the Sanyasi, seems to defy that involvement with others upon which the European order is based. Hermit or Sanyasi, their autonomy seems presumptuous, their truths too distant, their love a pretense unless demonstrably realized in loving the suffering as well as the rich and the incorrigible nuisance next door. When the Sanyasi's discoveries and techniques enter the European ambience, they do so mainly as auxiliaries to the efficiencies of community pursuits. A few minutes of yoga after a heavy day at the office makes one fitter for tomorrow's day at the office.

Though the European hermit may be sought after as a kind of wizard or wise man, a curiosity, a tourist attraction (as Father Thomas Merton became for a while) he stands aside from the community and is—unless under the discipline of others—in principle an affront to the community he seems to have rejected. No explicit niche exists for him, he has to make his own way. And the Sanyasi, too, can sometimes be just such an affront to Hindu caste society. Still, an explicit niche is provided for him. In principle—following Dumont (1966)—the institution of *sanyasan* is in a complementary relationship with Hindu caste society. The two go together. Formally separated from political and economic power, the hierarchies of caste society may be described as sets of relationships determined by relative ritual purity and impurity. While relative purity indicates a superior or higher caste than relative impurity, a higher caste is not necessarily politically dominant or economically more powerful in a situation than a lower caste. Though there can be disagreements as to which caste in a local hierarchy is the superior, dispute and resolution turn on given criteria of relative purity and impurity. And these criteria go to the circumstances of birth, modes of behavior in interaction with others, forms of work, and relationships to artifacts, flora, fauna, and their products. Born, growing up, and maturing within the rules of a particular caste, a person's identity and whole ambience of social relationships is determined by them. To be expelled from one's caste is a denial of moral being, a kind of death. But to choose to leave the world of caste and become a Sanyasi gains esteem.

Any man could or can leave his caste and become a Sanyasi. And this entails, as with the Shaman, a ritual funeral and initiation into *sanyasan*. That is, symbolically dead to the world of caste, freed from the prescriptions and restrictions of life within caste society, the Sanyasi becomes free to pursue the truth and realize himself in any one of numerous ways open to him. Apart from and outside of caste, the Sanyasi is not independent of caste: he is sustained with food and shelter by persons within caste society. Belonging to the total society, from his point of vantage outside the community of mutually interacting persons the Sanyasi is expected to perceive, realize, and communicate the kinds of truths not easily perceived from, let alone realized within the world of caste. His being and position are prime values in the Hindu social order. In revealing the contraries between freedom and restriction within the total social order, the Sanyasi is clearly a symbol. On the other hand, he did not and does not often deal in or mediate the moralities. In quitting the arena of caste relationships, he leaves the world of moralities behind him and embarks on a quest for truth and the union of the self with *Brahma*, the absolute All-being.

Such a journey is open to many kinds of abuse, and abuses by particular Sanyasis or pseudo-Sanyasis have been and are notoriously frequent and many. Indeed, aside from the fact that the authentic is bound to be accompanied by frauds and charlatans, from a moral standpoint the whole conception of the Sanyasi must be instinct with the inherent potential of abuses. Yet for those within caste society, for those whose moralities were and are formally unchangeable and as closely and rigorously prescribed as those of Australians under the traditional Law, individuality is next to impossible. Realization of the self within or in spite of the rules must appear as overwhelmingly important. The Sanyasi was and is a reservoir of spiritual truths, an invaluable resource and exemplar for those in the process of realizing the self within the confining moralities prescribed by caste. Formally, a Sanyasi is as free of moral rules as he chooses to be—he makes his own rules, and, in authenticity, subjects himself to discipline—while a member of caste is as subject to rules not of his making as anyone could possibly be.

The mutual antitheses yield a sure identity. Caste and the Sanyasi predicate and define each other. The aging householder who becomes a Sanyasi may be presumed to have realized the moralities relevant to him. And it is possible that in leaving the world of moralities behind him he has also transcended them. But unless, in Kierkegaard's terms, he can from his position of withdrawal influence and change the moralities of caste, he surely fails in full individuality. Nevertheless, there are many examples in history of Sanyasis who have felt themselves compelled to move from a preoccupation with the self, absolute truth, and the spiritual toward and into a concern with the moral. What offended their moral sense were the confining rigidities of caste, particularly the spiritual pride and moral exclusiveness of the Brahmins in relation to final redemption or *moksha*. And so far as a Sanyasi has been able to carry significant numbers of others with him in his transcension of caste moralities, so far is he surely an individual in the sense determined here. Mostly, however, this kind of activity has been initiated from the ranks of the Kshatriyas and has been concerned with the relations between Brahmin and Ksatriya castes (cf. Burridge 1969a: 86-96). Mahatma Ghandi has been one of the very few who has addressed himself to the destruction of caste itself by going to the very roots of the whole system: the polar opposition and complementarity between Brahmins and Harijans or outcastes. But despite the activist critiques, the caste system as a continuing moral framework has endured. Identities are assured. Each knows his place and space, may realize the self.

Realizing the self in the person, conforming, becoming someone, is less lonely and in a sense more satisfying than attempting to be an individual. Moving into the unstructured no one and tilling fields of implicitness beyond conformity without losing the desire and ability to participate in the beings of others carries its own costs. The current interest in the Western world in itinerant Sanyasis is undoubtedly part of the characteristic reach into, and impulse to absorb, varieties of otherness. But the new and often confused desire for self-realization as a kind of Sanyasi seems more intimately related to the permeative growth of bureaucratic procedures. These create much the same certain identities as does the caste system, bring the person into prominence. Indeed, accepting the operation of complementary oppositions, it is likely that as bureaucratic procedures and work routines make the person more and more prescriptive, so withdrawals and attempts to realize the self will become more common and the realization of the individual more difficult. If most of the varieties of "counter-culture" in the Western world today seem to be more or less untutored entries into an unstructured unknown which lead into self-indulgence rather than self-realization or new moralities, there is little doubt that sometimes—because in such instances there are explicit disciplines—a spiritual as distinct from a procedural self is in fact realized. Yet it is also possible now and again to identify the search for a freer and more suitable community ambience in which the self might once again find its traditional metier oscillating between the person and the individual.

Five examples do not make a case. But apart from prophets and charismatic leaders, obvious individuals, if all the other figures of the ethnographic experience had been included the final result would not have been very different. As it is, most of the occasions and moments of individuality have been displayed. While persons confirm the given system of roles and statuses, reiterating the structure, the relations between them and individuals or their likenesses or refractions make the structure evident and indicate the possibilities of moral variation and innovation.

In contrast to the examples cited, and indeed to most other cultures which, more occupied with the self and person than with the individual, have prescribed the parts and refractions of individuality to selected positions and roles in particular circumstances, European or Western society has generalized individuality, making it a desideratum for each member of community. The self is directed to integrate the assertion to autonomy with the participatory values and the given moralities so as to produce moral innovation. Except in rare and singular circumstances, self-realization apart from the participatory values has been secondary when not positively eschewed. Whether generalized or prescribed, however, individuality and/or its semblances go along with some kind of initial separation or alienation from the interacting moral community of persons. By prescribing individuality or its parts to selected positions, individuality—and so the seeds of change and moral innovation—is controlled, and a traditional structure is maintained and renewed but not necessarily changed. Generalized individuality, on the other hand, implies continuing restructuring and change.

Generalized individuality is clearly unsafe. It is a standing temptation to charlatans and "men of movement," and even in authenticity invites continuing disruptions of the social order, putting the normative moralities at hazard. And although, of the components of human being (animality, cultural faculties, morality, spirituality), the normative moralities are the most variable, they remain the only firm and basic framework for determining the truth of things. Survival requires a satisfactory mediation of the moralities within an ambience of stable continuities and, also, some mode of changing the moralities, becoming another culture when and if necessary. But why, in the absence of dire and obvious emergency, invite changes in what has been tested and has sufficed?

Given culture, articulate thought, and the assertion to autonomy, nowhere can it be impossible to realize the self. Both culturally and in relation to the gene pool, a social order which completely thwarted self-realization could not survive for long. Some cultures, to be sure, are less tolerant than others. Yet it is difficult to conceive of self-realization outside a discipline, a context of rules. The Shaman, subject to the rules of his calling, might realize individuality as well as the self. In Hindu caste society, where self-realization is a prime value, the self can be realized either within the normative rules, submerging itself in the person, or in contraposition to them. Those Sanyasis who do not order their lives by any rules at all abuse their calling. If some cultures have become extinct, it was not because there was no way of realizing the self. On the other hand, apart from wars, famine, pestilence, and cataclysm, peoples and cultures have certainly foundered because there was no adequate way of mediating or changing the moralities. Moral variation and innovation are as essential to human survival as genetic variation. And the instrument of this variation and innovation is some kind of individuality.

The examples offered have been called "prescribed positions" because, in contrast to the European situation, they are open to only a few in the community. Ordering their likenesses and differences into some sort of evolutionary or developmental series in relation to the individuality of the

European experience defies conviction. If each example seems to be peculiarly suited to the social order in which it has been located, this is only to be expected, no more than a "just so" story. Produced by and reproducing and maintaining and re-newing the social order, each example is an integral part of the social order and emerges as an independent variant of the thematic in culture. The Shaman masters lesions of loneliness and the self's disintegration to communicate wholeness in so-cial orders where unique interests (as among the Inuit) or mutual competitiveness (as among the Indians of the North-west coast) contradict the values of communitas—together-ness, being members one of another. Yet in Australia the Shaman would be considered a sorcerer or just crazy. For there, given the Law, organization into groups, and shared in-terests, the task is how to realize communitas without being an automaton. And this the Man of High Degree does by dis-ciplining the assertion to autonomy so as to reconcile inner and outer conditions within the Law. The Australian sor-cerer, on the other hand, gives free rein to the assertion to au-tonomy, desiring personal power over others rather than power from and within the Law. Placing the self in truth where otherwise all social relationships are prescriptive and depend on appearance, the Sanyasi provides hope: he is the exemplar of freedom and self-realization within strict disci-pline. The Manager, in command of conscience and tempted to sorcery, reveals the dilemmas of morality which each must resolve for himself. The Leopard-skin chief displays and ma-nipulates the symbols of communitas in situations where as-sertions to autonomy and opposed interests must necessarily negate them. Each distinct set of moments spells survival, provides the social order with that which is life-giving, at-tempts to reconcile the search for the self's integration in the values of communitas with the demands of community and assertions to autonomy. Yet in each case—excepting the Leopard-skin chief—turn the coin and evil is discovered.

In principle, permuting and combining the moments of in-dividuality as they have been identified here could produce an almost infinite number of institutional variants: a fact of immense evolutionary significance. Still, European individuality seems exceptional if only because it is generalized and combines most of the moments contained in the examples above. And the question why this should be so can only be suggestively answered, and then only partly, by a recourse to history, to the social ambience of events in Palestine at the beginning of our era.

The conditions of the Roman hegemony—good communications and reasonably safe travel, trade, much business, money, peoples of different cultures and traditions encountering one another, intellectual curiosity, a choice of many philosophies and cults combined with a willingness to experiment with them, but withal a certain boredom and ennui—were well suited to the growth of a vital and dynamic movement such as Christianity turned out to be (cf. Nock 1933). Much more important than these enabling conditions in the present context, however, were the events exampled by Peter's change of heart, conversion or, more technically, metanoia when without hesitation and standing on a truth perceived, he chose to abandon his livelihood and become a fisher of men; Paul's reversal, enlightenment, conversion, and metanoia on the road to Damascus; and the Pentecostal experience. For these events, providing exemplars, seem to have generalized and institutionalized the specialized experience of many Old Testament prophets: clear individuals who, if not exactly prescribed, were fully within the range of expectations. They became, in Christian eyes, models and precedents carrying an instructional burden and message which, realized in the figure of Christ whose complexities of perceived universality reached back and through what the prophets had said and done, was for each and all. As exemplars exhorting each and all to change heart and mind toward a specific realization, the prophets have always been an integral part of the developing Christian ambience. They laid the basis for that deeply ingrained if often muffled cultural and moral imperative to continue in transformations of heart and mind until the

Christian message was realized in its entirety. Generalized individuality, the suggestion is, started with Christianity and has spread with it, metamorphosing its idioms of expression but, nevertheless, retaining its links with these and, as we shall see in due course, other related exemplars.

Allowing that there are particular kinds of events and occasions which, experiencing and experienced by the self, are sources of truth in that through them a given governance of being is confirmed or denied and, perhaps, new principles of governance initiated—What kinds of occasion, regularly encountered, tend to bring about a critique and rethinking? What kinds of sources of truth are capable of making a new man in whom a new structure of moral discriminations becomes evident and manifest? What kinds of experience, soberly rationalized, bring about a conversion, a metanoia, that significant change of heart and mind which knows it must take a path whose end dips out of sight?

7 OCCASIONS AND SOURCES OF TRUTH

Generally, the truth of things comes into cognizance in two main ways: by means of deliberate and systematic processes of investigation; and by a variety of phenomena (dreams, visions, etc.) or procedures (meditation, trance, etc.) which permit a truth to impose itself, intervene and insist upon an awareness or intuition of itself. And although the two modes, metaphorically if inexactly the science and the *satori*, are normally in a dialectical relationship, the truth of a *satori* can stand by itself, is *sui generis*, has no need of the science. On the other hand, if the science is to develop it needs the truths of a *satori* if only at the level of the intuitive. Still, a truth revealed, a truth intervening and imposing itself, requires some buttressing by the science, some systematic rationalizing, if skeptics to whom the truth has not been directly revealed are to be persuaded. And while those who hold to given or traditional truths appear reasonable, seem safe, and have the comforting support of others, he or she who stands on a truth newly perceived stands alone and risks varieties of obloquy and exclusion. Allowing that the moralities can be and often are changed by truths discovered by systematic processes of investigation, by the science, what is important in the present context are the ways in which truths arrived at by the events and procedures covered by a *satori* are acknowledged and rationalized, modify existing and investigatory truths, and give rise to new moralities—or are ignored or obfuscated by traditional rationalizations and moralities.

To many—and they are probably right—the truths of a *satori* are plain deceptions, product of a disturbed mind or psyche in an inimical or discomfiting ambience. But if, following Cassirer (1946: 7), all mental processes fail to grasp reality itself, for such approximations as they do make they seem dependent on some kind of intervention, bestowed, fortuitous, serendipitous, or invited. Even then only the alert and expectant mind can seize the event and make it work for him. By contrast, symbolic and ritual activities focus attention on given cultural truths, seem to seal off avenues to truths which lie outside those overtly prescribed by society, appear to cut the channels of seminal interventions. And though for Cassirer (*idem*) symbols are paradoxical in that they obscure what they seek to reveal, the very ambivalences of symbolic and ritual activities render them capable of yielding up their latencies.

Mary Douglas (1970: 1-18) has traced and criticized the European movement away from ritual and symbolic activity, and both in the same work and elsewhere (1966) she has pointed out what these activities really do. Most importantly, they indicate the lineaments of order and also serve to maintain it. They tell us what to do and provide the routines which keep us doing. They map the world of ideas and values, mark the borders, and, by showing where an opposition merges into unity, indicate the moments wherein competitive interests are subsumed in a whole. But in doing these things they also point to those areas where truths not apparent in the overt presentation of culture are to be found. By drawing attention to the variety of levels of being within culture, rituals indicate the possibilities of interaction between them. In working to remedy the gap between actual experience and the idealized social categories, straying sheep are nudged back into the flock. But these very processes indicate to the apperceptive where truths are to be found. In this way the ambivalences of symbolic and ritual activities provide an idiom of intervention. The conformist grasps the obvious and overt, regarding it as instruction. A would-be individual perceives a hidden message and accepts the invitation to explore. Moving away from rituals reveals a distaste for ambivalences and the deeper complexities of being in culture, and displays a preference for the linear simplicities which a machine can deal with.

The ambivalences of ritual are perhaps at their clearest in male pubertal rites of passage. More often than the pen can acknowledge, ethnographers have stressed that these rites prepare a youth for adulthood and forcibly inculcate the moralities didactically as well as by a series of physical ordeals. Great emphasis is laid upon the trauma of circumcision, its consequences in conformism and socialization—even its symbolic emasculation: he who has been circumcised will be an immovable pillar of the law, an inflexible guardian of the established moralities. The assertion to autonomy is socialized. And yet, for obvious reasons, information is scanty on what happens in the beings of initiates in the periods of isolation, so often enforced on them. What *can* happen to initiates during these periods, and what are they implicitly invited to do? The young North American Indian was forced to go out into the wilderness alone, encounter a world lying outside the confines of culture as overtly presented to him, and seize his own reality, métier, or guardian spirit. In similar vein, an Australian youth had to face the world of nature alone and discover in the deed what had been taught him. Few families in our own environment do not encourage their sons to go out into the world, pit hazard against safety and order, and so "find themselves" before they shoulder the responsibilities of adulthood. Again and again across the ethnographic spectrum pubertal rites place the initiand in a pivotal position between the orderliness of cultural instructions and the chaos of a unique perception. The process of ritual socialization itself invites a new integration.

For many years since Van Gennep's masterpiece (1909/60) this pivotal position, one of isolation and liminality, was regarded as a mechanical entailment in the movement from one status to another. Yet as Turner (1967: 93-111; 1969: 94-130) and Eliade (1964: 64ff.) have pointed out, it is perhaps the most important part of the rite. The liminal period becomes an introduction to, and test of, moral being. Generally reenacting the transformation from nature to culture, pubertal rites bring the components of being together and confront the cultural faculties with the oppositions and correspondences between animal, moral, and spiritual being. To use another idiom, the initiand is asked to measure communitas and anti-structure (Turner: 1969)—wherein human beings, stripped of their roles, statuses, memberships, and moralities, are in communion as human selves—against the demands of organization and structure.

In this situation most initiands, responding to the past pressures of kinsfolk and conformists, yield to the more obvious and overt side of the ritual. Some, intuitively grasping that symbols and symbolic activities contain a mysterium—a latency, a promissory note, an invitation to realize that which lies behind the obvious and overt—may perceive and order a truth which, because they cannot withstand conformist pressures, they will hold in their hearts all the years of their lives. Others lose themselves in the chaos, unable to bring it to order. A few persevere and are led into areas which the overtness of the cultural symbols hide from most. But while the affirmation of a truth discovered calls a halt, one negation breeds another and discovery becomes a continuing journey. Truth's center seems to grow more distant with each successive launch from closing peripheries. Each arrival entails a further moral choice if it is to make a new point of departure, and each departure requires a further transformation of the self in relation to otherness. In Turner's phrase (1969: 203), "man grows through anti-structure and conserves through structure."

Social relationships, roles, and statuses ordered by the moralities are perforce ritual or ritualized relationships. By adhering to the explicit in ritual, by sticking to the cultural categories as they are overtly presented, life becomes lineal, logical, and apparently more explicable. Traditional and well-worn logics apply, the person is in his heaven. The only significant distinction between a ritualized relationship and one that is not resides in individuality. And only an individual, one with an indeterminate identity who enters the mysterium by moving to no one, can understand and make the distinction. From this position, however arrived at, apperceptions of roles and statuses necessarily separate the self from the person, lead into the rejection or transcendence of current rituals of relationship, and demand a reintegration of the components of being. In turn, there follows an exploration into that chaos and disorder whose potential, censored and shunned by the person, finds extreme expression in the images and fantasies of the insane. If truth and reality are to be found in the mysterium, in those deeper and hidden recesses of culture which must tend to be currently represented as outside culture, these are the areas which an individual should penetrate—continually negating a given order so as to seek new principles of order in the unordered or disorderly. They are areas of turbulence. If a truth is not found and articulated, the seeker must become as confused as his ambience. For persons, mouthpieces of the given and overt forms and principles of order, a life of ordered illusions provides anxieties enough. Those deeper recesses are either a void or filled with deceptions. Why pull aside the veil?

Every initiation presupposes renewal, wider comprehensions, and concomitant responsibilities. The main overt dialectic is between an extant prescribed being and a prescribed new being. And, to be sure, this may be broken down into several subordinate dialectics. But the latter simply add texture to two significant features: that in the essentially disintegrative liminal period the initiand is given an opportunity to apperceive the terms of the dialectic and so touch a truth; and the presence of an underlying dialectic between prescribed beings and new and alternative not-yet-prescribed beings. To work, to enable both mind and imagination to complete an apperception, both features require a living semantic environment of rationalizations contained in the myths, legends, folktales, and stories which accompany the ritual and procedures of initiation. Characteristically, the narrative contexts provided by these myths and folktales first evoke the lived experiences and derived attitudes of the listeners, then render the events and relationships they deal with ambiguous or oracular. Apperceptions grow out of the process of resorting and ordering the conflicts and ambiguities between experiences and rationalizations. And since the narratives usually deal with particular dyadic relationships which the initiand either knows about or has actually experienced, these relationships become dialectically constructed avenues to truth.

Perhaps the most important of these dyads is that between the person and the Hero, antitheses whose successful resolution is surely the most that can be asked of anyone. Entering the dialectic generates, and its resolution is dependent upon, accurate perceptions of truth and resolving several subsidiary dyads. The father-son (mother-daughter, mother-son, and father-daughter are usually of much lesser significance), generalized into senior and junior male generations, entails in a Subsistence economy not only a nonreciprocal relationship of "dominance/subordination" but that juniors should replace and succeed to the prerogatives of their seniors without actually killing them: the reverse of the Frazerian theme of the divine king. That is, succession depends on resolving and reversing dominance/subordination and coming to terms with killing/not killing. Husband-wife and brother-sister (generalized into men/women)—of particular significance in communities where so much of the dynamic of social life turns on exchanges and transactions between affines—are pairs which, in themselves governed by authority/service and responsibility/impulsiveness, are related to each other as reproductive unit/nonreproductive unit. Which is to say that animal and cultural continuities are dependent on resolving the tension between proscribed and prescribed sexual relations. Elder and younger sibling are usually figured in a relationship of self-restraint and responsibility contrasted to self-willedness and rashness where the elder, being responsible for, and in self-image exemplar to the younger, attempts to curb the initiatives of younger who responds with further excesses. Summing up the relationship as corresponding with responsibility/impulsiveness, survival appears as dependent on resolving "conservation of tradition/new initiatives." Finally, in some societies—particularly among the Indians of North America—the cunning of the Hero is differentiated into the figure of the trickster, yielding much the same dialectic as between elder and younger sibling: survival is dependent upon resolving "given wisdoms/resourceful initiatives."

In Complex societies the force of these dyads, each of which entails some sort of concrete confrontation with contradiction, consequent critique, and the opportunity for brushes with truths not already given, tends to be diffused and distributed in a variety of relationships which need never be crucially engaged. Homicide, sexuality, survival, traditional responsibility, and resourceful initiatives are in the end not simply words or ideas but activities and events which, because they constitute the core of what human beings have to deal with within themselves in relation to others, generate the moralities through attempted resolutions of the triangular conflict between the self's perceptions of truth, the cultural instructions and constraints of others, and the assertion to autonomy. In Subsistence communities the moralities are continually regenerated and reexpressed by exchanges and other interactions within a context determined by traditional constraints and the situational objections and agreements of interested others. In Complex societies, however, the main burden of personal confrontation is appropriated by and diffused in a variety of bureaucratic procedures. The sorts of truth which can be perceived only through prolonged and enforced interactions between people—whom the social order compels to communicate their parts to each other—become lost in a myriad of opportunities for avoidance or buried in procedural arrangements. Literacy and book learning—which go along with bureaucracy—may provide a wider and deeper vicarious experience and opportunity for perceptions of truth. But how far the vicarious experience is any substitute for the direct experience must depend on the impact of that experience on the self's integrations.

Perhaps the most significant confrontation with truth and reality among traditional or preindustrialized societies, Subsistence or Complex, is death. Experiencing the death of another or thinking about one's own death invite, first, repugnance and opposition, then acceptance of given rationalizations. These are etched in the mind, construct purposes in living and, ultimately, vindicate the traditional order. Nevertheless, in that initial repugnance and opposition lie the seeds of that which may change the traditional order. Death predicates life as often as it follows.

When the momentum of a social order is carried by the people who comprise it, as in a Subsistence community, each death is an invitation to think again, attempt to pierce the screens of tradition and rerationalize. Rarely regarded as due to what we might call "natural" causes, a simple biological extinction, death was referred to moral lesion both in the deceased and in the community: sorcery and/or witchcraft. And subsequent procedures led inevitably into that rearrangement of roles and statuses which had the potential of turning tradition into new paths. The death of a Polynesian chief ushered in a period of anomie: old truths were dead. Out of the chaos of weeping, wailing, wounding, and the destruction of property and crops, new ways appropriate to the succeeding chief would be fashioned. Nor is the situation very different in more sophisticated traditional social orders. Christian beginnings in the Roman world were in no small way linked to a preoccupation with death on the one hand, and the promise of salvation and resurrection on the other. Eternal life was in a sense part of the bargain entailed in conversion. Christ's conquest of death was the climax to centuries of speculation. Where indeed was death's sting? The last enemy had been beaten, absorbed into love.

It is not easy for us today to appreciate the force of this climax. Inevitably confounded and eclipsed by killings, selfish self-destruction, and the all too often egotistical search for varieties of martyrdom, the death absorbed into love has become its opposite: the horror reported and pictured from

far and near in all its grotesque variety. The pause which fructifies in refractions of love has been appropriated by the
momentum and purposes of the social order itself. Disburse-
ments of money seize the mind, the urgent and strident automaticisms of life and the living crowd the mind's eye and
the heart's care. Gilgamesh's pursuit of immortality survives
in a faint curiosity, in the concrete evidences of vanity and
self-justification. The last enemy has become a fraud, a
cardboard grimace. A half-century ago Maeterlinck (1913: 12)
could write that "death is the one event that counts in our life
and in our universe." Depriving lives to be of their lives to
come is now an uncertain ideal. Mora's (1965: 142) "death renews life, elicits certain possibilities without which certain
forms would never come to life" seems scientific but out of
touch with the faith we can derive from our own social experience. When we read that the Dinka master of the fishing
spear conquers death by choosing his time (Lienhardt 1961:
298ff.), we are amazed, even awed. If there is merit in such
foolishness we assign it to a misguided courage. We may read
of its effects and significances among the Dinka themselves,
but the event itself is difficult for us to enter and experience
vicariously. For most of us, human death has become a purely
biological event: its traditional association with an awakening
or growth of the psyche or spirit no longer affects us.

Having learned to accommodate death, we are carried forward on industrial and commercial leitmotifs, enveloped and
dominated by our affairs, routines, and ambitions. We reserve
our energies, interest, and sorrow for other kinds of death:
the death of God, of European civilization, of Christianity;
the death of this or that political idealism, policy, or party; the
social death of a hostess or climber who has made a mistake;
the death of a career, or of a tradition, a custom, an idea; the
demise of the tram, good workmanship, roccoco theaters,
and the like. The transference of human emotions to the level
of the category and institution makes an ordinary human
death simply an incident. It may be that news of famines,
floods, wars, and massacres have numbed us. It is more likely

that bureaucracy has led us into identifying our lives with those of the social categories. The memories of one who once lived, his ghost, the pricklings of conscience that the dead arouse in the living—these may occasionally pierce our vitals but, carried along by the programs of institutional life, we tend to brush the questions aside.

For traditional anarchists and assassins a human death was regarded as important because human beings were assumed to manage and manipulate the system. An assassination once catalyzed the descent into world war. Today even lesser gestures against the system are trodden into institutionalized prisons and asylums. Appropriated by the state or the categories of the social order—as in modern industrialized society, or as in Hindu caste society where the notion of transmigration reinforces the appropriation—human emotions and responsibilities, particularly concern for the well-being of others, must atrophy. Because in such societies human beings are no longer masters of a system directed to more transcendent ends, but simply serve the system, today's anarchists and esoterics are surely consistent in seeking to destroy the institutions and those who maintain them.

For Hegel death was the sovereign master of the world. It has become another statistic. The pain and reality are briefly confined to a narrow domestic circle, the procedures soon dust them away. Yet in traditional societies each death reverberated through networks of kin and political alliances and oppositions, assessed obligations, and punctuated the continuities. Each life stood poised for reshaping. Death was not "simply the end of life but an event which shapes and constitutes life" (Mora 1965: 172).

If thinkers such as Hegel, Mora, and Maeterlinck were simply reiterating the rationalizations typical of traditional societies—rationalizations which the conditions and systemics of industrialized society portray as illusory in that context—then in industrialized society death ceases to be the predicative change in animal condition which engages the dialectics between varieties of being and nonbeing, and is no longer the event out of which the human being, exercising free will, creates purposes, makes a moral choice, and snatches immortality out of extinction. In such circumstances, preventing each life from becoming purely one of selfishness and greed requires the binding systemics of an anthill. Defeating death by choosing one's own time becomes not only nonsensical but also impugns the state which has appropriated both life and death. An organic dialectic between being and nonbeing becomes a series of artificial discontinuities and alternations: the dialectic is engaged like a mesh of cogwheels with broken teeth. Some, perceiving too much connectedness, disarm themselves and die with each death. Others, perceiving no purpose, deny themselves a moral choice. Death wins.

Appropriated by the state or social order—which may occur in the historical phases of a traditional society as well as in industrialized society—death as a source of truth is neutralized. It ceases to cry for a critique of that order. People disappear, others take their places. The machine is served, carries its servitors. Still, since what is ultimately at stake is ontological status, and so the ordering of social relationships, the quest for truths about death will not be denied. Scientific nonsense they may be but rationalizations such as "resurrection," "metempsychosis" and "life after death" continue in currency. Modes of direct access to the departed proliferate. Some are sincerely interested in what may happen to themselves after death. Most, on the other hand, are much more obviously interested in what may happen to those who survive them. Which is to betray an interest and concern not in or for the self alone but in others and the social order they will be involved in. In turn, this interest in others indicates that despite the appropriations of bureaucracies there still exists that sense of human communion which, distinct and free from the oppositions and bondedness of community life, forms at least a part of what may be understood by communitas. Further, since such a sense of community can only arise from a sense of communitas—in which the conflicts and oppositions of community are resolved—the interest in others, intimately connected as it must be to given rationalizations about death, revivifies and qualifies those rationalizations. They deny the power of the machine, return the human to the predicament of the event and its rationalization, defeat the state, take the "finis" out of death and place it in a context of kinds of being: which allows the individual to posit moral choice and seek to preserve the truth in the moralities. Indeed, unless what happens after death is rationalized as some kind of being, the moralities become mere norms of convenience: a pleasing hedonism which quickly dwindles when those with power decree convenience.

The given truth of things tends to converge with power, and competing or differentiated kinds of powers go along with competing or differentiated grounds of truth. While the power that predicates the truth of things can be obnoxious, the power that is predicated by the truth of things is desirable. Unless made mystical or sacred, rationalized and thought of as derived from and subject to the truth of things located in divinities, visionary experiences, dreams, or abstract ideas or formulations capable of varieties of rationalization, power wielded by rather than mediated through humans tends to brutalize and dehumanize. Power and truth become one, alternatives residing in differing perceptions of truth become twin to what is.

The most common modes for bypassing rationally mediated systemics of power and order so as to obtain another, more direct access to the truth of things are dreams, visionary experiences, trance, possession, and the orgiastic dance. They provide for a usually cyclical dynamic, normally feed into and confirm tradition, but may also change tradition. Nor is the European or Western tradition exceptional thus far. It becomes exceptional in the mode described here as the pentecostal experience and/or its simulacra, derived from the historical exemplar of Pentecost. For in this mode transcending the given is explicit. It involves a change in animal or physiological condition. It is a mode of access to the truth of things which, when coupled to a metanoia as it is supposed to be, is expected to yield new or refurbished moralities. The springboard for countless millenarian, reformist, utopian, and revolutionary movements in European and Western history, pentecostal experiences and the metanoias that are supposed to go with them still decisively inform institutionalized modes of recognizing or bringing about changes in the moralities. And though both pentecostal experiences and metanoias as they have come down to us have their roots in another, the Hebraic tradition, and are universal human possibilities, they have, characteristically, become authentic to the European or Western. Only within the Christian cultural tradition have pentecostal experiences and metanoias been regular expectations with well-defined niches.

Normative in the sense that it occurs frequently, is positively institutionalized in certain subcultures and denominations, and is otherwise acceptable albeit only after exhaustive systematic critique, a pentecostal experience is usually communal and participatory as in the historical exemplar, but may also occur to single persons by themselves. It may involve visionary experiences, receiving audible instructions, glossolalia, and/or a genuine spiritual experience or "descent of the Spirit," each or all of which can result in that change of heart and mind which, in determining a new and positive moral direction, is known as a metanoia. And although a metanoia can occur without actually undergoing a pentecostal experience, it cannot be wholly accounted for without invoking a pentecostal experience at some time in some place. Ultimately, the events and background of the New Testament, particularly Pentecost itself, its social ambience, and the activities and teachings of St. John the Baptist, Christ, St. Peter, and St. Paul, stand as warrant for both metanoia and the pentecostal experience. Conversely, metanoia and the pentecostal experience contain and are expected to redistribute the essential social significances of those events, teachings, and experiences: transcendence, spiritual and moral renewal in love, the defeat of death. One might add much more. It suffices that

what is involved is a continuing critique of the moralities as
they happen to exist at any particular time or place, the institutionalized containment of moral renewal and regeneration.

Until recently and before the great increase of "pentecos-
talism" among the Christian denominations, particularly in
North America, most descriptions of pentecostal experiences
were inclined, perversely, to dismiss them as psychological
aberrations, forms of hysteria, soft imaginings, and the like.
And for quite different reasons the established denominations
have also regarded them with suspicion, even hostility. Now,
however, more sober and penetrating evaluations are being
published, and the established denominations, concerned for
renewal and revivification in the face of dwindling numbers
of adherents, have become receptive and permissive. The
overwhelming recent evidence is that those who have had the
experience know or are aware of something real or true
which, whether or not others think it hallucinatory, is abso-
lutely compelling and more than capable of holding out
against the massed batteries of skepticism. At the least the experience seems in fact to open channels between heart and
mind, psyche and intellect. Censors are dismissed, structures
forgotten, communitas invoked. The boundaries of given
cultural categories are transcended, fresh rationalizations and
new moralities may emerge. Yet these features and more are
rooted in the historical and creative exemplar. And the events
of Pentecost inform the cultural tradition both at and below
the level of the conscious, on secular as well as sacred occasions. We imitate them, try to relive them. From them are derived all those inspired—the very word takes us back to
them—penetrations into truth and reality which we associate
with our greatest scientists, philsophers, writers, poets, musi-
cians, and artists. Through and because of them we expect
persons to become individuals, transcend the given, penetrate
to truth, and bring their discoveries into the culture.

It would be oversimplistic though not wholly misleading
to think of a pentecostal experience as an intervention of truth

or reality from *outside* the culture or social order, or an intervention *into* the cultural categories arising out of the psychophysiological experience involved. Nevertheless, some kind of intervention, which is not necessarily manifested as ecstasy or hysteria, which does not necessarily involve loss of control of the self, and which yet seems to grace the situation with glimpses into truth and reality, seems to occur. Unlike the investigatory procedures of science and the intellect, which subordinate an initial intuition to method and move systematically and purposefully into the unknown from what the culture has already determined as known, the pentecostal experience entails a direct perception and a subordination of the intellect to the soul such that the mind is the willing servant of the soul or psyche. And unlike drug-taking or spiritual or meditational exercises, the charisms of the experience can be "withheld" when apparently desired, or bestowed when apparently undesired.

Institutionalized in the sacramental life, or in prayer meetings where pentecostal experiences are sought, the events of Pentecost itself, and the charisms, graces, and truths taken to flow from them, represent the primary focus in the European or Western tradition in which is made manifest the instruction that man is a reality absorbed in truth only when heart and mind interact freely in union with the triune Godhead. The view that it was only by freeing ourselves from the clutches of this kind of obscurantism that the achievements of the European intellect, particularly science, have become possible is countered by the equally dogmatic assertion that pentecostal experiences created and continue to create the conditions in which systematic investigatory techniques can be pursued within morality. Yet it is more constructive to focus on the interaction between the two modes, the dialectical relationship which, when engaged, must include successive negations of current notions of ordered truth. Change and perhaps new moralities then become implicit in the process, if not always entirely realized.

While a pentecostal experience or its less dramatic analogues along the scale to what we call an "intuition" can change the experiencer and result in a new moral order, there are no sure means of having or obtaining them. They are gifts of the spirit or Spirit (or the hidden inherencies of biocultural being) to which all humans are vulnerable, but which European tradition has both explicitly solicited and attempted to confine and regulate. And a part of this regulation is contained in the notion of metanoia: that change of heart and mind which, upon an inspired appreciation of the truth of things, entails a quite different integration of own being in relation to others and the given moralities. Usually associated with another event, an otherwise commonplace encounter with someone or something, or, more dramatically, a vision, a dream, the sudden comprehension of the interior meaning of a myth, instruction, or statement, or a traumatic psychic experience, a metanoia may also come about more slowly, through regular spiritual or moral exercises, as a gradually dawning enlightenment. Entailing both a repentance and sorrow for past deeds not in accord with the newly perceived truth of things, and a resolve to go in the way of the newly perceived truths, a metanoia indicates the start of a developmental process in the self in relation to others, the moralities, and the truth of things. Informing the conversion which may involve heart or mind but not necessarily both, rooted in communitas or anti-structure and distinct from the change that comes about on the assumption of another given role or status, a metanoia grows the person so that the self may be realized more fully, embarks the individual on a voyage of moral and spiritual development, and requires the positive decision to be so grown and developed.

Disagreements over the theological requirements of a true metanoia, we may remind ourselves, played a major part in the onset of the reformation, from which Max Weber (1958a: 105) traced the beginnings of modern European "individualism." Yet all the varieties of ways in which it becomes possible, in the European or Western environment, to change one's mind or attempt to persuade others to change their minds are surely to be derived from the Christian encounter with the Roman world. Tradition and law were sacrosanct only so far as they could not be transcended or changed through a pentecostal experience and/or metanoia. Plato's counsel that normative moralities should be changed so as to accord with the truly Moral Idea became, in Christian hands, a positive instruction. Within the ambience of the varieties of conversion and initiation that were possible in the Roman world of Paul and his successors (cf. Nock 1933), Christianity gave focus and direction to hitherto diffused currents of intellectual and religious quest. Becoming necessary aspects of each other, the events of Pentecost and the idea of metanoia deepened the relevance of a conversion into a commitment in which social change and the emergence of new moralities are always explicit.

Prima facie, given particular conditions, a metanoia or something like it can take place anywhere at any time. In fact, outside the Christian ambience it occurs only rarely. Disassociated from the events of Pentecost and the cultural instructions derived from them, an incipient metanoia is a lonely cry in the dark: myth and tradition rule, preserve the continuities; given roles, statuses, identities, and group memberships are maintained; deviants and nonconformists are shunted into given and prescribed positions or eliminated. In the European or Western tradition, on the other hand, the continuities are preserved in history, in the documentation of strings of significant change and conflict whose interconnections, thought of as cause and effect, rest more snugly in the mythopoeic relevances of Pentecost and metanoia. The normative lifestyles, routines, and moralities of one generation exist to be transcended and changed in the next. The ordered stabilities of given roles, statuses, and identities are in dynamic tension with the instruction to abandon current boundaries, enter a communitas or anti-structure, and remake the moralities. And as events move persons to become individuals, they engender the conflicts which make further moral choice and decision necessary.

In all cultures high status, influence, and achieving or possessing what is considered valuable depends not only on locally prescribed, generally overt and understood skills and capacities, but also on certain abilities which, in one idiom described as the favor of the gods, may also be described as the successful passage of risk, chance, and hazard. These last punctuate the road to fame, and where they do not exist in nature they are built into the cultural fabric. We have noted two examples: the Naga man who wished to put the seal on high status with the slaughter of *mithan* cattle had to range his beasts in the forest where they were prey for tigers and panthers; the Yap islander risked storm and a multitude of accidents to get his stone disk back to his village. Yet allowing that there is always a residuum of the mystical—which allows one man to be described as "lucky" and another of apparently equal ability as "unlucky"—after inspection much of the mystery evaporates.

A successful Melanesian manager, for example, certainly has to have things going for him. But he can also be shown to be one who, besides having acute perceptions of social situations and how others will react to them, knows himself and is able to handle his father's (or elder brother's) ghost—which last can be shown to mean or correspond with command over or enjoyment of satisfactory relations with his conscience (Burridge 1969b: 434ff.). Similarly, the able and successful in other cultures can usually be shown to be remarkably skillful not only at manipulating and construing the future possibilities of what is overt in a situation, but in the way in which, often with the aid of particular techniques or through encounters with spirits, ghosts, dreams, familiars, and the like, they are able to sense or interpret what is implicit or covert in the situation. This foresight or, at a deeper level, prescience of the possibilities and probabilities contained in the personalities, characters, and interests of those involved in relation to what is normative and overtly expectable, is usually phrased in a mystical idiom. As it must be: in the end there can be no rational accounting for "luck." Nevertheless, so far as that kind of "luck" may be accounted for, it is worth noting that the mediating feature—ghost, spirit, or familiar—hauls the seeker out of the boundedness of structures, elicits freedoms of insight and association, and permits apperceptions. Some sort of reintegration of the components of being which results in an access to knowledge or truths not available to others may be assumed. Further, although the knowledge gained may be said to be implicit in the deeper recesses of culture, it can be and usually is described as coming or gained from outside of what is overtly and generally known in the culture.

Shamanic ecstasies, trances, certain psychic experiences, visions, dreams, and the like, whether experienced unexpectedly and without invitation or engineered by drugs, meditational, moral, or spiritual exercises, entail changes in animal or physiological condition, a different kind of integration of the components of being and, perhaps, an access to supposed truths whose validity or usefulness is not normally judged on their intrinsic properties but by the mode of access. Skeptics, embedded in the overt expressions of culture, disallow them because they have not been obtained through what they regard as an appropriate systematic. Believers tend to give them more value than is perhaps their due. Either way, the supposed truths, even though they may in fact be derived from the recesses of the implicit or covert in culture, can be said to have been derived from outside the culture. And both versions carry their measures of validity. Nevertheless, without denying the true mystery of what actually happens, much appears to be contained in a movement from the structured to the unstructured and back again to the structured. Subsequent articulations by the experiencer of what has happened must stand as some sort of critique of the given, overt, and structured.

Sacred scriptures, regarded as derived from peculiarly significant mystical experiences (or movements from the structured to the unstructured) may be systematically studied for guidance or as scholarly pursuit, or simply opened at random so that, at second hand as it were, the original inspiration may, through the apparent happenstance linking seeker and words, provide the kind of guidance that the overt norms of the culture have not been able to give. Those who follow the first procedure scorn the second. Yet the latter may result in a decision to do this rather than that, a renewal of the given moralities, a mediation of the moralities, the resolution of a conflict within the given moralities—or even a determination to change the moralities. That is, assuming Ego has a problem which, apparently, cannot be resolved within the relationship between his current integration of the components of being and the overt cultural norms, there is a resort to an appropriate surprise confrontation. Implicitly if not explicitly, embedded in the procedure is the hope that cultural norms and components of being will fall apart and reintegrate into that fruitful relationship which will resolve the problem. The essential ingredient is an interruption—easily phrased as a mystical intervention—of the automaticism of cultural programming. The albeit momentary liminality it engenders provides the opportunity for a reassessment.

In much the same way, varieties of meteorological and celestial phenomena, astrologies, I-Ching slips, playing and tarot cards, as well as unusual bisociations and juxtapositions or encounters with ghosts, spirits, fairies, monsters, magical animals, and the like, can be made to mediate between the self and the overt programming of the cultural categories. Through surprise confrontations, that integration of the components of being which is the self accommodated to the cultural categories is given pause, placed in a liminality, perhaps jerked out of accustomed thought-tracks. Opportunities are presented to cut the gordian knot of traditional rationalizations and intellectualizations with a direct perception of the truth of things. The anxious, troubled, uncertain, alert, or inquiring mind is placed in a liminal position between the ordered regularities of the overt in culture on the one hand and the chaos of the disorderly and anomalous on the other. Perhaps, too, if the shock is sufficient, a seeker may experience a sloughing off roles and statuses and, thereby, perceive a disinterested truth. In contrast, systematic investigatory procedures, which are rarely disinterested, move in an ordered way from the known and ordered into the unknown and as yet unordered. They widen the ambience of order, broaden the horizon of knowledge. But because new data are usually rationalized and intellectualized in traditional patterns, the scope of the given moralities is enlarged but only rarely changed in content and axis. Overcoming the inertial momentum of traditionally patterned modes of rationalization so that new data will engender new rationalizations and new moralities requires a movement into the liminal or unstructured, whence inspiration comes.

When, among the simpler peoples of the world, exposure to Christianity, Complex economy, and the colonial and industrial apparatus have come so fast as to outpace the capacity to order and moralize, mystical interventions such as visions and dreams—shifts into the liminal or unstructured—have energized movements which have sought to reorder new knowledge and new experiences in new moralities. Naive in their beginnings, these movements have developed greatly in moral and political sophistication: intellectual systematics have ordered the turbulent and often confused inspirations and aspirations gathered in the liminal or unstructured situation. Yet such developments can only continue to take place and transform themselves into further developments if events are habitually confronted as opportunities for moral choice and decision. And for this an acceptable device for entering the liminal appears to be necessary: as soon as rationalizations and intellectualizations are allowed to concretize, they dominate and imprison.

Traditionally in Europe and the Western world this dilemma has been resolved by the liminalities inhering in generalized individuality, ultimately derived from Pentecost and metanoia. A continuing process of discovery and reordering entails standing aside from the structured cultural program and entering the liminal, and requires that disintegration-reintegration of the components of being which, heeding the promptings of the event, can wrest a new morality from a perception of truth. And this is what happens with each movement between person and individual.

When Zimmer (1956: 151) remarks that within the Hindu caste system the "individual," being totally identified with group tasks and roles, is compelled to become "anonymous," the mute assumption is that particularity of being arises from the dialectic between person and individual of the European experience. Similarly, when Max Weber (1958b: 132) observes that as soon as the "individual" in the caste system raises the question of meaning in his life he could experience it as dreadful, the implicit conviction is that "meaning" is derived from the same dialectic. The quest for truth, the surrender to love, and the belief that a new heaven and a new earth can be realized in the here and now, form the core of our European or Western notions of the individual. They entail entering a liminality—stripping off given roles and statuses—a willingness to ride the event into moral choice and new rationalizations, accepting that today's new moralities will become rituals which will in time give way to further new moralities at the instance of other individuals. They are the implicit but nonetheless predicative yardstick when considering other cultures.

The brief survey of general and normative orders and occasions seems to indicate that the viability and developmental potential of a moral order depends upon interaction between a positive preservation of the moralities as they are on the one hand, and varieties of intervention which, in positing new moral choice, may disturb, alter, or negate those moralities on the other. Some of these interventions may be construed as originating from some source outside culture, and described as mystical or supernatural, others are much more clearly built into what is overt and known and arise from particular kinds of relationships or from the latencies in the symbolic structure. Mostly, however, because a plethora of new discriminations would threaten too many, and without a secure anchorage in tradition a culture drifts and people become confused, interventions are ignored, traditional moralities are maintained, and new data are rationalized in traditional patterns. Still, without modes of mediating the moralities no culture can remain viable, and without modes of changing the moralities no culture can develop internally or remain viable in altered circumstances.

Though an individual posits the dilemma of moral choice, in most cultures the decision rests with the powerful, the established, the guardians of morality—so often the bonded community of adult and responsible males. And within such a context women become interventions. But the more women are disfranchised, the closer men have to bind themselves together. As the moralities become more artificial and exterior, and the culture becomes less viable, the more urgent it becomes to build in indirect interventions arising from women: feud, war, and fighting over adulteries. But in any case, since the groups which comprise a community have opposed and competitive interests, there must be some way or ways of mediating the moralities. Oracular devices, offices, or roles which perform the task are no less than built-in sources of intervention; and those who execute the task are interveners. And, as we have seen, this kind of man or woman, realizing something of individuality, is set apart from the community of interacting persons. He or she is marked and identified: on the one hand a standing contrast to the smooth functioning of the moralities, on the other hand a necessary complement to them.

Identifying and setting the human intervener apart from others seems necessary because the frequency and number of interventions which a community can suffer and yet remain a coherent community must clearly be limited and controlled. The moralities are the only ordered stability, the regulators of stable social relationships. Though they have an inertial momentum of their own, they are positively maintained and defended by those in power, the guardians, who preserve the continuities in terms of a sacrosanct tradition. A steady state is implied and found, moral changes tend to come about slowly if at all, and then they are folded into tradition. The generalized individuality of European or Western civilization contradicts this model. It demands changes in the moralities, and steady states cannot be maintained for long. Standing on love as a value to be developed for its own sake, the continuities are found in moral initiatives and changes, not in moral stasis. A transcendence of the given moralities, contained in the historical exemplars of Pentecost and famous metanoias and repeated in countless episodes through the middle ages and since, was and still is (though institutionalized and secularized in a variety of derivative and differentiated forms) the generative fount of the culture. Intellectually fixed in the platonic search for an ideal and universal moral order which, in turn, reinforces and has been reinforced by Christian universalism and love, generalized individuality becomes evident in that process of negation and moral hesitation followed by a positive affirmation which, in a diversity of cultural ambiences, seeks the power to make truth apparent in morality and, further, attempts to realize and generalize itself in those new moralities which will conserve the newly discovered truths.

It is tempting to lay generalized individuality at the feet of capitalism, urbanization, industrialization, and a burgeoning egalitarianism. Indeed, when consequences are taken to be their own causes the case is irrefutable. But, de Tocqueville notwithstanding, according to the ethnographic record, without generalized individuality egalitarianism goes along with a fierce criticism of others and rigorous conformities. It inhibits exploration of other kinds of truth, needs—and obtains—frequent encounters with ghosts and spirits, and otherwise relies on outside interventions to shift into a new key. Urbanization secures identities, may loosen the person from the matrix of kinship, but does not necessarily turn persons into individuals. There were many cities before the advent of Christianity but, so far as we know, no individuality as we think of it. To the extent that caste relations still hold strong in Indian industrialized cities, industrialization of itself cannot be an adequate cause or correlate. So far as caste relations have been weakened in the same context, it should be borne in mind that modern industrialization is a European product, that ideas and values travel with a product, and that large parts of India have been under direct European administration for many years. If personal capitalism and individuality seem to go hand in hand, corporate capitalism is inimical to it. Individuality existed before capitalism was institutionalized and, being antithetical to a given order, seeks so to change the given economic framework that the latter will conform to its newly discovered moralities. Nurtured in the medieval *societas*, individuality flowered in the varieties of opportunity offered by the renaissance and is as easily recognizable in its differing cultural modes and expressions in the hierarchies of enlightenment Europe as in egalitarian America. Successive industrial and technological revolutions have not yet expunged it. And if it can lead into the criminal as well as the saintly, the vicious as well as the gracious, that is the moral challenge. Individuality is not necessarily a prescription for a locally perceived good. It is a mode of reapperceiving the twisted interpenetrations of good and evil so as to redraw the lines of discrimination.

Whether truth or reality be regarded as secreted or contained within a dialectic of the spirit, as the differentials of coercive power attaching to status or wealth or control of resources, as emerging from revelatory experiences, or as latencies inherent in the sociocultural process, in individuality the resultants are articulated. Yet the logic of a given set of moralities or system of roles and statuses seems to require moments of truth derived from some source other than themselves if they are to remain viable. Outside the European or Western ambience the semblances or refractions of individuality which grasp these moments tend to be confined to and insulated in peculiarly marked or prescribed positions. Within the European experience, on the other hand, seeking such moments of truth to renew or change the moralities is incumbent on all. And this feature, generalized individuality, seems rooted in the earliest Christian experience which generalized the Hebraic prophet tradition.

PART III

INDIVIDUALITY
AND POWER

8 GUARDIANS AND THEIR ENEMIES

The human impulse to know the truth of things, manifest in attempts to articulate the real and true, is also a search for the springs of power. Whether in the curved beak of a hawk, the armed divisions and industrial base of a nation-state, a child's innocent brown eyes, or revelatory experience, power moves to realize its own inherencies, determines. What is sought of and from the moralities, on the other hand, is an equilibrium of order, a harmonious balance of powers grounded in reciprocities: for each right a duty or obligation, for every privilege a responsibility, for every good given or service rendered an equivalent return. Constraining, the moralities breed further constraints. Mutual obligations and responsibilities, from which rights and privileges may be derived, accrue through time as an increasingly heavy burden. Unopposed, unenlivened by the quest for truth which, in measuring own experience against the representations of culture, must be seized with the potential for disrupting, degrading, renewing, or changing the moralities, the moralities would defeat themselves and extinguish the culture. But without an order imposed by the moralities there would be no culture.

Those who maintain the moralities are guardians. They appreciate and treasure the culturally prescribed realities, are derisive and scornful of any other. Thoroughly socialized, they are both creatures and masters of their culture and its moralities. Theirs the appeal to justice, to a current ethic. Identifying themselves with the given moralities and their maintenance, guardians draw upon all the power inherent in a framework of order. Their initiatives and arrangements give life its textures, make it worthwhile or otherwise. They possess the hunting, fishing, farming, navigational, building, engineering, and manufacturing techniques, skills, and experience on which the culture depends. Controlling material resources, they may secure this control with armed force, command the allegiance of those who would like to succeed them in time. The mainstays of established religion, cults, clubs, secret societies, rituals, and symbolic activities, they react forcefully to any attempted innovations, strive to maintain the cultural symbols. Familiar with the different kinds of social situation that take shape, they know how to handle them with skill, dignity, and decorum. Long practice has made them aware of motives and natures; avoiding the disrupting and damaging confrontation is their forte. Intellectually and in wisdom they are the storehouses of all that the culture can provide.

Leading participation in all the varied activities of a culture provides guardians with the networks of allies and associates necessary to their collective control of political life. Because they have spent much of their lives learning the skills and techniques of management, they do not willingly relax their hold or take kindly to new ways the complexities of which they may not be able to master. The law and administrative and bureaucratic procedures are their delight, the framework of their aesthetic. Roles, ranks, and statuses, each in place and conserved in rituals of protocol, are imperatives. Maintaining an equilibrium of ordered social relationships are the guardians' best skills and interests. Continually reiterating and reestablishing the precepts and activities whose ordered relations shape the structure of society, that structure is their being. Under stable conditions, guardians are authentic to a culture, realize a local universal, preserve the good. They are admired and respected, sometimes envied and feared. Under conditions of change, particularly when a traditional culture is changing, fading guardians are to others within the community authentic only to the past: figures of fun as new guardians take their places. To the stranger, however, particularly to the

European or Westerner, those same figures of fun can excite admiration. Whatever they might be now, they had fulfilled the categories and were authentic to something at some time. We know that a culture is changing when we perceive that a new authenticity is being sought. And in such a situation only those who are presently as no one can be authentic.

Given the order maintained and imposed by the guardians, society becomes an almost sensible fabric, seems to maintain itself, appears to defeat evil. Without order all hopes become fears. Order is good, the good is secreted in order, what is orderly is good and vice versa: disorder is bad, and disorder and evil tend to be equated. If evil can show its face in order as well as disorder, guardians would say, with order evil may at least be identified. In disorder nothing can be identified. And because an order and the ethic which the normative moralities indicate are closely identified, guardians maintain the order so as to defeat evil and preserve the moralities and ethic. They maintain the rules, concern themselves with rules for changing the rules, are alert to features which disturb the smooth operation of the rules, and counter regularly occurring disturbances by institutionalizing them. Devices for doing these things normally keep order and ethic from drifting too far apart. But internal contradictions there must be. The moral order that is not sharpened by opposition loses its creative edge. And when guardians use their powers to maintain order against the quest for truth and the emergence of new moralities they begin to manifest evil. Ultimately, without mediation the moralities must founder; and an order unable to metamorphose must extinguish itself.

There seems to be no culture in which the guardians are unaware of the assertion to autonomy. They are able to articulate the fact that the assertion to autonomy and ordered moral reciprocities are in antithesis, and that human beings do not take to reciprocities as a matter of course. Moral sense and awareness have to be explicitly inculcated. But whether at or below the level of the articulate, and even though responsibility starts with an explicit presumption of awareness, socialization—molding to conformity—is not something that is achieved at a particular point in the life cycle but is, rather, a continuing process in which the assertion to autonomy and self-willedness are pitted against the rules, the moralities. In dynamic tension the antitheses bear fruit. An excessive proliferation of rules stifles the culture. Though self-willedness may enliven the culture, without adequate controls it may destroy the culture. Within these extremes the limits and modes of tolerance tend to become institutionalized, insulating or isolating expectable and repetitive disturbances from the mainstream of the general moralities.

The careful control in traditional societies of assertions to autonomy and self-willedness in pubertal and subsequent symbolic activities illustrate one model. General normative responsibilities are emphasized, and the greater responsibilities of taking initiatives are opened to those who can appreciate and handle them. Specifying occasions and periods of particular license, sexual license for example, is another model: if nothing very positive is achieved, thwarted energies are bled out of the system. But in contrast with these and other disturbances which run an expectable course, the presentation of a new idea has a random potential. A saint or genius may be exiled, hanged, or burned. Insanity, the rearrangement of categories of appropriateness such that the culturally prescribed versions of reality appear to have no validity, may be shut away in asylums, banged like a recalcitrant television set, shocked with starving, scourging, drugs, and electrical devices, suffered in love, tolerated, used, or watched. The arctic madness which, as identified and treated by many a Western clinician must surely have made an ordered life in northern climes next to impossible, was perceived quite differently by the peoples of boreal cultures. They chose to master it so that, through the shaman, transformation agent and crosser of boundaries, madness could become the means of revealing to all the fully rounded potential of the human.

The difference between perceiving and grasping opportunity, and identifying and lamenting psycho-physiological lesion, may thus make the whole difference between survival and extinction. More pointedly, the difference marks the confrontation between the optimisms of anthropocentricism and the pessimisms of environmental apperceptions. Perceiving the outer world through the lens of cultural prescriptions, what might have been loss was turned to advantage. Opposing the potential of the whole human to the merely moral, together with the explicit notion that to be thus whole it is necessary in some way to die or to transcend morality, reveals the apperceptive diagnosis of arctic madness as relevant only to the higher incidence of shamans in arctic regions than is found elsewhere. As it happens, the psycho-physiological lesion that might have, and at times may have, resulted in general anomie and disaster is objectified, mastered, and made to become a source of strength for the whole community by bringing that mastery into an institutionalized complementary opposition to and separation from the regularly interacting moral community. The latter stands secure. Its members are shown how the moralities can only order a segment of the totality that is human life and being in culture. The whole of human being in a particular culture is contraposed to the variety of specializations, interests, and partial being typical of the moral community. Mastery over an affliction that anyone might suffer, crossing the boundaries between levels and contexts of being, revealing the continuities, showing forth the transformational process, mediating the moralities, curing the souls or the moral or spiritual sicknesses of others, being "rounder" or "more than" others, all carry their own compulsions. And these the guardians must attempt to keep within bounds.

The anthropocentric concern for the significance of life and the world which Max Weber (1958b: 330-31), writing of Indian and other Asian religious systems, contrasted with the European address to "the things of this world, the everyday events of nature and social life, and the laws or principles which determine their unfolding" is as true of the Hindu sanyasi as of the shaman. In the case of the sanyasi, however, it is not so much psycho-physiological lesion of itself that is dealt with. Rather is it the much more self-conscious and direct assertion to autonomy manifested in the explicit demand for self-realization within a discipline of own choice in relation to a moral order that rigorously prescribes particular modes. The resultant corresponds with the relationship between the shaman and the mutually interacting moral community. The caste system holds firm by virtue of the variety of exemplars of life outside caste that are objectified in an oppositional relationship. Accepting that the sanyasi may as effectively curse as bless, may steal, eat or copulate with corpses, and is often a fraudulent and intolerable burden on the productive capacity and patience of the moral community, he nonetheless represents an overarching ideal of the self made whole to which any man might aspire. This and the sacrifices entailed in being authentic seem to make tolerable and even worthwhile the quite different sacrifices and satisfactions of the caste-bound. The choice is clear-cut. What another social experience might regard as an evil is formally and can in fact be transformed into a good.

As exemplars participating in the Hero, both the shaman and sanyasi can initiate and present new ideas because, though in opposition to the interacting community, they are insulated from it. Their mastery is idealized and accorded power, but rendered safe. The new idea may be taken up by particular persons, or simply ignored. Even when a new idea begins to inform the moralities, the latter grind it to fit. The diviner, Leopard-skin chief, and others in their substantive positions are, on the other hand, much more clearly and specifically moral devices produced by the operation of the moralities themselves. In their situations new ideas must be seen as dangerous, often evil. While shaman and sanyasi represent the wholeness of human being in contrast to the acknowledgedly partial, moral person, the mediator is *per se* a buffer between opposed but similar and roughly equivalent forces of morality. He is necessary to a social order or context dependent on mutually opposed and competitive segments and interests. He is, to be sure, objectified, separated off, insulated and institutionalized. But his powers are carefully defined by the moralities. Sacralization and the ascription of symbolic and ritual powers protect him. And though some may bring more to their office than others, becoming the interstitial figure that a mediator is does not necessarily flow either from an aspiration to realize the self or from the assertion to autonomy. The office is derived from the order imposed by the moralities, the latter prescribe modes of recruiting the incumbents. And though a mediator of this sort may become an exemplar, participate in the Hero, even realize some sort of individuality, the kind of social order which requires such an office is clearly one in which the moralities are emphasized against the whole human being. Evil then grows out of the moralities themselves and is countered by them through the office.

The Melanesian manager and Australian Man of High Degree are not insulated from the interacting moral community. In presenting new ideas and initiatives they risk their personal selves and their identities. Generally the servants of the moralities, in the crucial situation they are asked to rise above morality and produce initiatives for which the moral community may in fact destroy them. If the representation of the whole human is, again, sacrificed to the moralities, new ideas and initiatives are subjected to the test of working moralities and not permitted to exist as ideals which the members of the community find generally unrealizable. Evil is now manifest as envy which grows out of fear, thwarted ambitions, the anxiety that another may override the moralities and still remain secure, and the active manipulation of these features by the sorcerer. While in the Melanesian situation wholeness of being is a representation of myth to which some may aspire but which the community rarely allows for the living, among the Australians wholeness is to be found in a full realization of the moralities themselves.

Within the European or Western ambience of generalized individuality the cultural instructions to surrender to love, transcend given moralities, create a new heaven and new earth, and find a true or ideal and universal morality requires that guardians supervise orderly moral changes and transform varieties of new experience into new authenticities. So far as they fulfill these requirements fading guardians are admired and respected. In so far as they fail to do so they tend to appear comical—albeit authentic to a past. On the surface moving towards an analogue of the Australian situation, wholeness of being becomes an aspiration for each in terms of that morality which can encompass the totality of human experience. As multifaceted as the good, evil is secreted in the selfishness and self-concern that deny both true self-interest and the quest for truth in love.

Because they are grounded in reciprocities, the given moralities which guardians seek to maintain and extend are an imposition on a natural world that is in continual and dynamic recreation. Meteorological phenomena, climatic variations that result in bad harvests or a scarcity of game, the proximity of aggressive and more powerful peoples, sickness, death, injury, murder, malice, arrogance, contempt, contumaciousness, the assertion to autonomy, pubertal self-willedness, the abrasions arising out of particular relationships such as those between men and women or senior and junior, the articulated experience of psychological trauma, dreams, visions, trances and the like constitute evidence of the nonreciprocal both in nature and in culture. Guardians identify them, bring them to order in clusters of rules, taboos, and rationalizations, and so exert a measure of control over them. Where wholeness of being—which must include the nonreciprocal—or its likeness is insulated or controlled in prescribed positions, the relations between the reciprocal and nonreciprocal maintain culture and the moralities in a viable dynamic. Without such insulation, and unless (as in the Australian case) wholeness of being is contained in the moralities themselves, the attempt to be whole is obnoxious, negates the ordinary workaday relationships of the moral community and engenders a reaction that insists on the moralities.

This last, indeed, is the dilemma of generalized individuality. Even given the cultural instructions of the European or Western ambience, the moral initiatives inherent in the movement to wholeness must start as seeming arrogance and, in any case, are a threat to the given moralities. Three kinds of reaction are invited: first rejection, then perhaps a temporary insulation followed by, in some cases, acceptance into the moralities. Going the whole course depends, in the short run, on the political power the initiative can recruit and, in the end, on the relation of the new initiative to the manifest truth of things. Without the instruction to transcend, all movement would be returned to the given moralities. Without the surrender to love transcendence would hardly occur, and would be vain if it did. Conversely, without generalized individuality and the instruction to transcend, that development of the idea and activity of love in all its colors which is unique to Western civilization would have been impossible. Loving and transcending inform and develop each other.

Though there is no sweeter and more sublime deliverance from the automaticisms of given moralities, love yet disturbs, frightens, is even repulsive to dedicated upholders of the law, tradition, and the given moralities. All that such people have given their lives to be and attain is set at nought: sense of justice, fair play, deserving merit, moral indignation—all derived from reciprocities—are defeated. If, ideally, a moral cause is a unidirectional refraction of love, love in its blindness may transgress or transcend the moralities, violate or renew an ethic. Because love is fundamentally opposed to the roles, statuses, and associated ethic of a social organization, and may discount or ignore them, guardians attempt to control love by permitting it a bounded range of expressions appropriate to an ethic and idea of justice secreted by the moralities. Held fast by the local ethic, love and its betrayal are in constant embrace. Breaking the embrace requires a reentry into or renewed surrender to love, which is what a proper individual does or should do. Love makes whole.

Within the European or Western tradition love between man and woman is but one facet of the relationship between self and other which makes whole. The other may be of the same or opposite sex, related or unrelated, a generalized many, a group or collectivity, an idea, expression or activity, or deity. In most cultures, however, the notion of wholeness is figured and almost completely exhausted in the union of male and female categories and, though otherwise also aspired to, is most frequently focused in the union of man and woman in marriage. Thus, for example, while the shaman who crosses the divide between male and female—so experiencing or containing most of both categories in his or her being—approximates wholeness irrespective of marriage, the sweet and fruitful marriage in which each partner has fulfilled the appropriate categories and also, through the marriage, participated fully in the being of the other, approximates that wholeness which the culture and its moralities provide for the members of the moral community. Formally and inclusive of the division of labor that follows from this fundamental and most elementary cultural and moral discrimination, the relations between men and women can be summed up as complementary and cooperative—descriptions so often more accurately rendered as oppressive and subservient. And though the one set does not necessarily exclude the other, the former is always vulnerable to the latter.

It is a commonplace around the world through time that the distribution of explicit and overt powers in most cultures leaves women relatively disfranchised. Not that women do not have power. It is simply that the power they have is generally exercised through men, is covert and not often explicit. On the whole, the more rigorous, sharply defined, and intellectualized the moralities, the more are women relatively disfranchised, and the more are they oppressed whether or not they are conscious of the oppression. Where these conditions obtain, moreover, women are generally regarded as threats to the moralities. And since women are not burdened with explicit and overt responsibilities to the extent that men are, they may indeed, in particular contexts, stand as threats—a situation recognized by most cultures with a host of taboos, symbolic attachments, and restrictions on their activities, particularly during menstruation and childbirth, animal or natural events. But again, while these and other arrangements—such as the confinement of women to the home and to particular tasks and locales—mark out and insulate the threat, protecting the moralities, the breach, occasioning swift reaction, points up and resharpens the moralities. The cycle is closed.

Given rigorous moralities, men often hold women to be instinctual rather than logical; intuitive rather than methodical and systematic; sound in heart rather than mind; excellent at routine tasks, poor at extemporization, at initiating and facing an emergency or unfamiliar social situation; and naturally adapted to drudgery. And where these stereotypes obtain it is usually the case that women are not given the opportunity to be logical, methodical, and systematic, and are debarred from positions which require extemporization and initiative. In such circumstances the women's assertion to autonomy finds three main channels if the self is to be realized outside simple acceptance: copy the man, become a guardian—than which nothing could be more draconian—and reinforce the state of affairs; take to varieties of sexual abandon; turn to mysticism and ecstatic activities (cf. Lewis 1971). And since the first choice is a congruence, and the second and third are easily institutionalized and insulated, the cycle is closed yet again.

Generalized individuality together with the love which ideally goes along with it breaks the cycle and provides a way out. It becomes possible both collectively and in particular instances to overcome oppression and subservience and renew the complementarities and cooperative values. But only temporarily. Those with more resources, energy, resourcefulness, and opportunity inevitably begin to demand and enforce. Complementarity and cooperation become the breeding ground of oppression and subservience. Only a rare and complete surrender to love can prevent this. A love that is not mutual may as easily oppress as liberate. Still, informed with love, generalized individuality's renewal of the moralities defeats their tendency to proliferate, harden, become purely systemic and grind the life out of culture. Yet wholeness must include the spiritual. And whatever the spiritual actually *is*, it is not the animal nor the moral, though it must contain and, through the cultural faculties, transcend them both. Allowing that the relations between men and women may be epitomized in the sexual act, what might have been mere copulation becomes so informed with the cultural faculties that, through a marriage in which the complementarities and cooperation may be expressed, an animal act becomes moral and may go on from there to transcend morality in a flight into the spiritual. Not only in English does a single word, worship, refer to a disposition appropriate both to sexual relations and relations with the deity.

The vehicle for realizing the spiritual, and the least stable of the components of being, the moralities tend to conceal the realities which might change them. So they drift into illusion. Nonetheless, the realities of the nonreciprocal continually intervene. Reality is that which *does* intervene to demand rerationalization and renewal or change in the moralities. To remain viable they must be able to deal with regularly occurring and expectable interventions—the assertion to autonomy, pubertal self-willedness, sickness, death and the like. It is in this sense that the moralities, through symbolic activities, rituals, taboos, and varieties of modes of separation and insulation, come nearest to "reflecting" the realities that are considered to matter in a particular context. But new realities, new discoveries about the external world or the nature of human being, require new moralities.

Moral rigors which engage the critical faculties and give rise to low thresholds of indignation seem to go hand in hand with witchcrafts, sorcery, and/or feud and war: reassertions of the reciprocities of morality within an ordered framework. If the moralities are weak or uncertain—such that the guardians cannot exert their authority or neither know nor care what to do—tolerance is extended to the point of lawlessness and anomie: fighting and violence occur within an unordered framework, and "men of movement" have the field to themselves. It then becomes easy to short-circuit the very real sociological problem by asserting that man is an aggressive animal, a natural killer and instinctual warmonger. Human being is as inevitably cultural, moral, and spiritual as it is animal. At the level of the collective—where motives are contained in rationalizations which mobilize—all fighting and violence have to do with the reassertion of moralities which are believed to have been breached or in danger of breakdown. Order and the moralities are theses which beget their antitheses, and wholeness is found in their synthesis. Choosing the confrontation with death, as does the Dinka master of the fishing spear, takes being out of the systemic and yields hope. The moralities are confronted with that in human being which can transcend them. Though the animal in the human is a continuing challenge to the moralities, maintaining the tension fructifies and makes possible a transcension of the moralities into the spiritual. Submerging the animal or destroying the moral invite disaster and make entry into the spiritual impossible. Mystics, who have engaged the animal, transcended morality, and entered the spiritual, and so approximated wholeness, do not fear death. They have resolved the paradox of being. Fear belongs to those bound tight in local moralities and unable to transcend them.

In all cultures the tendency, reinforced by the guardians, is to make moral, moralize, and stabilize the moralities. Occurrences and occasions which threaten the moralities are marked, insulated, institutionalized, and made to work for the moralities. People are constrained to be persons. Incipient individuals, deviants, nonconformists, and outsiders are shunted into positions where they can be watched, do little harm, and perhaps be of benefit. From these prescribed and

insulated positions they may mediate the moralities, reinvig-
orate them, or reveal the whole of human being in relation to
the moralities. No culture can do without them. Conversely,
the greatest threat to any stable and coherent moral system is
generalized individuality, the continuing emergence in each
generation of individuals and "men of movement" who, concerned to change the moralities, cannot and will not be
pushed into insulated positions.

Some of the circumstances which enabled and indeed
forced European or Western civilization not only to court this
peril but, through generalized individuality, to ensure continuing changes in the moralities have already been suggested.
Christian beginnings and their ambience provided an exemplar which, despite successive contrary movements directed
towards stabilization and consolidation—wholeness now!—
has endured. Each attempted stability has given way to the
values contained in the exemplar. And the social conditions
resulting from the operation of the exemplar have, in turn,
themselves been necessarily vulnerable to the values of the
exemplar. Continuing change is written into the program. As
a diverse collection of peoples, cultures, cults, and moralities
held together by an administrative, legal, trading, and military structure, the Roman empire provided complementary
conditions for the kind of revolutionary movement that early
Christianity was. The decay of the empire and the growth of
Christianity went together with barbarian invasions and the
splitting of the old hegemony into many different and opposed political units. Though Christianity was enabled to
move and develop along the old trade routes, it was characterized by schisms, heresies, and movements of a millenarian
kind. At once holding to and attempting to transcend its only
models of order—the tatters of Roman administrative
threads, and a law which had started to crumble as soon as it
was rigidly codified—Christianity in the Western world
hardly achieved a viable and organized structure until about
the twelfth century. The stress laid by medieval scholars and
theologians, guardians all, on the coherence and universality

of the Church hardly corresponded with the social circumstances as we know them. Their supposed coherence and universality were an unrealized neo-platonic ideal carrying its own contradiction: each achieved morality should give way to a better and more ideal universal. As guardians, these scholars seem to have allied themselves with the given moralities and moved towards their concretization. On the other hand, themselves participating in generalized individuality, they were at pains to emphasize that the single person was a universal, and that this universal should embody that morality which inhered in the mystical body of Christ, represented by the Church. And this entailed an ongoing and continuing process of perfecting the moralities: a continuing revolutionary process which, through generalized individuality, was nonetheless more or less orderly.

Not until the thirteenth century, with St. Thomas Aquinas, did Christianity attain any coherence. And that coherence and supposed universality were at the intellectual and theological levels only. Until then (and indeed since) it had been a number of developing but converging as well as diverging coherences held together by a few Biblical, chiefly New Testament exemplars most generally conflated in the Nicene creed. Competing interests within the Church itself were accompanied by attempts by various polities to rout the Church temporal and so take control of its centralized and permeative administrative structure. Despite the common use of Latin, diverse local customs and social organizations and differences of opinion regarding the interpretation of the sacred texts in relation to quite distinct native situational contexts and idioms of understanding added to the varieties of difference. It is true that within the Church itself, among the religious, whether ordained or unordained clerks, the growing intellectual and theological coherence was reflected in those rules held in common by the varieties of religious orders and secular clergy. But again, the differences between these kinds of churchmen on the human level of working, doing, and the organization of intra- and inter-community relations were, as

they still are, as significant as the liturgies and rules of principle held in common. Besides, no sooner had Aquinas
achieved his largely aristotelian synthetic coherence than the
renaissance and reformation, obedient to the exemplar in social projection, were plunging Europe into further moral, religious, and political ferment.

Whether the values inherent in the exemplar of Christian
beginnings were predicative of, or simply found their opportunity in, the conditions of the ongoing situation may for the
moment be left to one side. What matters is that the conditions one would associate with generalized individuality are in
fact found in the medieval period as well as since those times.
New heavens and new earths have been and are being continually sought. Generalized individuality was indeed, as
Dumont has said (1970: 32) a "mental revolution." But (con-
tra Dumont, *ibid.*) it is surely rooted in the first century.
Within the civilized ambiences of the time, three alternative
general forms of governing large urban populations and their
rural dependencies had been devised: the authoritarian
tyranny involving a devolution of power from the apex
downwards, a distribution of power which could only be
modified by rivals and the threat of armed rebellion; democracy based upon slavery; and, through the Hebrews, subordination to a given set of laws which (corresponding with the
Australian model) were not to be set aside. In contrast, essentially antisystemic and invoking a sociological nullity in its instructions to love, and transcend the law, Christianity was
forced to organize itself partly on the these models and partly
in antithesis. In principle opposed to the unidirectional coercions of political authority, the organized Church nevertheless conformed to the known model for maintaining order
while also holding to principle or the law. Itself demo-
cratically organized without slaves, authority conferred
tended toward absoluteness. If given laws were to be transcended, there had to be laws to transcend. Caught in these
ambivalences, the Church generated moral and spiritual
power distinct from the purely political.

In spite of expectable and perhaps necessary corruptions on either hand the duality of Church and State provided the necessary framework for ensuring and conserving generalized institutionalized individuality. The conformities resulting from political coercion were countered in the Church's critique: individual and person corresponded with Church and State. And even in the betrayal of allying itself with the political authority, the Church could not destroy what had given it its authenticity. For though the renaissance and reformation certainly accelerated the process of individuation, and the secularization of the Church's organization into explicitly democratic political forms replaced in some part the functions of the division between Church and State, these developments in themselves appear as further expressions of the possibilities entailed in the generalized individuality which had already been established with the Graeco-Christian synthesis. This it was that initiated the ongoing dialectic between the tendency of guardians to gather and concentrate power, restrict, conserve, concretize, and stabilize the moral order and its intellectualizations, and that instruction contained in the exemplar of Christian beginnings to liberate the spirit, transcend the given, and make new and more perfect.

De Tocqueville correlated the individuality, egalitarianism, and democratic forms of American life with discontinuities. And he contrasted the freedoms of this mix with the restrictiveness of European hierarchical orders which, however, provided continuities. That is, in a particular idiom and context, he reiterated the dialectic initiated by the Graeco-Christian synthesis. He could scarcely do otherwise. Refracted and projected onto varieties of arcs of relevance, *person* ⇌ *individual, identity* ⇌ *nonidentity, someone* ⇌ *no one* are at the center of European or Western being.

While it is clear that democracy and egalitarianism have had much to do with the further development and generalization of individuality, so soon as a particular form becomes restrictive and concretized it must be challenged by that which is liberating and new. It should be remembered that Christianity as a political force started as a democratic and egalitarian movement and found acceptance, as it does today, among slaves, outcasts, and the disfranchised over against established hierarchies. Moreover, Christianity itself is subject to the same dialectic. If, over the years, established denominations have frequently had to come to terms with and surrender to restrictive and hierarchical political forms, European and Western democratic forms, we may remind ourselves, are not derived from Athens, which depended on forms of slavery, but from the modes developed by the Church and its religious orders. Millenarian and similar movements as well as reformist movements within the Church itself have always started by emphasizing egalitarian and democratic forms. Their later corruption and betrayal is as endemic and necessary to the process as is Judas to the Last Supper.

As we have seen, urbanization of itself has little to do with the generalization of individuality. What matters—the Graeco-Christian inheritance aside for the moment—is money in opposition to prescribed exchange. The latter insists that people be persons, allows only a marginal individuality. Money encourages ego-centered social relations, loosens group and moral allegiances, invites the person to be an individual: its atomizing effects can only be reined by rigorous traditional moralities such as the caste system, or by overarching and tightly knit bureaucracies. Initiated and taking root in a moneyed environment, Christianity in its social aspects has always been deeply affected by the tension between *giving* ⇔ *receiving* and *giving* ≠ *receiving*. It reexpresses the tensions between morality and love, person and individual, the law and its transcendence. Yet if money can provide the opportunity for that kind of decision which, affecting oneself and others, some (cf. Levy 1962: 226) regard as definitive of individuality, to perceive and grasp the opportunity there must be some preexisting imperative, proclivity, or attitude which stands poised to discover it and is ready, not simply to take advantage, but to make it moral.

This preexisting imperative or proclivity has been located in the idea of metanoia: the development of the Hebrew notion of repentance for past deeds coupled with the determination to eschew sinful ways and walk in the paths of the Lord. As developed by Christianity, a missionary faith, metanoia was not simply the basis for conversion. It represented an institutionalization of the putative capacity in each human being to change his or her mind about the nature of the world and the truth of things: a transformational act or process, a crossing of the boundary between one kind of being and another which entails a continuing process of developing awareness. While revelation, faith, dogma, the discoveries of science and the intellect, love, service to others, and a variety of institutional arrangements have provided the framework or environment for changing the mind, it has never been wholly forgotten that the burden is ultimately borne by the conscience in each single human being. The Christian conscience, that is, is not a matter of custom, group feeling, and the like, but a question of what one believes to be true and real in relation to the Godhead on the one hand, and the information and experience conveyed by the social environment on the other. And here, because it goes together with the notion of metanoia, we must add the idea of free will: a further emphasis on the single human being as responsible agent. Not custom, tradition, or the system are responsible; oneself is responsible.

Both metanoia and free will sum up sets of rationalizations which, in ordering and moralizing the assertion to autonomy, channel its power and energy into individuality and so into the moral community. Where other cultures and civilizations have insulated this power and energy, Christianity made them integral parts of the moral community and, through its particular notions of conscience and responsibility, provided them with their own restraints. So far as typical guardians are concerned this is and was a dangerous innovation. The integration of Hebrew faith and adherence to the law, Greek imagination, and Roman administrative genius injected with love and platonic idealism made up an unstable explosive.

With each generation in Christianity's tortured history the exemplar of Pentecost exerts its force. The tension between the system and the self's perceptions of truth, or between guardians and persons becoming individuals, has to be resolved again in new moralities. The paradox of organized Christianity is that within each of its differing denominational moral systems there is secreted that impulse to liberation which defies being organized. Given that a change of mind is but a prevaricating infirmity, that free will is a chimera, that conscience is a coward's excuse, that love has no divisions and an ideal no firepower, these weaknesses can combine in the predicative power of individuality.

9 CHARISMA

The respect accorded to shamans and sanyasis seems to rest
on that control and mastery of themselves which, through an
integration of the components of being, can transform what
appear as animal and moral ailments, lesions, or weaknesses
into sources of power of benefit to the community at large.
Demonstrating wholeness of being in relation to the necessarily partial truths of the moralities, the shaman's and sanyasi's
many capacities make them "more than" those in community. Their beings are rounder and fuller, they are nearer than
others to the truth of things. But apart from their apprentices
neither shaman nor sanyasi normally commands *people*. They
command abilities—spiritual, psychic, imaginative, intellectual, scientific, or quasi-scientific. Insulated, these capacities
either fructify or at least do no hurt to the moral and political
powers of the guardians who command the loyalty and allegiance of people.

Lacking an environment of stable security predicated by the
moralities, neither shaman nor sanyasi would have being or
value. And by insulating their powers, which are opposed to
the moralities, a culture gains the advantages of stability. But
when these powers are recruited by particular political and
moral interests a culture begins to change: it may develop a
new equilibrium, or it may after a while revert to the former
balance of oppositions. Conversely, if the means of penetrating closer to the truth of things become accessible to sufficient
numbers, wholeness of being comes under the control of the
moralities—with all that that means—and confers explicit authority. As an example, Strehlow (1971: 677) writes of the
Aranda and Loritja speaking peoples of Central Australia that

their songs—which encapsulated their mythological lore,
their rituals and intellectual and imaginative capital, and
brought them into touch with the truth of things—were
"venerated," the greatest treasures any man could aspire to,
taking the place of private wealth, and conferring "supreme
social prestige." "The men held in universal esteem, who had
been invested with the power of making life and death decisions while sitting in the councils of elders, were not the phys-
ically most powerful men or the most experienced hunters in
the community, but the local ceremonial chiefs who had
learned all that there was to be known of the sacred songs and
rituals in their area."

Through the gamut of cultures as we know them, whether
the truth of things, reality, is figured as residing in God, the
Great Spirit, the Spirit of the Universe, All-being, a written
text, or variously distributed between numerous gods, giants,
spirits, ancestors, ghosts, familiars, demons, and the rest, the
more closely in touch with these representations of the
sources of truth a man or woman is considered to be the more
respect he or she commands. In all sorts of ways he or she
who has some grasp on the truth of things, which must include the covert or hidden or implicit in culture, is considered
to have greater capacities than, is "more than," those whose
beings are predicated by the overt in culture, the moralities
alone. As we have seen (pp. 161-63), it is the necessary basis
of high status. But whether such capacities are regarded with
awe, admiration, or fear, a guardian's imperative is that they
should be controlled by the moralities, the fundamental predicates of community life. And, allied as they are to each other,
tradition, and the intellectualized modes in which custom is
conserved, guardians usually have the last word. In principle,
generalized individuality abandons such control. Responsibility for restraint is on the single human being in relation to
others: each becomes a guardian with a duty to conserve and
stabilize, each is also charged to change and transform. Some
group themselves together to emphasize conservation and
stability, others combine to emphasize change and transfor-

mation: a continuing dialectic between stability and moral innovation.

Interstitial roles or positions such as mediator or judge, standing between opposed segments, are not necessarily regarded as being "more than" others. Frequently, as in the case of the Leopard-skin chief, they are thought of as in many ways "less than" others. Still, they are generally protected and insulated, most usually by devices or ideas converging in the sacred or forbidden. By contrast and in principle, generalized individuality negates such selectively protective devices, and holds each sacrosanct, equally vulnerable. Despite the insistence of guardians that only current moralities be mediated, the general expectation is that new moralities, new laws, will emerge. Generalized individuality contains that residuum of the ancient Hebrew notion of repentance which, integral to the idea of metanoia, enables the person to say "no" to current moralities and, becoming an individual, seek new ones. Whether in a particular instance the negation of given moralities is a simple negation of morality itself or that transcendence of the given which gives rise to new moralities is usually a *post hoc* judgment. Nevertheless, when in the act of negation and positing new alternatives others are persuaded that the truth of things lies therein, command over people and perceptive grasp may come together in charisma and charismatic leadership.

Max Weber's translation of the charisms of Christian theology into the charisma and charismatic qualities of sociology (1947: 358ff.) has had a mixed history. For although analyses of charisma and charismatic qualities can show empirically determinable kinds of effectiveness related to the social ambience, the synthesis that is charisma—spelling success where ambience and aspiration seem to invite failure—can only as yet be accounted for or explained by the mysterium of charisma itself: a gift from God. Like *mana* and similar words in the ethnographic record, it may be that, as Lévi-Strauss has suggested (1966: xliv, l), charisma is essentially without specific meaning or *sens* and used to "explain" what otherwise cannot rationally (in terms of the culturally overt) be accounted for. On the other hand, it is surely possible to confront the mysterium, resist the temptation to go along with the *a priori* loading of the word, and examine the determinable features contained in that "gift from God."

Charismatic qualities may in the first instance be physical, located in the animal: glowing or hypnotic eyes, the presence that turns all heads, commands silence, compels attention. No doubt cultural attributes add to, even predicate the animal presence. Combining the cultural and animal, the spoken word, so often utterly banal when written, contains a coercive resonance. And so far as the words and their resonances coming from a particular mouth are effective and successful, move others to action, and continue to command their fates and destinies, thus far may the combination be described as charismatic. When, however, the combination begins to fail to move and command, charisma dwindles. Charisma seems authentic in, and defined by, success. Yet those who define "success" in political terms—command over people rather than ideas and capacities of perception—have only themselves to blame if charismatic qualities often appear as exercises in irrational futility. Rather should one attempt to penetrate the layers of superstitious mysteriosity that surround a true mysterium by looking for the kinds of success that, in the empirical situation, the use of the word charisma seems to indicate.

Many attempts have been made to spell out the particularities of the social ambience in which charismatic activities, centered on one with charismatic qualities, begin to form and are reinforced (e.g., Burridge 1960, 1969a; Fuchs 1965; Lanternari 1960/65; Lawrence 1964; Wilson 1973; Worsley 1957/68). But for a variety of reasons having to do with the fieldwork situation—only rarely is an investigator on hand when a charismatic leader goes about his business—studies of charismatic activities at first hand have been few. One such, however, an analysis by Johannes Fabian (1971) of the *Jamaa*, a movement which emerged in the Congo during the late 'forties under the charismatic impulse of Father Placide Tempels, a Franciscan missionary, illustrates the issues involved and takes us to the heart of the matter in hand.

Like many missionaries, Father Tempels had begun to find to his acute dismay that he was talking to air. For him Christianity breathed the realities of love, life, and truth into an environment that was otherwise constructed of illusions—job descriptions, economic relationships, statuses, authorities, recreational activities—unreal activities and relationships because uninformed by the unitive purposes and relevances which indicated the truth of things. For those to whom he preached, and for whom he had pastoral responsibilities, Christianity appeared as a series of liturgies and rituals together with, most importantly, schools and institutes which provided the necessary basic training for jobs, posts, and an illusory social advancement. . . . Deep in the African bush, towns had sprung up. Hunting and agricultural peoples had been catapulted into the bureaucratically and closely controlled, moneyed, disciplined, and mechanically ordered urban-industrial conditions engendered by the Union Minière and its ancillary companies and activities. On the one hand Father Tempels felt that neither he nor Christianity were penetrating into the lives of the people, on the other hand people seemed to be following their noses into jobs, money, and temporary or adventitious social relationships held together by little more than the bureaucratic colonial-industrial apparatus.

Then, with genuine sociological apperception, Father Tempels became aware of his own Christianity as distinct from his European-ness, and sought to understand the underlying values of the Bantu people. He wrote a book on the theme (Tempels 1945), translated his Christianity into Bantu categories, and made his insights work for him (and Christ) in his preaching and teaching. He articulated his understanding of Christianity in terms which his audience had already interiorized, which were integral to their being. More, intuitively or more purposefully, Father Tempels seems to have comprehended the aspirations of his audience and to have articu-

lated those aspirations in terms which members of that
audience were groping for, feeling for, and which they themselves, given time, might or would have used. Of particular
importance to Father Tempels—doubly important, sociologi-
cally, in an environment of transient social relationships—was
the outflow from the concrete events entailed in the encounter
between one human being and another. For in such situations,
stripped of given roles and statuses, each might and could experience the other as a fellow human being. And it was precisely this kind of participatory experience informed with
love that Father Tempels' audience seems to have been looking for. The many almost adventitious confrontations between job categories, roles, and statuses now became suffused
with meaning and relationship. Each could feel and recognize
the other as at least partly oneself. Formal structures were
transcended. So, as it happened, under Father Tempels' guidance the encounters between pairs and small groups matured
into the movement known as the *Jamaa*, Katanga Swahili for
"family." Pooling the experiences derived from the liminality
of their encounters, articulating a sense of communitas, participants began to develop a shared understanding of the relevances of their encounters. Brought together and objectified
in and as *umuntu*, being man (human), these understandings
became the central tenets of what was to become a coherent
system of belief and action (Fabian 1971: 148).

For a variety of reasons which need not detain us here,
Father Tempels eventually had to return to his native Belgium. From there he regularly wrote to, and advised, those
who regarded him as their spiritual leader and adviser. Although members of the *Jamaa* seem never to have regarded
themselves, nor were regarded by others, as outside the
Roman communion, Fabian is in the end convincing in
demonstrating—through linguistic evidence, the manuscripts
and letters of Father Tempels, published manuals, and what
was said and done by members of the movement in meetings
and in conversations—that the *Jamaa* was no ordinary pious
movement within the Church but represented an integrated

and complete system in itself. For going along with the development of doctrine—a gradually cohering environment of words and meanings, rationalizations, extracted from the experience of the encounters—went a felt necessity for realizing and fixing the doctrine in particular kinds of behavior and social relationships. Encounters and their outflow became ritualized, a communitas was becoming a community. A gathering of the pious who had found new meaning in their lives in their discoveries about themselves, who had developed a sense of communitas within the Church, began to develop into a distinct politico-moral movement.

The concretization of rationalizations about experience which made the Jamaa communitas into a community is not always inevitable. Father Tempels seems to have wanted the movement to remain in a steady state of germinative exploration. He had always stressed, and at the time of the investigation continued to stress in his letters from Belgium, that "power, leadership, kills the doctrine" (Fabian 1971: 92). Whether this maxim was born of an intuitive insight or a grasp of history makes no matter. When selves interact and find they have the same or similar basic assumptions and aspirations, they draw together, organize themselves and so put on roles and statuses. And once this process starts, relative status, leadership, and authority become crucial concerns. Incipient moralities have to be informed with an ethic, an idea of justice emerges, and the parable of the workers in the vineyard, who received equal pay for unequal amounts of work, becomes subject to tortuous reinterpretation. Any gathering together of selves, or of those who simply love one another, is sure sooner rather than later to generate the man or woman who makes comparisons and so introduces envy: "I am (doing) more than he, am more deserving, and yet. . . ." In that moment a standard of what is fair and deserving, an ethic, an idea of justice are born. Love, overleaping what is deserving, finds a refuge from envy in morality which alone can *order* envy.

In organizing themselves as a collective body the members

of the *Jamaa* illustrated the original Christian dilemma: those who love one another are compelled to put on the corruption of organization, assume roles, and compete for status and power: the communitas of selves becomes a community of roles and statuses. Only by transcending the corruption can those who have become so organized fulfill themselves within the mystical body. That kernel of the antisystemic which is firmly embedded in the Pentecostal exemplar continually reasserts itself to negate the given order—only to be reimprisoned in a new order. Realizing the Christian message and being organized constitutes the central tension of Christianity. From first beginnings (e.g., 1 Cor. 3:3ff.) into the present, clergy and the informed laity have always been sensitive to the potential of fission and schism inherent in the tension. Human beings live in an environment of words with meanings, and these meanings are mainly and substantially derived from the content, arrangement, and particular contexts of social relationships. Together, words, meanings, and social relations (moralities) yield a culturally prescribed truth and reality. But for some key words there is a penumbra of meanings derived from a patina of experience not wholly consistent with what is culturally prescribed. When the circumstances are such that both penumbra and patina not only seem more relevant but are shared, then this divergent if only tentative reality and those who subscribe to it cry out for organization. The lone voice may be coherent (or organized) or incoherent (unorganized). But once that lone voice is joined by others, organization becomes imperative: not only must relative status be made explicit, but the criteria require some kind of acknowledgment.

Despite Father Tempels' continuing insistence that the doctrine of the *Jamaa* could not survive organization, the *Jamaa* has become organized and constitutes a "total definition of reality" (Fabian 1971: 162). Nevertheless, Father Tempels continues to be regarded as the prime source of truth and doctrine. His authority, clearly, is symbolic rather than positive. He has authority and is listened to because of rather than in spite of his distance and separation from the scene of action. Had he remained in the Congo he would have been compelled to take one of three courses: obstruct organization—and so take his chance in a power struggle, corrupt himself, and perhaps lose his authority; insist more positively upon an unorganized status quo—which would have had much the same result; or corrupt himself by lending his authority to particular currents of power or influence within the developing organization. His initial authority was derived not only from the fact of being a European in an ambience where Europeans generally enjoyed high status, and from the way in which he provided and articulated just the right answers for those who were seeking them, but from his embodiment of the antisystemic, nonstructural, or anti-structural. This last was the necessary Archimedean point from which Father Tempels' charisma could grow. Thus positioned, he "mobilized ideas" (Fabian 1971: 172) which defined a perceived and desired reality. Having entered a mysterium, he "objectified aspirations" (Fabian 1971: 120), provided what Fabian calls a "privileged approach" to the causes of cultural change, and gave the new orientations a vital impetus (*ibid.*).

The fact that Father Tempels no longer positively controls the *Jamaa* as a coherent set of activities and social relationships, though remaining its guide and mentor from a distance, is a commonplace of charismatic action. When granted, charismatic authority becomes absolute. Yet roles and statuses and leadership within an organized community must be based on moralities which are informed by reciprocities. Further, and particularly within the Christian or European heritage, the pragmatic requirements of a politico-economic order can rarely coincide with an idealized morality—even though precisely this seems to be the burden of charismatic action. If in a particular instance charismatic powers, ideally based in love and the nonstructured or antisystemic—in a sense returning the location of charisma nearer the animal—are transformed into organized politico-economic powers which exert a direct command over people, the grace is corrupted. Still, a working compromise is usually achieved. In that charisma is essentially unorganized or unstructured power, its promise cannot be wholly realized within the constraints which organization demands. So it must nearly always seem to fail. But so far as the residues of charisma emerge in new moralities it succeeds. When those with charismatic qualities or powers eschew organization, as they often must do if they are to retain the integrity of their charisma, the guardians must take over. And in that moment truth is shivered. Both in myth and in life organization comes from corruption and corruption grows out of organization.

The treasure of the *Jamaa*, the direct encounter between human selves stripped of the automated responses of roles and statuses—corresponding with the love and sense of communitas exemplified by St. Francis or, in our own day, by Mother Teresa in India—has been transformed into, and so been corrupted by, an ethic. The moralities have begun to control and order love. On the other hand, the participants in the *Jamaa* have exchanged an anomic or liminal or unstructured condition for one that has become structured, ordered. What effected the transformation of communitas into community was—in outward manifestation at least—the way in which words, rationalizations of the experience of communitas, began so to cohere and concretize that they predicated a community. Father Tempels would have preferred to maintain the state of communitas as a continuing and generative fount informing and affecting the outer and overarching social order. In fact, the words jelled together and bespoke a community. The *Jamaa* has (all but) become a separate sect. As Fabian puts it (1971: 80), *Jamaa* doctrine has transferred interaction from the instrumental to the symbolic level. Or, the moralities and their symbolic attachments now prescribe truth and reality under the supervision of guardians. The truths of the encounters must now be quarried out of the symbols into which organization and the moralities have necessarily forced them. In an evolutionary idiom, the internal features of the process—the formation of a sense of com-

munitas through the experience of encounters with others un-
encumbered with the predicates of roles and statuses—have
become externalized and rationalized in explicit but new
symbols, roles, and statuses. A new community together
with its necessary corruptions has been created.

Though the people involved and the circumstances might
seem unusual, the *Jamaa* movement reveals the principal characteristics of other charismatic movements. It emerged from
an ambience most economically described as one significantly
informed or predicated by the contradictions and ambiguities
inherent in the coexistence of *giving* ≈ *receiving* and *giving* ≠
receiving. Entailing uncertainty and doubt, the coexistence of
these opposed sets of moralities also provides unstructured
opportunities. Entering the unstructured, a would-be charismatic figure stands on a truth or truths perceived, and ra-
tionalizes it or them in the form of a set of new moralities
which, ideally, reconcile or transcend the ambiguities and
contradictions in *giving* ≈ / ≠ *receiving*. And here uncounted
numbers of would-be charismatic figures often founder. At
its simplest there has been no contact. The posited truths and
rationalizations have struck no spark in others. The drama
that might have been collapses. Nevertheless, the apparent
failure is not necessarily total. Empirically, if not in principle,
few charismatic movements do not rest on foundations prepared by precursors whose efforts seem to have been in vain.
    Why there should be a positive response, why a spark
should be struck when it is struck, is not on the whole difficult to account for. The event itself indicates features in the
socio-historical ambience which an observer, with the advantages of hindsight, may afterwards appreciate as significant
and contributive. The source or mode of access to truth, usually enshrined in tradition, is patently acceptable; the posited
relations between the perceived truths and their rationalizations clearly transcend or reconcile ambiguities and contradictions, providing a greater or more desirable coherence than
had been given; and the new rationalizations or moralities

provide obvious and positive advantage. Nor is it hard to account for many of the negative instances, when no spark is
struck. The source or mode of access to truth appears as defi-
nitely aberrant, the truths perceived do not make the sense
they ought to make, the new rationalizations or moralities are
not seen to provide sufficient advantage over what is extant,
there are too many risks involved, coherence is lacking, the
relations between the truths perceived and their rationalizations are seen as inappropriate. The lonely voice, so convinced of its own rightness and coherence, is to others at least
touched with madness or the insane: the not uncommon fate
of individuals as well as charismatic leaders.

Other negative instances, however, and they are the crucial
ones, defy an adequate accounting. For until more is known
of the interactions between physical presences, perceived
truths, and rationalizations the difference between spark and
no spark can only be returned to the predicative and cohesive
or integrative powers or properties of charisma. Thaumaturgies, exhortations, threats of disaster, and promises of better
things to come certainly play their parts, helping to persuade
the doubters. But since these features are also present in the
seeming failures, we are again returned to an effective or in-
sufficient charisma. That is, given that the initial situation is
one characterized by contradiction and ambiguity, a situation
entirely suited and appropriate to the interaction and transformation of rationalizations and/or symbols, charisma both
starts and gives direction to a process of rationalization and
rerationalization which, like myth and as myth, overcomes
contradiction and resolves ambiguity. At the least, contradiction and ambiguity are shifted into contexts where they seem
resolved. Further, charisma appears as the agent integrating
the relations between the ways in which symbols and/or rationalizations interact and are transformed, and selves which
integrate both biological and cultural parts.

Both contradiction and ambiguity can make for uncertainty
and anxiety, leading into psychosomatic lesion: the self in
disintegrative or disintegrated mode. They can also simulta-

neously or alternatively present the integrating self with ma-
neuverability and choice. The question why one and not the
other is only partly answered in terms of the address of the
audience—the perception of advantage of one kind or other.
There is also the fact that the grammar, the principles by
which symbols and rationalizations are transformed, impose
their own discipline and set limits to the kinds and numbers of
transformations and recombinations that selves can integrate.
Rejecting the impossible or ridiculous, selves test the possible
and plausible until that which appears appropriate is integrated. Yet it has to be remembered that in attempting to describe a state of disintegration, the unstructured, a chaos from
which an order may emerge, one is imposing an order on that
which is what it is because it is unordered. Addressed to
psychosomatic lesion, ritual curing procedures involve disin-
tegrating the self, breaking down attitudes toward reality and
the ordering of social relationships which have resulted in lesion. And this entry into the unstructured, a liminality, is followed by a reintegration of the parts either in relation to identified harmful elements, which may be concentrated into a
given concrete form and disposed of, or in relation to positively identified goals, or both. If much seems to go begging
with that "reintegration," it is precisely in the movement toward and out of the unstructured or liminal that ritual curing
procedures, modes of access to truth, rites of passage, individuality, charismatic activity, and the central rite of most
religions, sacrifice, and indeed all learning processes, converge in the realization of new being.

   The significance of an ambiguity is its ambiguity, and the
point of a contradiction is that it is a contradiction. Potentially
creative as well as destructive, neither the creative nor the destructive potential of an ambiguity or a contradiction can be
resolved into the logic of a linear progression unless and until,
having entered the unstructured and through a process of rationalizing and rerationalizing, the contradictions and ambiguities can appear as resolved. But before that happens, before a specific direction is accepted and taken, the activities

must appear as irrational. The unstructured or liminal have no order of themselves. They instance the chaos where order is not. The person is to no one as the structured is to the unstructured, as the rational is to the chaos or unordered. With integration, a new order emerges, new rationalities reign. When this does not happen, either the tensions implied in the original ambiguities and contradictions continue in potential, or they result in various forms of withdrawal—the self in muted disintegration—or even anomie.

When a charisma succeeds in integration, when a spark is struck, when there is a positive response, the audience follows the example of their leader. Through some device for entering the unstructured—it may be encounters as in the *Jamaa*, or it may be an orgiastic dance, stripping naked, promiscuous sexual relations, the inducing of trance states, the use of drugs—participants attempt to gain a sense of communitas and perceive truths about human being which are then rationalized either in conformity with or in relation to the rationalizations of the leader. And this, as we shall see presently, and as Father Tempels would have preferred it, can become a continuing state. Most often, however, an endpoint is reached when, in an integration of physical presences, perceptions of truth, and rationalizations, rationalizing ceases to generate further rationalizations. At this point, with ambiguities and contradictions resolved into seeming certainties and coherences, the truths perceived become fixed and contained in their rationalizations and/or moralities. Order is plucked out of disorder, social relations become governed by morality, roles and statuses become defined or ritualized into regulated interrelations, a communitas becomes a community. Nor does the process itself seem to be any different in the case where the order and moralities achieved seem to an outsider to be thoroughly immoral and depraved. A charismatic leader is not bound by extant discriminations. Hitler's moralities commanded consent from sufficient numbers to enforce compliance from others. New moralities rarely find favor among the uninvolved. The obvious peril in charis-

matic activities is that the "special individual" may turn out to
be a mere "man of movement." The new may be "worse"
rather than "better." Hence the wariness and hostility of
guardians to charismatic activities.

The Rastafarians of Jamaica (Yawney 1977) provide an
example of how a sense of communitas can be maintained
without becoming a wholly organized community. First, the
use of marijuana enables participants temporarily to slough
off roles and statuses, thereby creating an albeit artificial sense
of communitas. Second, Rastafarians refuse to allow words
and rationalizations to gain specific and concretized meanings
in particular contexts. In their meetings, now become rituals
as the marijuana is ceremonially passed round, a variety of
topics are discussed. Meanings are drawn out of words
through associative and false etymologies, new words are
coined, and sounds and perceived connotations are transposed
from one word to another in an almost infinite variety of puns
and other kinds of word play. By these means Rastafarians
achieve a sense of possibility, a liminal open-endedness
punctuated by well organized activities such as demonstra-
tions, public speeches, and short-term charitable programs.
These concrete activities seem to offset the anxiety and uncertainty that usually go along with prolonged periods of liminality. Since, too, the explicit major aim of the Rastafarians
was, as it still is, to establish black Jamaicans in utopian communities in Ethiopia, an aim now become for all practical
purposes impossible to achieve, it could be said that maintaining the sense of possibility has become institutionalized, a
positive value, an end in itself. The movement continues to
move and regenerate the membership to a variety of ends.

Might a charismatic personality transform the possibility
and associated activities into a more cohesive and directional
movement by, for example, positing another but realizable
major aim? In fact, the Rastafarians do not lack charismatic
leaders. But since the membership, mainly drawn from the
poor and disfranchised, also includes signficant numbers in

varieties of established jobs and positions, to substitute an alternative aim apparently realizable in the local circumstances would likely split the membership and, perhaps, ultimately destroy the whole force and potential of their activities. And these last, of worth and supported and applauded by other elements of the population, are also satisfying to the members. For though the thaumaturgies frequently associated with charismatic activity are useful recruiting devices, rationalizations which mobilize energies and interests, the political power of a charismatic leader—no doubt bolstered by the claim or supposal to be speaking for deity or the transcendent—rests on the fact that followers form a solidarity in relation to objectives and posited moral categories of obligation and mutual aid. And this command over people bound together in positive aspiration tends to open access to necessary material resources. But where this solidarity is lacking—and a membership drawn from different walks of life often entails just this—a charismatic leader is rarely able to exert a positive and unidirectional political suasion.

If it be argued that it is precisely this solidarity of effort that a charismatic leader is expected or supposed to create, the response must be not simply that some things are impossible even for charisma, but that while some charismatic leaders positively create such a solidarity, others in more passive mode are enabled to, some do not or prefer not to, and others cannot. The conditions for any one of the possibilities must be presumed to be inherent in a congruence or otherwise of perceptions, rationalizations, and that truth of things which relates the politically possible to the transcendent. When the rationalizing that attempts to create a new semantic environment of meaning and significance strays from the truth of things, as it often does, the creative process collapses. A fresh start may be made at some later date. Compounded of past experiences as well as perceptions of what might be, the truth of things is as firm or infirm as faith and indicated in the inherencies of community as well as communitas. The movement between community and communitas, framing the authentic in religious experience, is very essentially not endowed with the automaticisms of magic, science, and technology. Evident in rites of passage, life crises, changes in status, the activities of Shaman, Manager, Sanyasi and Leopard-skin chief—if only marginally in the Australian Man of High Degree—as well as in individuality and charismatic activities, the movement between community and communitas is a recipe of risk, hesitation, and uncertainty of outcome. Nor could it be otherwise. Movement between on the one hand a knowledge and experience of obligation and opposition inherent in the roles and statuses of community—necessitating diplomacy in the conduct of social relationships—and on the other hand a sense and experience of unobligedness, freedom, and at-oneness is, in principle, fraught with infinite possibility.

Limitation, containment, and control of the possibilities reside in the ways in which the process of rationalization, the manipulation of signs and symbols, relate to the truth of things. Yet if figures of speech such as metaphor, metonym, synecdoche, periphrasis, directness, and other devices of rhetoric may be held to account for one result, the very same tropes—now regarded as, perhaps, "mistimed"—may also be posited as accounting for a quite different result. Action is suited to word when the word is suited to action. And the conditions for a specific integration must involve all aspects of being human. Even then, the integration may not be viable in relation to exterior conditions. Employing a mode of rationalization which, by its very nature as well as in relation to the heterogeneous membership and lack of an overall and realizable objective, cannot jell into a positive and unidirectional decision binding on the whole membership, the Rastafarians seem as responsive to the truths of the limbo they have created and recreate for themselves as the *Jamaa* people were to the certainties produced by their rationalizations. Loyal to his Church, Father Tempels wanted and prescribed for the *Jamaa* people something similar to the Rastafarian creation within the organized denominational community: an institutionalized mode of moving between community and communitas which the Church in its local expression should have been but was not providing. Perhaps there were many *Jamaa* people who also thought they desired just what Father Tempels wanted. Nevertheless, their rationalizing, both creating and guided by the truths in themselves and their situation, led them into an integration which bespoke a distinct community.

Within the specifically Christian ambience, charisma and the charismatic refer not to kinds of politico-moral authority, influence, power, or suasion but to graces from God bestowed on particular people. Whether seen as an insight or perception or intellection about the wholeness of truth and reality, or as a quality of character, or as bestowing spirituality, or as a redemptive attribute, in most people so delicate a gift as a grace cannot in the end withstand the constraints of the given moralities without corruption—though itself may enliven those same moralities. From the point when the grace is bestowed, free will, different perceptions of relevance, and the corruption inherent in normative community moralities begin to operate. If the grace is to retain its authenticity it must either transcend the moralities, or be isolated and separated from the moralities. The same is substantially and correspondingly true of charisma, charisms in their Weberian sense: its command over the thoughts and activities of others (seen as moral authority but actually rooted in the reverse, the provision of opportunity to strip selves of moralities) is eroded and betrayed when captured by the moralities. The implicit dilemma for the participants in charismatic activities is whether to retain the charisma and continue as no one, or sacrifice the charisma and, wrenching certainty out of uncertainty, become someone.

The encounter between charisma and the given moralities within the European or Christian ambience usually leaves its residue of new moralities. And although much the same kinds of process have also occurred outside the Christian ambience, it would take a specialist some time to come up with more

than a dozen instances which, looking like charismatic authority, and specifically outside the Christian ambience and heritage, have given birth to new moralities. No doubt there are
scores of instances which have gone unrecorded. So that, although there can be no absolute correlation, it has to be con-
ceded that, statistically, charismatic authority yielding new
moralities seems characteristic of the European or Western
ambience, and goes along with generalized individuality. One
cannot but be impressed with the numbers. Millenarianisms,
enthusiasms, pietistic movements, and adjustment, accom-
modative, vitalistic, militant, and reformative movements—
there are so many (cf. Burridge 1969a: 97ff.). And they have
for the most part occurred in ambiences either determined by
Christian missionaries or in which Christian missionaries
have been active.

Was Father Tempels a typical missionary? In personal
makeup, character, temperament, origins, and background,
Christian missionaries comprise a far wider spectrum of possibilities than that connoted by European or Western civilization. As a class or group of persons their ethnic and cultural
origins are as diverse as humanity itself. Their characters,
idiosyncracies, and capacities run the whole gamut of human
traits, abilities, and knowledge. They comprise the widest,
most varied international and intercultural of classes. Though
internally organized into large numbers of bodies within each
of the numerous denominations, every missionary nonetheless brings to the scene and attempts to realize a basic set of
objectives. And central to these objectives is a metanoia: that
those who are addressed should say "no" to the past, change
their minds, and enter into new ways with a positive "yes."
The methods adopted to bring about this transformation and
spiritual renewal vary widely, as do the forms and substance
of repentance, what particular traditional ways should be rejected, how a change of mind may be authenticated, how the
entry into new ways may be expressed. Consequently, the results of missionary activities—seen simply as modes of cul-

tural expression—tend to be even more diverse than the varieties of missionaries.

Despite this diversity of cultural expression, however, and although many of those who enter Christianity later leave the fold, what is significant here is not whether such converts are "true" Christians from this or that subjective point of view, but that each missionary explicitly teaches the possibility of changing one's mind about significant truth and reality, and attempts to realize this possibility, insisting, moreover, that it be manifested at the moral as well as spiritual level. Because of the Christian heritage, those within the European or Western environment tend to take this possibility for granted. It comes with some sense of shock to learn that outside that environment this change of mind is either rare or unknown. Certainly it is not institutionalized. Truth and reality are the sacred prescriptions of tradition and the current moralities. It is one thing to change one's mind about this or that within a given framework of reality; another to experience or be experienced by some more or less traumatic psychic disturbance. But a metanoia, deliberately and soberly changing one's mind about the nature of truth and reality, whether or not consequent upon a vision, dream, or psychic experience, but in any case in response to an ambience of explicit teaching, is something else again.

A metanoia connotes a change of state, a change of being, a transformation. Truth and reality are not what they were, the change predicates a different kind of being, the change in being feeds back into and confirms the change in truth and reality. Further, indelibly stamped as it is with a notion of linear time, an idea of History unfolding itself, a true metanoia is unlikely in a Subsistence economy where cyclical notions of time predominate or are decisive. Although a change in status—movement from one stasis to another—is often mistaken for metanoia, what is contained in the meaning of the word is a continuing and ongoing series of developmental transformations leading into more and more complete appreciations and realization of Christian truth and reality: wholeness as a universal as distinct from wholeness within a particular culture. With each transformation the given moralities are seen in different perspective, new moralities are envisaged. To this the lives of the better authenticated saints bear witness. Christianity evokes and demands the continuing development of psyche and intellect, insists that this development not be isolated or separated from the moral community but be moralized to the greater perfection of the moralities, and invites each person to make his or her contribution. The initial metanoia leading into the Christian life is but the first step. Even if there had been no Greek, particularly platonic injection, Christianity would have had to be developmental—as indeed the New Testament frequently illustrates—to survive. That, once started, the ongoing developmental process should often lead out of a particular denominational fold need occasion no surprise. Once the possibility of changing one's mind about significant reality and truth has been appreciated and realized, it becomes possible to do so again, and free will and circumstances select the direction. Whether the developmental process ceases upon eschewing Christianity or its cultural residua is open to question. It suffices that, suffused as it is with the optimisms of Christian doctrines of hope and salvation—in which all or most welfare and social retrieval schemes seem rooted—the European or Western tradition (which includes those who have espoused it) cannot rest content with things as they are, but is impelled to change and develop.

Attempting to bring about precisely those transformations which lead into just such a developmental frame of mind, missionaries nurture them when they see the signs, and endeavor, through education, to indicate specific directions. Mostly, however, like Father Tempels in his earlier years, they fail. The initial transformation or, more usually, transference, has absorbed most of the convert's imaginative energies. One set of routines has been exchanged for another. But the seeds of generalized individuality—the social outgrowth or projection of metanoia—have been sown, and the next generation may do better. Sometimes, though, there is a true metanoia. And as most missionaries will confirm, the circumstance is accompanied by a noticeable change in physical aspect or animal condition. Yet from this point, replaying the charismatic experience in both the Christian and Weberian or sociological senses, the directions of the developmental process are hardly predictable. Some achieve a certain saintliness, some become churchmen, others become or follow "men of movement." Few leaders of newly emergent nations have not had a specifically Christian background in a missionary school. If it would be too sweeping to assert that no nation that has emerged from the European colonial world has not been seeded by Christianity or its residues, it would not be easy to argue the contrary.

This circumstance has many implications. For present purposes it is sufficient to note that a metanoia, generalized individuality, charisma, and charismatic qualities converge, are rationalizations or intellectualizations referring to particular aspects or refractions of the same phenomenon or event. Analyzing the meaning or empirical content of any one of the terms by working from the rationalization to the actual event is bound to involve the others. And, since the capacity to change one's mind about truth and reality, say "no" to traditional ways, reject current moralities, and infuse others with an articulate notion of new moralities must entail some initial distancing from, and distaste for, the truths and realities predicated by the given moralities at a particular time, some sort of alienation is also entailed.

10 ALIENATION, ANOMIE, AND THE RECREATIVE CYCLE

Because the guardians identify themselves with the given moralities, they have moral authority and can provide moral leadership. The active preservation of an environment of order which, because it is ordered, provides meaning and becomes idealized, is the basis of their power. Collectively, the guardians represent and make explicit to others that consensus to prescribed truths and realities which makes community life possible. They conserve the reciprocities which enable each to be fulfilled in and through others. Survival, whether in animal, cultural, moral, or spiritual terms, depends upon the consensus which is, too, the environment providing access to truth and reality. When the moralities appear to be going awry, so that truth and reality become a shifting kaleidoscope of opinions, the demand for a moral authority that will stabilize the situation increases. And charismatic qualities may provide such authority. That is, when it appears that the guardians are disunited, are abdicating their responsibility, no longer control truth and reality through the moralities; when the discrepancies between experience and the prescribed moralities compel a rejection of the latter; when the differences between what is experienced and what is prescribed are shared—then charismatic qualities are evoked. On the other hand, where there are other, institutionalized means for regaining an equilibrium, the guardians usually reassert themselves and claims to charisma are rejected.

In either case, however, a situation in which the moralities are awry implies that persons are alienated from them. The variety of meanings of alienation converge in a relationship of

opposition to the given moralities. When the (usually varying) oppositional content becomes such as to render the
moralities uncertain, weak, lacking in authority or compulsion, individuality becomes available to those who can enter
into it whether it was previously generalized or particularized. Without adequate moral restraints, the assertion to
autonomy is given more or less free rein. For a while there
may be confusion or, more familiarly, anomie: a state of lawlessness and disorder, a state in which varieties of oppositional
relationships to the given moralities have succeeded in neu-
tralizing them without having yet provided a substitute.
Power becomes wild, ready to slip into the hands of those
who can create order out of chaos and disorder.

If an "order" often seems more apparent than a "morality,"
order and morality are obverse and reverse of the same coin,
and if either is awry and left unremedied the ensuing alienations often lead into anomie. Anomie is the word we use to
describe a particular development of alienation. If the kinds of
alienation are so diverse that they cannot, collectively, neutralize the given moralities, then there is no anomie: however
disenchanted they may be, people cling to the only tested environment of meaning and order they know. Anomie exists
when there is sufficient common ground of opposition to
neutralize the given moralities, in which case the period of
anomie is usually short; when there is sufficient strength of
diverse oppositions, in which case the period of anomie may
be prolonged; or when the guardians cast doubt upon or
themselves start dismantling the given moralities. But in each
case charismatic qualities stand as a remedy, as they may remedy alienation before the point of anomie is reached. Thus
though individuality, in criticism and opposition to the given
moralities, is symptomatic of and produces alienation leading
into anomie, individuality and charismatic qualities stand as
remedy.

If this seems to be a paradox it is more apparent than real.
Metanoia, individuality, alienation, anomie, and charisma
refer to different and even processual points on an arc opposi-

tional to the given moralities. Metanoia is a renunciation of the given moralities when it is not a transcending of them. It connotes a change of mind envisaging new moralities, it appears as the basis of, and may lead into, individuality. Even when individuals are guardians, individuality entails some sort of qualification or development of the given moralities: a basic opposition to, and critique of, culturally prescribed truth and reality. Alienation comes about when, with the help of the assertion to autonomy, the critique of the reciprocities predicated by the given moralities is such that in relation to the truth of things its validity or usefulness seems to outweigh what is prescribed: actual experiences and/or perceptions of the truth of things are positively opposed to or alienated from the moralities inherent in given sets of roles and statuses. In anomie these relations spread to greater numbers and destroy the consensus necessary for order. In this situation human selves, stripped of the roles and statuses which now have no consensual warrant, and ideally drawing on the inner shapelessness of love, life, and truth in their relationships but otherwise looking for mere personal advantage, seek that order without which their experience is meaningless. Charismatic qualities, the particular development and dramatization of what happens each time the person moves into the individual, provide that order. They resolve the situation, albeit only temporarily. Having a positive set of goals or aspirations, one with charismatic qualities redefines reality by antithesizing the anomie and its apparent causes, then engaging a dialectic between goals or aspiration and what has been given in tradition. The critique is both explicit and implicit, and an achieved synthesis emerges as a new and ordered set of moralities—which may, however, break down and call for further charismatic action if the synthesis is not acceptably coherent.

Generalized individuality entails continuing alienations at both the collective and personal levels. In turn, the alienations lead into recurrent situations of anomie or near-anomie. And these are remedied by the individual and/or charismatic activity whose rerationalizations, positing new moralities, attempt that reordering which, derived from a new sense of communitas, will make present alienations unnecessary and, temporarily, put an end to the anomie. Yet the anomie, far from being the disaster that guardians and addicts of order generally paint it, is in effect the seminal commencement. For by definition anomie denotes a state of lawlessness, the unstructured. And just such a movement into the unstructured is, as we have seen, the basis of that charisma which, unselfish, persuades others into the same movement. The process, a cycle constitutive of our own being and into whose vortices we are inevitably drawn, may be summed up in the formula *someone→no one→someone*. Or, more briefly, *someone⇋no one*. Where individuality is not generalized, alienation is rare, anomie correspondingly so, and charismatic activity unusual.

Metanoia, individuality, alienation, anomie, and charisma are rationalizations which, returned to the experience of the peculiar and exceptional events of the New Testament and converging in the exemplar of Pentecost, comprise a particular kind of set: the least number of most inclusive terms by which those who share the European or Western cultural heritage attempt to grasp, describe, and analyze a social process that, in varying degrees of intensity and dramatic expression, is fundamental to that heritage and constitutes its armature. Each of the terms has numerous synonyms and analogues, and in the endeavor to be more accurate about the subtleties, intensities, effectiveness, and dramatic dimensions of this basic social process, each term and its synonyms and analogues have generated yet more terms and their analogues. The scale, impact upon others, consequences, and particular historical events attendant on, say, the activities of Father Tempels, or James Naylor, the early Christians, or the French revolution are scarcely comparable. Each fall of rain is different from another in scale, impact, consequences and historical context. But whether it be a thunderstorm, deluge, or light shower, the same few elementary relations suffice to account for each manifestation. Similarly, a permuting and combining of the varied textures of European or Western cultures at given times within the terms of a few primary relations may, without being simplistic, be held to lie behind much or most of what has happened in their history.

Whether as conversion or transformation, metanoia represents the movemental relation between one state of being and another: the emergence of a new man. It is empirically verifiable physiologically (Sargant 1957/63), behaviorally, and linguistically. It is the basis of all those equivalents in European languages of *credo*, I believe. Because it is essentially a movemental relationship between states of being ($B_1 \rightarrow B_2$, $B_2 \rightarrow B_3$, $B_3 \rightarrow B_4$ . . . n) the articulated "credo" must indicate a transitional mode or state, a continuing hesitancy derived from the experience of changing social orders and moralities. From time to time, however, now in one place then in another, certainties have to be pulled out of the anxiety of uncertainty and hesitancy. Hence the diversity of connotations—from extreme doubt to absolute conviction—which can be conveyed by or read into "I believe . . ." Both "believe" and "transcend" draw meaning from the convergences in situational contexts of individuality, metanoia, alienation, anomie, charisma: an experience of flux and change which yields the apperception of an unfolding or developmental process in which identities are never wholly secure. In most other cultures perceptions of stasis—that relations are given and thus, providing secure identities—overwhelm perceptions of flux and make it inaccurate but easy in ethnocentric assumption of translate statements of existential relations into statements of belief.* The fact that Christianity entered an ambience in which changing one's mind and being converted to one or other cult or philosophy was common and habitual surely had much to do with a particular "credo" being probably temporary if not transitional.

---

*Compare Rodney Needham 1973 where, however, the conclusions are different.

On the other hand, the charisma of the Pentecostal experience, grounded in love as well as repentance, seems to have given specific direction to varieties of choice and, moreover, transformed doubt and prevarication into an ongoing developmental process.

The transitional mode indicated by an experience whose relations are rationalized by a "credo" implies an equivocation between retreat on the one hand, and reaching out for a more comprehensive understanding and articulation on the other. Both reveal an uneasy fit with the identities or roles and statuses provided by the extant social order. Only the self grasping at relations of transformation has permanence and authenticity. But whereas the retreat leads into something less than identity, the reach leads into those continuing transformations in the relationship between the self and other which is the essence of metanoia. And being readied to expand awareness and shift belief, to transform oneself, emerges as preliminary and necessary to that part of the structure of individuality which, entailing a relation between the self and truth, moves to transcend the given moralities. Charismatic qualities, individuality intensified, add dimensions of drama and excitement. What is important is that the particular metanoia being experienced is successfully transmitted to others, received, and responded to so that many become implicated in the same transformation: converting at least a part of the love inherent in communitas into moralities which, characteristic of the community, seek to order that love. And again we are returned to the Pentecostal experience and/or its simulacra, the basic experience of the European or Western civilized tradition. That in contingent particularity this experience is often thought to be both illusory and delusory is one of those creative ironies which are equally a part of the tradition.

It has to be emphasized that the effects and influences of the Christian exemplars are not necessarily dependent on being a Christian. Christianity seems to have drawn upon certain human capacities—but not proclivities—and institutionalized them into social processes which have become the basis of the cultural tradition. The interplay between enthusiasms and skepticisms has resulted in a persisting resolve to transcend what is given—whether in the field of material artifacts, political forms, or the bounds of knowledge—and, ultimately, to reconcile the inherent antithesis between love and morality so as to achieve a morality in which love is perfectly reflected and ordered.

When the self cannot integrate the relations between truth and the given moralities, when love for the other is thwarted by the moralities, when life itself is barren because love and truth and the given moralities appear inconsistent with each other and cannot be integrated, alienation begins. The self rebels against and begins to erode the person. One remedy is psychiatric treatment: an attempt to reconstitute the normalcies of the self so as to reestablish the person as culturally prescribed. The traditional and more creative remedy—especially where the anomie, alienation, experiences, and perceptions of truth are shared—is to allow the self or selves to create a new person by means of charismatic activities. The exemplar is the Pentecostal experience the charisms of which, ideally, remove the barriers between the self and truth, allow truth free access, reintegrate the components of being, and slough off offensive moralities as new ones are realized.

Where generalized individuality does not obtain the recreative cycle indicated by individuality, alienation, anomie, charisma, and metanoia can occur only rarely, and then, as the ethnographic record shows, only after the intervention of Europeans, usually missionaries. Before the intervention occurs, tradition and the guardians, supported as they are by an overwhelming consensus, are much too strong to overcome. The self and the assertion to autonomy are subordinated to the given moralities in which terms they may develop themselves or, when recalcitrant, be allowed the semblances of individuality in prescribed and insulated positions. Otherwise and generally they are forced to find expression in a variety of nonconformities, self-willedness, arrogance, sorcerer-like activities, criminality and, in rare instances, tyranny. Identities are known, prescribed, and insisted upon. So are strict reciprocities. In such circumstances the relationship between, for example, altruism and egoism, product of generalized individuality and entailing an opposition between selflessness and selfishness, becomes almost meaningless. In a situation governed by *giving* ⇌ *receiving* the options are closed: altruism, acting on behalf of others independently of the moral obligation to act in relation to others, is indistinguishable from egoism. On the other hand, in a situation governed by *giving* ≠ *receiving* the options are open, altruism becomes distinguishable from egoism, love may be developed as a value in itself. Or again, where *giving* ⇌ *receiving* the moral system is closed; suspicions and accusations of witchcrafts and sorceries dominate; injury, sickness, and death are referred to moral lesion; chance, accident, coincidence, and the fortuitous have very restricted fields of meaning if, indeed, they exist as concepts at all. But where *giving* ≠ *receiving* chance, accident, coincidence, and the fortuitous play important and fructifying parts. It becomes possible to be charitable, to suppose that others in the same moral network might not necessarily be evilly intentioned. Love is given scope for development. If we refer back to the formulaic summary of the moments of the individual—

$$(self/others) + (self/moralities) + (self/truth) \rightarrow individual$$

—altruism refers to an emphasis on the second terms of the pairs and egoism to an emphasis on the first. Perceptions of truth, as we have seen, usually require some sort of surprise confrontation, encounter, accident, or coincidence to jerk the mind out of accustomed thought-tracks. Without love the relationships between the self and others and the self and the moralities must appear sorcerer-like, criminal, or just wrong. The dialectics implied in the pairs give rise to fluctuating or changing identities; and the same dialectics at a further point in development stabilize identities.

Generalized individuality is an open invitation to box the compass of human experience. The reach into the being of a new man or woman, new moralities, an appetite for power, veering into insanity and bending to outlawry, arrogance, the vicious and depraved sum up the varied projections or realizations. Stable identities become unstable and vice versa. Altruism and egoism are transformed into each other. Love, self-sacrifice, attention to the needs of others, and an unyielding hold on a perceived truth easily become selfishness, self-centeredness, self-righteousness, pride, arrogance, and contempt for others. Were it not for the guardians, whose firm identification with the given moralities combined with inertial tendencies to the securities of conformity maintain people as persons and ensure stability in community life, generalized individuality would make for continuing chaos and anomie. Guardians and persons regard institutions as the boundaries of social life. They strive to maintain those boundaries so as to make social life manageable and predictable. Their continued reiterations of the relations within those boundaries give the structure of society its sensible form. Antithetically, individuality takes the same institutions as points of departure and stands poised for change and the conflict which, in precipitating moral choice, may lead either to the introduction of new moralities or into confusion. Should the guardians loose their grip, break faith with the moralities through tyranny, or themselves attack the moralities which form the basis of their control and power, these very acts of self-destruction restart or accelerate the recreative cycle.

This recreative cycle entails a cost in human agony. Recurrent alienations and anomies remedied by metanoia and charismatic revelations are embedded in a matrix of discontents, thaumaturgies, mysticisms, violence, and attempts in myriad idioms to break out of or transcend the given. Much of what results may be described as varieties of brutalization or simple frustration. Nevertheless, emerging from this chaff are the grains which enliven the human spirit in new moralities. The continuing reach into otherness that is characteristic of the European or Western heritage, the quest for truths to be reflected in new moralities, and the progressive individuation of the parts of the whole into semiautonomous components—subcultures, differentiated fields of knowledge, an increasingly complex division of labor—are but aspects of generalized individuality projected onto different arcs of the cultural whole. And the energies generated by each individuation—temporary resolutions of the triple dialectic of individuality—require physical, social, and intellectual spaces in which to realize themselves. Lacking these spaces explosions are bound to occur. The cheapest and most easily available since the reformation has been physical space—now virtually closed. Yet creating further social and intellectual spaces without particular kinds of overarching and unitive foci must necessarily be precarious, initially disintegrative, and apparently destructive.

If within Dumont's (1970: 32) oppositional dichotomy of holism/individualism the European medieval period was holistic in relation to what came later, the same relation holds between other cultures or civilizations and medieval Europe, medieval Europe and the renaissance, and each earlier and later phase of European or Western history. The "increasing pace of change" is a cliché which, in referring mainly to technological change, obscures the process of individuation, that recreative cycle by which more and more subcultures and social spaces have been generated—to the point where they have begun to outrun coordinating organization and have become more and more isolated from each other. Guardians have become distanced from persons, and persons from one another. Greater ranges of social mobilities within the framework of an accelerating differentiation in the division of labor not only make for increasingly temporary social relationships, but isolate one kind of work from another, one intellectual or scientific endeavor from others, one morality from another.

The paradoxical result is that although larger and larger

numbers of persons are pushed more and more often into the structure of individuality, there is little advantage from it. Even if particular people are able to sustain the responsibility of being individuals, the audience is transitory. The community as an interacting and interparticipatory set of persons hardly exists. A particular set of moralities is as dispensable as a shrug of the shoulders. While media and bureaucracies prescribe, money has become synonymous with meaning, usurping the truth. Resources of money can override local moralities: what seems at first to be immoral can be made to look moral if and because the money is right. If each was willing to become the instrument of another's making money on the condition that such enrichment would serve the ends of each and all within the community, money could weld together varieties of diverse moralities. But the inherent ambiguities of money vitiate this, and the reciprocities that might have been entailed in a common allegiance to money can be flouted with impunity. To ameliorate or prevent what might become total disorder, bureaucracies appropriate the management of money, and those who wish to honor their reciprocities can only do so in impersonal ways: through the taxation structure, or by donations to those parts of the bureaucracy which claim to represent a community. Further, since these communities are merely transitory and only concretely discernible in those parts of the bureaucracy which claim to represent them, and since social mobilities entail transferring the realities of community life to its representations in the bureaucracy, the representation becomes the reality.

To this situation a fourfold response may be remarked. First, the traditional: the formation of small participatory communities which, under a variety of guiding ideas, preserve the structure of individuality in its traditional relations. Relatively few in numbers in relation to the greater society, these groups are nonetheless dependent on that greater society which, implicitly or explicitly, they would like, through their example, to permeate with their own moralities. Second, there are those who, taking their cue from Hindu *sanyasan*, either alone or in loose groups abjure most of the activities and routines of the greater society in order to engage in spiritual exercises and meditation. But again, though this entails a perception of the truth of things by and for, essentially, the self, few of those in this category are not also imbued with a missionary spirit: their truths and solutions are actively fed back into the greater society. Third, lacking the mutually participatory community, persons in the greater society who aspire to individuality take their given moralities from the bureaucratic structure and attempt to inform it with those moralities which reflect their perceptions of the truth of things.

The desire to enlighten others and create a new heaven and a new earth is not the only common feature in these three categories. While some have created new social and intellectual spaces for themselves, others have made traditional ones more viable. All, temporarily or more permanently and in a variety of ways have resolved the ambiguities of money. Wherever money may be placed on their several lists of priorities, they know what the latter are. Whether identifying with the greater society or in opposition to it, they know who their friends are and can interact with them on a reciprocal basis: their identities are secure, they may develop the self. And because they are secure but also aware of alternatives, they may venture into no one and become individuals. The remainder, the fourth and perhaps largest category, are the undecided who have failed to resolve the question of money. They exist in ill-defined social spaces in a condition of sustained or alternating alienations, implicitly waiting for the anomie and charisma which, ushering in a new morality, will enable them to become, first, individuals and then persons at one with a new morality. Prey to contradictory rationalizations and the victims of fickle money and bureaucracy, they lack the means and courage of decision: the event escapes them. Relatively powerless in an ambience that appears meaningless because without well-defined normative moralities,

they are sustained only by bureaucratic order and a will to
survive somehow.

Providing a framework for normative social relationships,
a well-defined and stable moral order renders experience of
others susceptible to objective or charitable interpretations.
The judgments of others, implicit in the way they enter into
and conduct their social relationships, qualify the subjective
evaluation and impress upon the person the necessity for
maintaining social and therefore participatory relationships in
spite of the personal and subjective prejudice. Steady normative moralities tend to enforce an acceptance of others on their
merits rather than a rejection on their faults. If there is a whole
truth about a particular person it is contained in the self, and
indications of the facets of that truth can only be obtained in
relation to the moralities, in the ways in which a person engages social relationships. The greater the consensus and the
tighter the moralities, the larger is the proportion of truth
about a person contained in the moralities themselves. Bereft
of that framework each must be perceived by another not as a
coparticipant but as actually or potentially hostile. Confused
moralities make others anonymous adversaries, encourage
the assertion to autonomy. And because all others become
alien, they may be temporarily induced to serve as a means to
one's own ends and then discarded. Which is as much an oppression of the person as an enforced set of moralities which
does not enjoy the free consent of those who are subject to
them.

If, ideally, freedom in community is to be found in that
moral order to which each freely assents in the full knowledge
that each participant should be the fulfillment of others, there
is more freedom in *any* moral order, however oppressive,
than in no moral order. Order, even that of a police state,
makes morality possible. Without it there can be no points of
departure, no bases for criticism or pertinent action. An oppression is discoverable and identifiable as such not because
the assertion to autonomy is enforcedly constrained in some
and allowed a free rein among those with privilege and

power—though this is the subjective experience—but because
the (enforced) normative moralities do not serve moral, that
is reciprocal ends. However, because it cannot be convinc-
ingly demonstrated or asserted that an appreciation of reciprocities is a natural human endowment, the critique of a
moral order that results in identifying it as oppressive cannot
necessarily arise from a moral spontaneity. It is much more
certainly rooted in the assertion to autonomy.

  The reciprocities found among Hunter-gatherers and Subsistence cultivators are neither natural nor spontaneous. They
are the relatively temporary but viable and purposive outcome of confrontations between equal and opposite assertions
to autonomy or nonreciprocal action: the attempt to arrogate
power to oneself. The reciprocities usually noted—normally
confined to those of the same sex and roughly the same
generation—derive from the nonreciprocal relations that exist
in any society between men and women, parents and children, older and younger, the more capable and less capable.
Experience within these relationships, from childhood on,
teaches nonreciprocal values. Only later, by exhortation and
in relationship to peers who are likewise imbued with nonreciprocal values, are reciprocal relations realized. If the maintenance of community life depends on well ordered reciprocities, the survival of the self as well as the community
depends on the command which the self, in asserting its autonomy, can responsibly exert over the reciprocities.
  Normally, authorities are fixed, responsibilities are attached to them, and situations and relationships within which
authoritative or reciprocal relations are proper are clearly prescribed and distinguished. Charismatic authority introduces
ambivalence. On one axis it provides for a new and more
satisfactory moral order based upon mutual reciprocities, and
on the other it does so authoritatively through nonreciprocity
and the assertion to autonomy reinforced by the subjective
representation of divine inspiration. In itself, charismatic authority contains and may resolve that opposition between rec-

iprocity and nonreciprocity, or between morality and the assertion to autonomy, which is the central problem of every culture. If there must always be room for the egalitarianism manifest in the observance or reciprocities, some kind of hierarchical arrangement linked to the assertion to autonomy and differing capacities is also required. The ways in which a community resolves these oppositions gives it its peculiar style and genius. And there are, clearly, as many varieties of style and genius as there are different cultures and communities. Here, however, the concern is with nonreciprocity in relation to the event and its rationalization. Some cultures emphasize and hold to their traditional rationalizations, intellectualizations, and symbols, ignoring new kinds of events; others look to the event and are prepared to rerationalize. Some examples will clarify the issue.

Traditional Melanesian society was, as we have seen, based upon exchanges of produce, artifacts, and valuables. And this was so whether the particular community was organized into ranks or loose statuses, achieved or ascribed, implicit or explicit. Loyalty to the group took second place to the responsibility on single persons to meet their exchange obligations. If everywhere each could count on the more or less axiomatic aid of a core of particularized kinsfolk, or neighbors, or allies, or association members, the crucial operational area in relation to advancing in status lay among those with whom social relationships were ambiguous. Resolving the ambiguity, knowing whether one had made an ally—whether as cooperator, exchange partner, or rival—or an enemy, and making use of the ambiguity of relationships obtaining among others, were of the highest importance. So important that even those whose aid could be relied upon as matter of axiom could be sacrificed to it. Since advancing in status depended on maintaining particular significant exchange relationships, and there was a limit to productive capacity, unprofitable exchange relationships had, perforce, to be dropped by a unilateral or nonreciprocal decision. Hence the reputation of Melanesians as "pragmatic."

Again, however skilled and industrious a man was, however shrewd or well laid his plans and stratagems, events in the shape of storms, sickness, feud, war, blighted crops, the failure of an expected wind or rain, or the caprice, treachery, or changed interests of others could always bring him down. Life hinged on events, particularly on the moralities derived from the contingencies of transactions. They invited non-reciprocal action and its counter. What oneself or others said was a complex and cleverly woven screen behind which the ambitious and shrewd should discern real interests, what was actually being done, and what was likely to happen in spite of the words. Custom and tradition ruled, but disaster lay in store for those who could not adapt a situation to the event, or who could not pull out of an event that which tradition required. Traditions were correspondingly flexible, knitted to the range of recurring events. Events were authoritative, habitual rationalizations were ambiguous and adapted to exigencies and emergencies, and the man who became a manager was one who could make events work for him. A "rubbish" man was one who consistently failed the event, who failed in reciprocities because he had not the nerve to be non-reciprocal when the event bade him be so.

Traditional Australian Aboriginal society illustrates the opposite. As we have seen, the emphasis was on category and group memberships, on the Law which, aided by rationalizations in paint and wood, made up an intellectual construct that impressed itself on and gave meaning to the features of the physical environment, cultural continuities, and the everyday experience of work and play in particular social relationships. Notoriously, this intellectual construct has held out against all manner of events,* and where events have not utterly destroyed a particular community they have been absorbed into the intellectual construct without significantly al-

---

*Because it was entirely outside the range of their experience and intellectualizations, the first Australian Aborigines to encounter Captain Cook's ship do not seem to have perceived it for some while (see Moorehead 1966: 104, quoting Sir Sidney Parkinson).

tering the relations predicated by that construct (cf. Tonkinson 1973). Authority and reciprocities were contained in the Law and mediated through a hierarchy in which relative position was determined by age, being male, and relative advancement in mastery of the Law. In this ambience, nonreciprocal action not permitted by the Law was swiftly countered, thus reemphasizing the power of the Law and expunging the significance of the event which triggered the nonreciprocal action.

Appreciations of the event invite nonreciprocal actions. And hewing closely to given rationalizations obscures the significance an event might have had. Through the intellectualized notion of order (*dharma*), Hindu caste society has provided for hierarchies of castes as well as for hierarchies, reciprocities, egalitarianism, and morality within castes. Identification with the prescriptions of caste yield an order of purity which positions the soul for the realization of a higher order of purity in the next life on earth. And though the cycle may be short-circuited and completed through *sanyasan*, the cycle itself invites conceptions of patience and time inconceivable to a European. Still, the intellectual construct—predicating order over vast spaces and huge and variegated populations—has survived. Events have had little or no impact on it. They have either been absorbed or rejected. Attempts to make use of events to change the construct—by Gautama, Mahavira, and many others since—have succumbed. The movements they initiated have become castes or subcastes, empirical reflections and variations of a set of integrated rationalizations which prescribe the modes of interaction.

Attempts to account for the survival of cultural forms or intellectual constructs are usually vain: they rehearse the features and ascribe survival value to them. In the end we have to accept the fact of survival and accept, too, that in particular cultures certain axioms seem to be written into the bearers. Given that in all cultures there are specified modes of mediating or manifesting social relationships, these modes are limited in number. And there can be few cultures which do not employ all or most of the available modes. But different cultures accord differing priorities and emphases to particular modes. Most African peoples, for example, accord priority to dogmas of descent: interactions become appropriate and manageable when descent and kinship have been made known. Australian Aborigines could only interact appropriately within an ordered framework when category and group membership, generally grounded in the circumstances of birth, were made explicit. By contrast, among Melanesians dogmas of descent, kinship, and group membership are of minor importance when set against the event, particularly the transaction, the exchange of foodstuffs and valuables: events whose relevances are inherently ambiguous, and whose rationalizations must differ with viewpoint and interest in the situation. Yet just these events mediate social relationships, make their nature manifest.

Tight bureaucratic controls coupled to, say, an intellectualized and strongly articulated tradition of family piety, as in traditional China, echo the Hindu situation. And the written constitution of the United States provides an interesting variant accounting, at least in part, for the many misunderstandings between that country and European states. For the history of European civilization is remarkable for the way in which—despite its dogmas of descent, lineage, class, rank, and status, and even when at its most obdurate as with the rigidly intellectualized authority of the Church just before and during the reformation—successive intellectual constructs or integrated rationalizations concerning order in the world and in social relationships have continually had to give way to the greater importance attached to the event. Perhaps things had to be thus opportunistic simply on account of the varieties of modes available for mediating or manifesting a relationship. At the same time, the governing exemplars can be seen in the Nativity, Resurrection, and Pentecost: animal-spiritual events or processes opposed to and defying an order and morality given by the intellect. If in the beginning was the word, the latter is constantly being renewed by disorderly events which contemporary sets of moralities are unable to rationalize satisfactorily. No social movement in European or Western history has not been steered by events or been obliged to qualify or change its initial framework in the light of subsequent events. Few novels within the tradition do not pit the event—emotional, physical, or spiritual—against an order of accepted usage and morality. Death, plague, love, war, and conspiracy presage the emergence of individuality which, often intensified into charismatic or quasi-charismatic qualities, eventually resolves the situation.

The *Jamaa* movement, as we have seen, centered on the human encounter: an encounter between beings stripped of roles and statuses. Presuming the occurrence, the experience must have included an awareness of being experienced by the other in that chaos which being deprived of given roles and statuses must imply. And an awareness of the meaning of that encounter and experience, articulated and so rationalized, gave rise to new kinds of ordered roles and statuses, a new definition of reality. The many charismatic-type movements reported from Melanesia, called "cargo" cults because of the general accent on the expected arrival of quantitites of manufactured goods, can certainly be related to the exposure to Christianity and the Western industrial, commercial, and colonial apparatus. But they—and particularly their incidence—should also be seen in the light of the Melanesians' general and keen appreciation of the event in relation to its rationalization. It surely cannot be thought accidental, with the African peoples' emphasis on descent and kinship, that the meaning of *Jamaa*, Congo Swahili for "family," should evoke the most important way of mediating social relationships; nor that Melanesians, giving priority to the transactional event, should engage in charismatic movements in which the accent is on having material goods to exchange.

It is one thing to say that some cultures are predisposed to the event, and others not, quite another to identify the reasons why either should be so. On the one hand sociological

analysis is forced into illustrating with more and more detailed data not *why* but *that* some societies are of one sort and
some another. On the other hand it is an evasion of the
sociological problem to attempt to escape the circular argument by trying to pin the predisposition to some natural fact
such as soil variations, climatic whimsies, sporadic dietary
poisons, and the like. Thus, though the incidence of shamans
in proportion to others in northerly climes may be accounted
for by arctic hysteria, since the institution of the Shaman occurs in many other kinds of climates and conditions, arctic
hysteria fails to account for the institution itself. The responses to outer physical conditions are so various that an-
choring a general "explanation" in those physical conditions
can only be vain, a "just so" story. Moreover, since in the
most general sense the "typical" response is a variety of
transformations of the effects of the physical conditions, the
transformations and their relations to other institutions must
become the objects of study. Giving close attention to the rationalizations involved, an "explanation" of the Shaman becomes apparent in the combination of relations inherent in
what he or she is and does in relation to other institutions,
persons, and the community as a whole.

Although analyses of rationalizations making up the whole
semantic environment have now become extremely sophisticated, so that we can the more appreciate the medieval
scholar's fine attention to the effects and consequences of the
living fabric of words and symbols, the common fate seems
to be a piling of Pelion on Ossa. Since analytical exposition
tends to convert events into rationalizations, the force of the
event itself is lost and rationalizations are themselves rationalized. The dramatic performance, the staged simulation
wherein the predicative power of the event in relation to the
programmed rationalizations of the actors is presented to an
audience to reinterpret, reviews and reanalyses the problem
only to return it to the mysterium from whence it emerged.
The fact that European or Western dramatic forms and traditions have been the most varied and changeable of any culture

or civilization is further evidence of the propensity to return a populace to the significance of the event. Rationalizations—words, signs, symbols, or representations—activate in particular ways because they refer to events which in fact do activate in those ways. Why some people should surrender to their given rationalizations, thus putting a virtual "finis" to the inventory of possible events and experiences, while others seek to enlarge or revise their rationalizations so as to take account of new events and experiences, is only partially answered in analyses of the properties and possibilities apparently inherent in the rationalizations. For sooner or later one is forced back to the conclusion that while the seemingly inherent properties of the rationalizations actually turn on given social interrelationships, the crucial innovation seems to arise from those integrations which particular selves, ready to innovate, make when they appreciate the event in the light of the reflections from other selves attempting to deal with it.

Confronted by the relations between events, people in relationships, and rationalizations and/or intellectualizations, we can say that some cultures tend to seize on events as the locus of truth while others, considering all events to have been properly rationalized in relation to given principle, cling to their given rationalizations and/or intellectualizations, and yet others employ both or alternate between the modes. To say that as cultural prescriptions the selection seems to be related to that which gives rise to social instabilities, or to that which enables a culture to remain stable, seems logically persuasive but is not in accord with the ethnographic record. If we resort to the nature of the physical environment to penetrate into the elusive "that which," we abandon the general, embrace the particular, and are still left with the difference between an instability which continues in the same mode and one which develops successive plateaus of new kinds of instability. The Spartans at Thermopylae were true to the prescriptions in which they had been nurtured, the Athenians were true to themselves in relation to the event. We cannot yet really account for the particular and specific integration that sets a culture on course and bequeathes it a preference—and so axioms and purposes.

Would European or Western civilization have taken the course it has taken without its historico-religious exemplars? Correspondences of relationship between these first beginnings and later developments have been shown or suggested. It happens that from these first beginnings European or Western civilization has continually tested its varying intellectual constructs against events, has tried to transcend the former in light of the latter, and has placed moral choice and responsibility squarely on the person to become an individual: one who tests given moralities and rationalizations against the truth of the event, and who is prepared to take the risk of initiating new moralities. This entails nonreciprocal action and a dialectic between the reciprocal and nonreciprocal turning on the event. Whether events are necessary to the development of a dialectical relationship, or whether the latter entails an appreciation of the event, is answered in the individual, without whom there could be neither perception nor apperception of a dialectical process at work.

Within the European or Western tradition the self, aware of its animal, cultural, moral, and spiritual nature, is set the task, through the series of rebirths ideally included in the idea of metanoia, of integrating truth, others, and more perfect moralities. Going along with generalized individuality, its intensification in charismatic activity, and the ongoing search for an ideal and universal morality, alienation and anomie become endemic: the assertion to autonomy, ideally and fruitfully controlled in relation to others and the moralities in a metanoia, cuts free for a while. Though many in the tradition have found spirituality, the cultural accent is on the perfection of the moralities: an inherently unstable set of relationships most vulnerable to the event. Especially is this so when, as is the case, morality is rooted in love, and moral responsibility is institutionally placed squarely on the single human being who must, as consequence, oscillate between person and individual. In all cultures, even though their references are by no means identical, analytical oppositions such as sacred/profane, mysterium/prosaic, *satori*/science, self-willedness/morality, nonreciprocity/reciprocity, anti-structure/structure, communitas/community, spiritual/moral, animal/moral, anomie/order, someone/no one, individual/person yet converge in the intuition, articulated and institutionalized in a variety of idioms, that though the ordered and moral and safe should always be asserted against the unordered and nonreciprocal and dangerous, the authenticities of the former are in every context dependent on the latter. The risk that man-in-culture takes in invoking the qualities and powers in the sacred or mysterium or their analogues is that they may as readily destroy as enliven. But unless the challenge is regularly accepted, culture and morality become moribund, the human spirit atrophied.

11 UNFOLDING AWARENESSES

Whether in some lonely jungle outpost, city slum, or desert of railway tracks, cheap tenements, and sleazy boarding houses bereft of love, the most obvious exponent of individuality is the Christian missionary. Concerned with moral regeneration, he or she is the bearer of that tradition which, moving out from the home environment, seeks the face of God and a universal morality in otherness. And this quest entails a dialectic between what is brought to that otherness and what is learned from it: a process of mutual communication and acceptance as, on both hands, horizons of awareness are widened. And a part of the product of attempting this is evidenced in libraries of ethnographic accounts. But the missionary who imposes or is imprisoned in his own morality, who cannot perceive the worthwhileness in otherness, fails his vocation. Envisaged as a mutual metanoia, a metanoia on both hands, renewal and transformation are ideally initiated in the unstructured and antisystemic kernel of Christian love which, because unstructured and therefore susceptible to being transformed into varieties of moral orderings, gives Christianity its transcultural developmental potential. A genuine dialectic is engaged when, following the liberating experience realized in the unstructured event—which a missionary should and in spite of himself often does embody—expanding awarenesses affected by differing pasts begin to articulate new orderings based upon new moralities.

Few missionaries realize the full extent of their vocation. It would be too much to ask. Intent as they are as individuals upon organizing their communities, they tend to forget that they should embody and communicate that unstructuredness which first made them into themselves and which, reexperienced, can lead into new moralities with a consensus. When on behalf of their communities they come into conflict with the political authority, they too often surrender the advantage of the moral and spiritual—which ultimately defeat political coercion—to adopt a political stance. And unless this last is demonstrably informed with moral or ethical and spiritual purpose, the individual becomes a mere "man of movement." Yet there are some missionaries who do realize their vocations—even though the eventual outcomes are rarely those originally envisaged. But rather than pursue the variety of failings—which but testify to the ideal—it is more useful to appreciate the collective endeavor: an ongoing dialectic process directed towards mutual metanoias which, projected onto different arcs of expression and resulting in the perception of continually widening horizons to be comprehended in relation to the truth of things, energizes the discovery and realization of the universals in human affairs.

Nor should this endeavor be regarded as necessarily attached to Church or denominational organizations. What once the single missionary tried to do, and in many areas of the world still attempts, has become differentiated into a host of professional specialisms—teacher, technical instructor, trader, doctor, anthropologist, linguist, and all that is contained in national and international aid and development programmes—each of which, carrying the instruction to learn, instruct, inform, and improve, is derived from and informed with the missionary purpose. Correspondingly, bringing the gifts of money, new techniques, and improved material conditions without also communicating the moments of individuality betrays a blind faith in the former to renew and transform: a peculiarly obtuse view of what it was in culture that created the product. Not that improved material conditions, mastering new techniques, and handling money necessarily depend on generalized individuality. But without some kind of (albeit secularized) mutual metanoia, the impulse to engage in a process of developing awareness is

lacking. Unless knitted into a framework of connected rationalizations adequate to their properties, material goods become things without meaning. And if there is no disposition
to rerationalize as new things are perceived, the new things
can only be rejected or constrained in traditional categories
which cannot adequately rationalize them.

In a variety of modes and degrees of explicitness and
didactic purpose, poets, sculptors, painters, architects, and
novelists of the European or Western tradition have sought to
grasp the event, then extended their imaginations and experience to contain and rationalize it. Where no events are perceived, there can only be intellectual vanities. And though
such vanities contain their own joys, the grass-roots response
is to be seen in the value placed upon the "happening" or "encounter group": staged events which invite persons to abandon their familiar repertoires of roles and, engaging the imaginative impulse, enter an unstructuredness from which new
kinds of relationships and experiences of being might emerge.
Though men and women continually reinvent themselves,
their gods, categories, rationalizations, and symbolic representations, they grow in awareness only through those rein-
ventions which arise from perceptions of truth in the
unstructuredness of what happens to them. Lacking the imperative to return continually to the event—and events fleet
by, irretrievable and lost forever unless caught in a symbol or
at least in a presently inarticulate memory—rationalizations
and intellectualizations grow rigid, and the mind is content to
move in preset grooves. Tradition reasserts itself, continuities
demand their due, the significance of events becomes
obscured.

Once accepted, intellectualizations are of their nature dura-
ble and tend to persist. And intellectual obfuscations of the
event are no stranger to the European or Western tradition.
Yet accepting that within that tradition events have a habit of
imposing themselves, the imperatives which push persons
into recognizing the event and becoming individuals do not
inhere in the events themselves but in the culturally deter-

mined predisposition to watch for it. Maintaining the continuities through the idea of history (the chronicling of events in relation to successive and differing rationalizations), change, development, and individuation come about through the interactions between events and persons who, poised to perceive significance in events and ready to become new men and new women, seize the truths revealed in events and transform them into moral rules. Becoming individuals, they seek a new allocation of powers, a different content and balance between reciprocal and nonreciprocal elements.

Within the meaning of "religion" adopted here (p. 49), a metanoia, whether secularized or thought of as contained within the specifically Christian tradition, cannot be other than definitional of the religious experience: a penetration into the truth of things which, in affirmation or critique giving rise to moral rules and assumptions about power, provides the basis for activities indicating the truth of the redemptive process. A truncated metanoia which results in a simple substitution is certainly not as deep a religious experience as a metanoia fully realized. Nonetheless, it has the potential of realizing a widened "universal." A metanoia more fully realized carries the awareness that each new heaven and new earth is but temporary, a step in the process being realized as one generation succeeds another. A metanoia wholly realized entails the surrender to love. This means significant interaction with others, but also involves detachment from prescribed positions and roles, from power, status, and the whole organizational apparatus, implicit or explicit, which determines persons' interrelations. Moving wholly into the category of no one, becoming Hero and exemplar, the surrender to love implies the abandonment of all those explicitly or implicitly prescribed dyadic relations which comprise a community. Each other is a reflection of all, all are contained in each. With this singularity it becomes possible to interact with others without necessarily entering specific and preset dyadic relations.

At this point, however, individuality begins to transcend

the moral to enter the spiritual or wholly unstructured. A St. Francis or Mother Teresa may found an organization without necessarily corrupting themselves because their beings are embodiments of the unstructured. The Order or organization is founded on precisely that singularity which, in eschewing particular attachments, enters a relation with all in the discovery that all is in each and each is mirrored in all. For such as these, cultural barriers do not exist. Since humanity is a universal, so must the Universal, God—under whatever other name—Who is love and life, be realized in all of mankind. But individuality is not quite wholly transcended. The European equivalent of the Sanyasi is surely the mystic and not one such as St. Francis. Like his counterpart in *sanyasan*, the Christian mystic looks and moves only to God. The self seeks union with the Godhead or All-being, with life and love in their totality. Into this pool, devoid of positive human interaction, the assertion to autonomy pours itself. Those such as St. Francis or Mother Teresa seek the realization of universal love and life in and through each of all others. The assertion to autonomy is swallowed in the needs of others, the self is released or constrained into a perfected morality. If often, regularly or more sporadically, animal being is transformed into spiritual being, what is most usually manifest is the perfected morality.

If this is the logical end-point of individuality as it has been defined here, only a few make it to the finish. Most fail to overcome the opposition between morality and spirituality and remain trapped in the moralities. Moving to no one and the unstructured, even becoming the unstructured for a while, they either return to the person or realize individuality. Seized by the event and perceiving a new truth of things, becoming new men and new women, in seeking to redeem themselves by realizing their newness in others, their objectives become changed assumptions about power and a renewal of the moralities. To accomplish these objectives they look for worldly or moral power and authority, become corrupted—often manipulating the moralities for selfish and partisan ends—and so deny themselves the franciscan access to the spiritual.

In recent essays Alex Inkeles (1970, 1975) has characterized "modernity" as, briefly, "keeping informed about the world and taking an active role as a citizen; valuing education and technical skills; a concern for economic advance; a stress on personal responsibility, planning in general and family planning in particular; approval of social change; being open to, and desirous of, new experiences including urbanism and industrial employment; sense of personal efficacy; freedom from submission to received authority whether in the context of family, tribe, or sect; keenness to develop non-parochial loyalties; and a readiness to grant autonomy and rights to minorities and lesser statuses." These characteristics, says Inkeles, form a coherent but complex and diffuse syndrome: together they make up what he calls a "measure of modernity" (1970: 61).

To anyone familiar with North American society the syndrome is remarkable for its mythic and symbolic qualities. Being "modern" in the terms set out appears in the context as a desideratum, an ideal, and while some criteria represent what actually is, others seem to refer to what average middle-class people would like to be. The syndrome is, in short, a mixture of what *is*, what *was*, and what *might* or *will* be, a manifestation of the perception of flux, of an unfolding, of developmental processes at work. What is becomes bearable because it is transitory, a temporary fixedness between what was and what will be. The ideas, ideals, material conditions, social relationships, and experience of the here-now were implicit in yesterday. Tomorrow is implicit in today. Each day is different, a movement between past and future. The central symbolic referent, which can occasion either approval or repulsion, is movement into another. "Today," a popular adage has it, "is the first day of the rest of your life."

Unlike most other cultures, including the great Eastern civilizations, the European or Western tradition is authentic in

the notion of continuing growth and development. Embedded in the matrix of the historic as well as the present social
experience, pervading all levels of both the conscious and un-
conscious, this notion and its variety of more precise expressions indicate an ultimate reality unfolding both within ourselves and the world around us. Identities are suffused with
hesitancy, transience, the reality of the other which shall be.
Each successive generation recognizes the existence of this reality, tries to grasp and define it in terms thought appropriate.
It is what makes us stretch out into otherness and ask, "What
is man?" And to answer that we have to ask, "Of what stuff is
all other?" The basic Christian tenet that Christ's presence on
earth was both a culmination of what had gone before and a
departure for the future is but one way of expressing or thinking about this ultimate reality. The details of dating, and the
precise mode of operation—whether or not the process was
set in motion, or merely accompanied, by a divine intervention—far from detracting from the principle that there was a
beginning or threshold, is a middle, and at some time or other
must be an end, only add substance to it. Attempts to join or
identify beginning and end-points have rarely found favor except as temporary relief from the dilemmas provoked by continuing growth and development. The idea of a "steady state"
always gives way to more specific formulations of the evolutionary process. An appreciation of the synchronic situation is
always a means of attempting to get at the diachrony.

The European or Western passion for documentation
coupled to the notion of History—itself arising from the attempt to make sense of, rationalize, the extraordinary and
anomic events of the sacred scriptures by annexing them to
Greek thought—are modes which not only express *that* processual growth and development are basic to ourselves and
our civilization: they also reveal a determination to find out
how that reality is operating. From Aristotle into the present,
varieties of formulations including, very loosely, evolutionary theories, have sought to articulate the nature of the
process which we are convinced is within us, is us, and per-

vades the world outside us. Our modes of dialectic argument, which we take to correspond with a dialectic inherent in the movements and developments of our social relationships, material conditions, and experience, are further examples of the way we attempt to give articulate expression to our awareness of the reality at work in and around us. We recognize and, because it seems indelibly real and true, even welcome the conflict that might open the gates.

The early Christians, seizing on the platonic ideal—and thereby giving morality its ambiguity between what is and might be—placed Morality in the Godhead, saw the Old Testament prophets as mappers of the way, and the events and sayings of the New Testament as truths indicating Truth. With the ambiguities of morality fixed in the Godhead, the Graeco-Christian synthesis seems not only to have expressed, but in its mode of expression entailed, a continuing attachment to the process of unfolding that seemed inherent in the world. Accepting that only an accurate knowledge of the concrete can lead into a worthwhile awareness of spirit, our machines and artifacts express what is sought and the modes of seeking it: having been made they become models of that which we know permeates our being, and which we seek to define and articulate more accurately. Isolating smaller and smaller particles of matter, we have come at last to the genes. And they appear to behave for all the world like a modern bureaucracy (cf. Medawar 1957)! With the advantage of hindsight we can perhaps appreciate that metanoia, alienation, anomie, charisma, and individuality are words by which we have sought not only to contain the epiphenomenal manifestations of the reality working within us, but, by so doing, reach into the truth itself.

Perhaps we need better tools. In the past, since man was deemed to be most significantly moral, the truth about him seemed appropriately discovered in a moral idiom. Now that we are beginning to know something of chemical exchanges and electrical impulses occurring in the body, other idioms may become necessary. Descriptions of ecstasies and spiritual conditions leave little doubt that they converge in much the same kinds of physiological conditions. But we still know very little about this intimacy between the spiritual and animal which transcends the moral. Dozens of close studies of charismatic or millenarian movements point to the truth of Fabian's (1971: 9) words: ". . . if one looks at its [the *Jamaa's*] various elements separately, every one of them can probably be traced to sources or models in the sociocultural environment. But we do insist on the fact that the *specific integration* of these elements cannot be reduced to the social and personality systems involved" (original italics). What makes this specific integration?

If we accept that movements such as the *Jamaa* both express and are in themselves epiphenomenal of that processual reality which, at another level and in varied but not wholly satisfactory idioms, we think of as the evolutionary process, somewhere in the complex of activities and words that we can observe and record something must be happening at the biological or animal level that anthropologists have indeed noticed but, in the circumstances, can scarcely investigate. Psychology, still a precarious bridge between physiology and sociology, has, despite its insights, so far led to more misunderstanding than clarity in transcultural contexts (cf. Burridge 1969a: 82). Because charismatic movements (and other expressions of individuality) engage the attention of authorities and are often a nuisance to bureaucracies, it has been convenient to slot them into given categories and diagnose them as due to mental disorders or lesions. Prison or a process of reeducation on the couch will reimpose conformity. Their realities as social process tend to escape us. On the other hand, because so many charismatic movements have taken place in specifically colonial ambiences, their politico-moral relevances have been more obvious. And while it is true that field studies have necessarily emphasized the fixedness, such synchronic studies have been but preliminary departures for understanding the developmental processes involved.

Understanding developmental processes is only partially

achieved by providing the historical background. A proper articulation and synthesis of the diachrony and synchrony requires much more. All we can presently do to transform the logic and principle of the here-now into that unfolding which we are culturally convinced is working in the world at large is to take a series of leaps in the dark. Our idioms of understanding lie as it were on the circumference. They indicate the center but neither wholly grasp nor fix it. Whether at the level of argument or in relation to concrete social relationships, thesis and antithesis move and engage. Synthesis appears, transient, and fresh oppositions have to be engaged. But the last step or steps by which the synthesis was reached are unclear. We nonetheless take the leap because, although we know the vehicle will not take us all the way, we know the direction and feel we can intuit the end. Not always right, the leap is taken because the reality that is in us, the not always explicit conviction that an unfolding is happening, bids us do so. If, generally, conformities to given intellectual constructs or rationalizations and bureaucratic and role and status requirements are regarded as healthy, few do not also respond to the impulse to change them. And the first step, which may lead in any of several directions, is an alienation from and critique of what happens to be given.

Social experience and commentary become sociology when, through the apperceptions which only individuality can provide, both the regularities and flux in social relations are transformed by the intellect into an ordered set which either corresponds with, or is a variant of, a given theoretical model. At this point, however, the predicative force of flux and ambiguity in social relations tends to be assimilated to the structure of orderliness perceived by the intellect. Individuals are turned into persons and, with a deft twist of the mind, the orderliness is transformed into an ideal which often becomes an ideology. Yet the apprehension of regularity and flux which gave rise to the process of finding order is not wholly lost in the apparent comprehension of an order which turns out to be but a wish or ideal. Seized by events, the individuality which perceived the structure as truth then turns on itself to ask whether truth resides in that structure, whether experience denies its validity. And the critique arises from discrepancies perceived in the relations between an event and its rationalization.

If they were always caught in the categories of current intellectualizations, events would pass us by. Individuality seizes the event that has escaped or been incompletely or wrongly rationalized. In individuality it becomes possible—to return to William James (1901-2: 492)—to "catch real fact in the making." Yet for that embryo to become relevant in the outer world it has to be so brought into engagement with the moralities that there is, as Fabian (1971: 9) has it, a *"specific integration."* Unless so engaged—and only the energies of an individual can bring the integration about—the moralities are indeed a screen of illusion. When so engaged—bringing all the components of being to the task—the moralities become the necessary medium through which the truth may be grasped. Without this continuing and creative thrust, the moralities become procedural programs. If there are latencies waiting to be realized, only an individual can perceive them and move to make them explicit and overt. Conversely, the person who happens to do so becomes an individual. Culture and the social order may make possible, but do not prescribe, a *"specific integration"* any more, or less, than the external factors in biological evolution prescribe that "co-ordinative condition" (Whyte 1965) of the internal factors in biological evolution so necessary to the process as a whole.

If there were no selves, no assertions to autonomy, human beings would be the automated creatures of their cultures. Indeed, such automata are frequently encountered. Through the cultural faculties and a communication below the level of the articulate, a self may integrate the moments of any cultural ambience. But an integration that is positively morally relevant requires the catalytic spark of individuality. If appropriate interactions with the symbols signify, in Turner's words

(1968: 270), "collective man's conquest of himself," what also seems required if the latencies of the symbols are to be realized is that *work be done* in the regions between experience and perception on the one hand and the formal institutionalized modes on the other. Tying the antitheses into temporary syntheses is what that work is about. Within the European or Western tradition creative work in these spaces turns on that experience of the event—and being experienced by the event—which traditional Christianity has represented as being contained in, primarily, the Nativity, the Resurrection, and Pentecost: the mystery of life and the creative processes entailed in conception and birth; the conquest of their antithesis, death; and the spiritual renewal which brings new life to moribund moralities and creates new ones. Their very enormity leads into the search for the more sensible events of ordinary life, all but necessitates turning outward to the world at large and the stars beyond. What we find out there is made to feed back and illumine what we feel in ourselves.

The Christian tradition does not wholly lack modes of integrating the self and realizing the self. But despite frequent attempts in history to establish those modes or create new ones—"wholeness now!"—the dominant aspiration to universality and a regard for the event, especially the new one, turn the gaze outward. The lives of the prophets and saints give some indication of the kinds of events which experience people, and which persons experience as they move into individuality. More mundane events suffice for most of us. But if seeking events is, therefore, a cultural prescription, the kinds of events and their whence, wherefore, and whither are unpredictable. Their one consistency is that they occur unexpectedly, as a surprise—commonplace, droll, dramatic, or freaky. Guesswork and an eye to fame and profit might seem to work as well. Seizing and being seized by the event is instinct with uncertainty. The tension between being borne on events and submitting to traditional moralities is hard to maintain. But that tension must be maintained if there is to be that synthesis which individuality can reveal. Usually, the tendency is either to dress events with an importance they do not deserve, or to lose them in given intellectualizations. When carried on events, all events become significant, providing an illusory momentum and energy. Surrendering to any one of the definitive orders prescribed by a variety of given intellectualizations—even though it may claim an ordered developmental unfolding—is equally defeating. If flux and disorder must be brought to order, it is only in continually realizing the unstructured and antisystemic event that a particular order can flourish and develop. This process, essentially one of spiritual, psychic, and moral growth, lies at the core of the European tradition.

EPILOGUE

Under the rubric of "individualism," individuality and the individual have been taking a beating. The movement away from a particular and passing "individualism" of greed, selfishness, and the exploitation of others toward the person and varieties of collective forms has been a necessary corrective. Too much had gone awry. Individuality had run wild. A reaction was bound to follow. Yet the individual never was authentic in autonomy, greed, selfishness, self-interest, and the exploitation of others. Those sorts of abuse are part of the risk entailed in generalized individuality. Overcorrection, on the other hand, puts on the straitjacket of the automated responses of group loyalties and interests, and substitutes dogmas and procedures for living morality. Anthropologists and sociologists, looking for order, have tended to idealize the orders—and so the persons—of other cultures and, as often, explicitly or implicitly criticized the order at home. And while the methods enabling them to find order have tended to become ideologies, reinforcing the person, both tendencies are in themselves characteristic of the individual: who wants persons to be of different kind.

Not an exploration of the sociology of the "single instance of the species," the relations and experiences and processes that have been discussed point to cultural variations of that disposition in being which is necessary for survival and growth of awareness: the positive affirmation, mediation, and reformulation of the moralities in relation to perceived truth and reality. In most cultures this task belongs to particularly prescribed roles and positions. In the European or Western tradition, however, the task became generalized. At a particular moment in history there appears to have occurred a synthesis of features none of which was unfamiliar and each of which could be accounted for in terms of the social ambience of the time. What is remarkable was its persistence and the way in which it prized the peculiar moral task from its protected and insulated position and bestowed it upon each involved human being. And this has meant that while each involved self could take refuge in the person, he or she was also obliged to move into individuality, make a moral choice and reformulate the moralities. Continuing and recurring alienations are implied. Whether caused by or finding their reconciliation in the Pentecostal experience and exemplar, the tensions inherent in the movement from acceptance through alienation and liminality to critic and a renewed acceptance appear to have generated most of the organizational forms with which European or Western civilization has been so well endowed. The core process has been a back and forth movement between the systemic or structured and the antisystemic or unstructured. In its outward and collective appearance, this process has taken the form of countless charismatic movements, repetitions of the Pentecostal exemplar. But it can also take place in solitudes of conscience reaching for truth.

The enabling material conditions would appear to be, primarily, not just money, but the implications of the contradiction between *giving* ≈ *receiving* and *giving* ≠ *receiving* generated by the presence of money. Yet these implications could hardly have endured productively if not joined to the injunction and experience that a metanoia is possible. Money tests morality as an exchange of goods and services cannot, continually queries the qualities of life and the value of being human. But without that sense of an unfolding which we try to capture in one or other evolutionary idiom or attempt to order in the form of a dialectic, and which the process indicated and predicated by a metanoia engenders and positively spurs into realization, there could only have been a series of successive retreats into traditional systemics. Constrained in the person, the self in each one of us must seem an irrelevance, the assertion to autonomy an unhappy frustration. Taking the responsibility of moral choice by perceiving and being seized by the event, generalized individuality implies a continuing search for the novel. Failing the moral task, other kinds of new things and discoveries emerge.

Material prosperities have brought individuality into association with developing technologies, commerce, industry, and entrepreneurial activity—byproducts of the central task of transforming the unstructured qualities of love, life, and the truth of things into ordered relations. Nor are these byproducts unnecessary. Without the concrete and material to house and conserve a thought or image, the human awareness of self and the relation to other would have been stillborn. Unless linked to the concrete and material, rationalizations become tricks curled in the entropy of impossible paradox. Failing the spiritual, the human mind requires the sensory experience of things to fix itself and take departures. In making and then distributing things, human beings model their relations with others, express their awareness of a given morality in concrete terms, and position themselves to change the moralities by changing the relations with things. And the more differentiated things there are, the more differentiated thoughts—and so the moralities—become. Conversely, the more differentiated the moralities, the more differentiated the relations with things.

As things and the uses and meanings of a limited vocabulary multiply, words begin to obscure the qualities, virtues, activities, and experiences to which they once referred. The truths of the unstructured retreat and become difficult to perceive. Bureaucracy-technocracy devours moral dilemma, becomes what matters. Shrouded by ideals and ethics linked to roles and statuses, spiritual truths become intangible and apparently impractical hinges of action. The conflict that begets real moral choice is shunted aside, ideals and ethics become obstacles to their own realization, the palliative rearrangement of roles and statuses seems fraught with promise. Hence the person: an identity, someone, declining both conflict and

choice, but keen on status advance—yet unless authentic in
the reach for a developing awareness, set in the insecurities
rather than stimulus of transience. To rescue the spirit and ex-
tricate the self from means become ends and the opiate tangle
of words, the self must be seized by events which, in renewing the words, gives them new meaning. If, inevitably, a
truth discovered must be translated into roles and statuses, the
quest for a truth independent of given roles and statuses cannot for long be wholly thwarted. Things and thoughts merge
into an awareness of what is happening in the heart, and this,
what happens to the self in the halflights of experience in spite
of the person, the praxis which escapes current modes of rationalization, is truth in the making. And even though it is in
the nature of a bureau-technocratic industrial order continually to absorb the energies of moral endeavor, twisting them
into its own likeness and purposes, individuality—and only
individuality—can in the end defeat it.

Where truth and reality are regarded as residing in the
differentials of coercive power, that kind of power must tend
to perpetuate itself in successive establishments of coercive
power. Reaffirming or deploring existing roles and statuses,
ideologies remain linked to the supposed truths and efficiencies of coercion and tend to prohibit that access to the unstructured which is essential to the growth and development of
human awareness. The frustrated self is then permitted either
to feed on the hope of gaining access to power or to withdraw
into mentations and images of purpose which generate more
amenable truths and realities: an epistemological islet which
can only perceive the moralities of the world outside as illusion, self-deception, and idolatry. And that outer world re-
ciprocates: uneasily tolerates or deplores the isolate or, in extreme cases, uses its coercive power to commit him or her to a
prison called home. Moving into the unstructured no one by
participating in the beings of others, on the other hand, not
only begins to create an individual, but keeps him or her on
course by avoiding a narcissistic concern with the self and engendering a keen regard for the rationalization that does not

square with the truth of the event. So that although a warped individuality can often lead into coercions that are an abuse of morality, or into epistemological confrontations that merely separate stubborn prejudice from simple pigheadedness, proper individuality stands as the remedy.

REFERENCES

Allport, Gordon W.
   1955: *Becoming*. Yale University Press, New Haven.
   1960: *The Individual and His Religion*. The Macmillan Company, New York.
Berndt, R. M.
   1962: *An Adjustment Movement in Arnhem Land, Northern Territory of Australia*. Cahiers de L'Homme, Mouton, Paris.
Borges, Jorge Luis
   1967: "Everything and Nothing," in *A Personal Anthropology*. Grove Press, New York.
Bradfield, Richard Maitland
   1973: *A Natural History of Associations*, Vols. I and II, Duckworth & Co., London.
Burridge, Kenelm
   1960: *Mambu*. Methuen, London.
   1969a: *New Heaven, New Earth*. Basil Blackwell, Oxford.
   1969b: *Tangu Traditions*. Clarendon Press, Oxford.
   1973a: *Encountering Aborigines*. Pergamon Press, London and New York.
   1973b: "Levels of Being," in *Religion and Morality* (Gene Outka and John P. Reeder Jr., eds.). Anchor Books, Doubleday, New York.
   1975: "The Melanesian Manager" in *Studies in Social Anthropology* (J.H.M. Beattie and R. G. Lienhardt, eds.), Clarendon Press, Oxford, pp. 86-104.
Carpenter, Edward
   1912: *The Drama of Love and Death*. Mitchell Kennedy, New York.

Cassirer, Ernst

1946: *Language and Myth* (trans. Suzanne K. Langer). Harper and Brothers, New York and London.

1951: *The Philosophy of the Enlightenment* (trans. Fritz C.A. Koelin and James P. Pettegrove). Beacon Press, Boston.

1963: *The Individual and the Cosmos in Renaissance Philosophy* (trans. Mario Domandi). Harper Torchbooks, New York.

Chang, Yunshik

1971: "The Urban Korean as Individual," *Korea Observer*, vol. 3, no. 3 (April), pp. 3-15.

Codrington, R. H.

1891: *The Melanesians*. Clarendon Press, Oxford.

Dostoyevsky, Fyodor

1871/1971: *The Devils* (trans. with introduction by David Mayarshack). Penguin Books, London.

Douglas, Mary

1966: *Purity and Danger*. Routledge and Kegan Paul, London.

1970: *Natural Symbols*. Barrie & Rockliff, The Cresset Press, London.

Dumont, Louis

1960: "World Renunciation in Indian Religions," *Contributions to Indian Sociology*, Vol. IV, pp. 33-62.

1965a: "The 'Individual' in two types of Society," *Contributions to Indian Sociology*, Vol. VIII, pp. 8-61.

1965b: "The functional equivalents of the Individual in Caste Society," *Contributions to Indian Sociology*, Vol. VIII, pp. 85-99.

1966: *Homo Hierarchicus*. Gallimard, Paris.

1967: "The Individual as an Impediment to Sociological Comparison and Indian History," in *Social and Economic Change* (Balgit Singh and V. B. Singh, eds.). Allied Publishers Private Limited, Bombay.

1970: "Religion, Politics, and Society in the Individualistic Universe." The Henry Myers Lecture, 1970. *Proceedings of the Royal Anthropological Institute*, pp. 31-41.

1958: *Rites and Symbols of Initiation*. Harper and Row, New York.

Eliade, Mircea
1964: *Shamanism: Archaic Techniques of Ecstasy*. Pantheon Books (Bollingen Series No. 76), New York.
1973: *Australian Religions*. Cornell University Press, Ithaca and London.

Elkin, A. P.
1944: *Aboriginal Men of High Degree*. Australian Publishing Company, Sydney.

Ellis, William
1829: *Polynesian Researches*, 2 vols., Fisher and Jackson, London.

Evans-Pritchard, E. E.
1940: *The Nuer*, Clarendon Press, Oxford.
1951: *The Sanusi of Cyrenaica*. Clarendon Press, Oxford.
1956: *Nuer Religion*. Clarendon Press, Oxford.
1965: *Theories of Primitive Religion*. Clarendon Press, Oxford.

Fabian, Johannes
1971: *Jamaa: A Charismatic Movement in Katanga*. Northwestern University Press, Evanston.

Firth, Raymond
1940: "The analysis of mana: An empirical approach," *Journal of the Polynesian Society*, vol. 49, pp. 483-510.

Fuchs, Stephen
1965: *Rebellious Prophets*. Asia Publishing House, Bombay.

Gennep, Arnold van
1960(1909): *The Rites of Passage* (trans. Monika B. Vizedom and Gabrielle L. Coffee). Routledge and Kegan Paul, London.

Girardi, Giulio
1968: *Marxism and Christianity* (trans. by Kevin Traynor). Gill and Son, Dublin.

Handy, E. S. Craighill
1927: *Polynesian Religion*. Bernice P. Bishop Museum Bulletin, No. 34, Honolulu, Hawaii.

Hayek, F. A.
  1946: *Individualism: True and False*. Basil Blackwell, Oxford.
Hogbin, H. Ian
  1951: *Transformation Scene*. Routledge and Kegan Paul, London.
Ibn Khaldun
  1958: *The Muquaddimah* (trans. by F. Rosenthal), Vols. I, II, III. Routledge and Kegan Paul, London.
Inkeles, Alex
  1970: "Becoming Modern," *et al.*, vol. 2, no. 3, pp. 58-73. And see also—
  1973: "A Model of Modern Man," *Social Science and the New Societies* (Nancy Hammon, ed.), Social Science Research Bureau, East Lansing.
  1975: "Becoming Modern," *Ethos*, vol. 3, no. 2, Summer, pp. 323-342.
James, William
  1901-2: *The Varieties of Religious Experience*. The Gifford Lectures, Edinburgh. Random House, New York.
  1920: *Talks to Teachers on Psychology and Life's Ideals*. Longmans Green & Co., London.
Kierkegaard, Søren
  1955: (orig. c. 1846) *On Authority and Revelation* (trans. with Introduction and Notes by Walter Lowrie). Princeton University Press, Princeton.
Lanternari, Vittorio
  1960/65: *The Religions of the Oppressed*. Mentor Books, New York.
Lawrence, Peter
  1964: *Road Belong Cargo*. Manchester University Press.
Lee, R. B.
  1968: "What hunters do for a living, or, How to make out on scarce resources," in *Man the Hunter* (R. B. Lee and I. DeVore, eds.), Chicago. pp. 30-48.
Lévi-Strauss, Claude
  1966(1950): "Introduction à L'Oeuvre de M. Mauss," in

Sociologie et Anthropologie (de Marcel Mauss). Presses Universitaires de France, Paris.

1966(1962): *The Savage Mind* (La Pensée Sauvage). Weidenfeld and Nicolson, London.

1969(1964): *The Raw and the Cooked* (trans. John and Doreen Weightman.) Harper and Row, New York.

Levy, Marion J.

1962: "Some Aspects of 'Individualism' and the Problem of Modernization in China and Japan." *Economic Development and Cultural Change*, vol. X, no. 3 (April), pp. 225-240.

Lewis, I. M.

1971: *Ecstatic Religion*. Penguin Books, London.

Lienhardt, R. G.

1961: *Divinity and Experience*. Clarendon Press, Oxford.

Lively, Jack

1962: *The Social and Political Thought of Alexis De Tocqueville*. Clarendon Press, Oxford.

Lukes, Stephen

1969: "Durkheim's 'Individualism and the Intellectuals,' " *Political Studies*, vol. 18, no. 1 (March), pp. 14-30.

1973: *Individualism*. Basil Blackwell, Oxford.

Maeterlinck, Maurice

1913: *Our Eternity* (trans. Alexander Teixeira de Mattos). Dodd, Mead & Co., New York.

Marett, R. R.

1914: *The Threshold of Religion*. Methuen, London.

M'Crindle, J. W.

1896/1969: *The Invasion of India by Alexander the Great*. Barnes and Noble, New York; Methuen, London.

Mead, George Herbert

1967(1934): *Mind, Self and Society* (edited with an Introduction by Charles W. Morris). University of Chicago Press, Chicago and London.

Medawar, P. B.

1957: *The Uniqueness of the Individual*. Basic Books, New York.

1960: *The Future of Man*. Methuen, London.

Merton, Thomas
1968: *The Geography of Lograire*. New Directions Publishing Corporation, New York.

Moorehead, Alan
1966: *The Fatal Impact*. Hamish Hamilton, London.

Mora, Jose Ferrater
1965: *Being and Death* (trans. from the Spanish). University of California Press, Berkeley.

Morris, Colin
1972: *The Discovery of the Individual, 1050-1200*. SPCK, London.

Nakamura, Hajime
1967: "Individualism in the East," *Hemisphere*, vol. 2, no. 9, pp. 8-11.

Needham, Rodney
1972: *Belief, Language, and Experience*. Basil Blackwell, Oxford.

Nisbet, Robert A.
1966: *The Sociological Tradition*. Heineman, London.

Nock, A. D.
1933: *Conversion. The Old and New in Religion from Alexander the Great to Augustine of Hippo*. Clarendon Press, Oxford.

Pareto, Vilfredo
1935: *The Mind and Society*. Dover Publications, New York.

Pilling, A. R. and Waterman, R. A.
1970: *Diprotodon to Detribalization*. Michigan State University Press, East Lansing.

Richter, Curt P.
1959: "The Phenomenon of Unexplained Sudden death in Animals and Man," in *The Meaning of Death* (Herman Feifel, ed.). McGraw Hill Book Company, New York.

Sargant, William
1957/63: *Battle for the Mind*. Pan Books, London.

Seeman, Melvin
   1959: "On the meaning of Alienation," *American Sociological Review*, vol. 24, December, pp. 783-791.
Simmel, Georg
   1959: *Sociology of Religion* (trans. by Curt Rosenthal). Philosophical Library, New York.
   1969: *The Sociology of George Simmel* (trans, edited, with an Introduction by Kurt A. Wolff). Collier-Macmillan Limited, The Free Press, Toronto.
   1971: *On Individuality and Social Forms* (ed. with an Introduction by Donald N. Levine). University of Chicago Press, Chicago.
Smith, Dorothy
   1973: "Women, the Family and Corporate Capitalism," in *Women in Canada* (Marylee Stephenson, ed.). New Press, Toronto, pp. 2-35.
Steiner, Franz
   1956: *Taboo*. Cohen and West, London.
Strehlow, T.G.H.
   1971: *Songs of Central Australia*. Angus & Robertson, Sydney.
Tempels, Placide
   1945: *La philosophie bantoue*. Lovania, Elizabethville.
Tocqueville, Alexis de
   1840: *Democracy in America* (trans. Henry Reeve). London.
Tonkinson, Robert
   1974: *The Jigalong Mob*. Cummings, Menlo Park, California.
Turner, Victor
   1967: *The Forest of Symbols*. Cornell University Press, Ithaca, New York.
   1968: *The Drums of Affliction*. Clarendon Press, Oxford.
   1969: *The Ritual Process*. Aldine Publishing Co., Chicago.
Watson, James B.
   1971: "Tairora: The Politics of Despotism in a Small Society," in *Politics in New Guinea* (Ronald M. Berndt and

Peter Lawrence, eds.). University of Western Australia Press, Perth.

Weber, Max

1947: *The Theory of Social and Economic Organization* (trans. by A. M. Henderson and Talcott Parsons). Collier-Macmillan Limited, London.

1948: *From Max Weber: Essays in Sociology* (trans. and edited with an introduction by H. H. Gertha and C. Wright Mills). Routledge and Kegan Paul, London.

1958a: *The Protestant Ethic and the Spirit of Capitalism* (trans. by Talcott Parsons). Charles Scribner's Sons, New York.

1958b: *The Religion of India*. The Free Press, Glencoe, Illinois.

White, Hayden V.

1959: "Ibn Khaldun in World Philosophy of History," *Comparative Studies in Society and History*, vol. 2, October.

White, W. G.

1922: *The Sea Gypsies of Malaya*. Seeley, Service & Co., London.

Whyte, L. L.

1965: *Internal Factors in Evolution*. George Braziller, New York.

Wilson, Bryan

1973: *Magic and the Millennium*. Harper & Row, New York.

Worsley, Peter

1957/68: *The Trumpet of Shall Sound*. MacGibbon & Ker, London.

Yawney, Carole

1977: "Lions in Babylon: The Rastafarians of Jamaica as a Visionary Front." Unpublished manuscript.

Zimmer, Heinrich

1956: *Philosophies of India* (ed. Joseph Campbell). The World Publishing Company, Cleveland.

INDEX

LIBRARY OF CONGRESS CATALOGING
IN PUBLICATION DATA

Burridge, Kenelm.
  Someone, no one.

  Includes bibliographical references and index.
  1. Individuality.   I. Title.
BF697.B863   301.11'3   79-83979
ISBN 0-691-09384-9